C

About The Author

Patrick Moore was born in 1970 and grew up in Athy, Co Kildare. He now lives in Galway where he has been working, amongst other things, as an actor for a number of years. He has written one other book, a self-published collection of poetry, 'This Man's Truth' (Blurb Inc., 2012).

PJ is available for one to one or group consultations and public talks, offering his views on a sustainable and financially balanced lifestyle. Enquiries are welcomed at pjmoore33@yahoo.co.uk

FINANCIAL FREEDOM ON A SHOESTRING

THE JUSTIFIED TIGHT BASTARD'S GUIDE TO LIFE

READ THIS BOOK AND REGARDLESS OF INCOME,
NEVER WORRY ABOUT BILLS, DEBTS OR A
SHORTAGE OF MONEY AGAIN.

PJ Moore

Requests to publish work from this book can be sent to the author at pjmoore33@yahoo.co.uk

Matador
9 Priory Business Park
Kibworth Beauchamp
Leicestershire LE8 0RX, UK
Tel: (+44) 116 279 2299
Fax: (+44) 116 279 2277
Email: books@troubador.co.uk
Web: www.troubador.co.uk/matador

332
ISBN 978 1783063 680
024

D216.516

British Library Cataloguing in Publication Data.
A catalogue record for this book is available from the British Library.

Typeset in Aldine by Troubador Publishing Ltd
Printed and bound in the UK by TJ International, Padstow, Cornwall

Matador is an imprint of Troubador Publishing Ltd

For Cáelum Joyner

Acknowledgements

This book would never have been completed – indeed might never have been attempted – without the love, support and encouragement of the long-suffering Joyners, namely Allison and Cáelum. Without their tireless and patient assistance in so many ways: practical, technical, emotional and artistic, my indulgent 18 month long undertaking would never have made the journey from a crazy idea nesting in the further reaches of what passes for my brain to its finished physical reality today. For that I cannot thank you both enough.

I would like to thank my parents for their contribution to the completion of my first prose project. Although they have both been dead for over fifteen years, without their contribution nothing would be possible for me, least of all the writing of a book. Thanks also are due in no small part to my editor Deirdre Eustace who went above and beyond her job description with helpful suggestions for many aspects of this project and to Penelope Rae Visser the talented artist whose sketches are used to enhance the text throughout. Special mention is also due to Sínead Hackett – my first critic of an early draft. Wishing to restrict my appreciative wanderings, let me wrap up my acknowledgements quickly and neatly by way of general thanks to all whose influence, through either direct or indirect contact, have helped shape and mould me into the unique and strange individual I am today; the one to whom it not only occurred to but who considered it a good idea to write this side-stream collection of fiscal musings. All of which is a longwinded way of delegating responsibility: the many people who played a part in my becoming the person I am today by extension share the responsibility for my creative offering. Therefore I can only reasonably accept as my due a tiny portion of the criticism this book will likely generate – I am however prepared to magnanimously shoulder the bulk of any praise proffered for my talents, despite this being the heavier burden of responsibility to carry!

'Money is like a sixth sense without which you cannot make a complete use of the other five.'

W. Somerset Maugham (1874 – 1965)

Contents

Introduction

In September, 2012 I began writing this book having listened, for over four years, to what seemed like the whole country predicting the end of civilisation as we know it: commentators warning that this was the recession to beat all recessions, that we were in the midst of the worst economic disaster since the great depression of the 1930's. I knew all this clap trap was utter nonsense (designed, one can only presume, to sell lots of newspapers and antidepressants) because, although at the tender age of forty two I wasn't quite old enough to remember the 30's or even the 60's, I could remember the 80's and I can say from firm experience that everyone has a proportionally greater income today when compared to that time. I'm no Einstein, just an average semi-observant five eights, but even I can see that everyone in the country receives enough money either through wages or social welfare payments to live, at the very least, in modest comfort. So, what's causing all the alarm? The answer: expectations and debt.

During the Celtic Tiger years our expectations grew faster than our wage packets and property prices combined. While the latter two have unceremoniously crash landed back to earth, our expectations are still riding high in outer space – somewhere just out of reach of the reasonable gravitational pull of logic. Allied to this, there would appear to be a financially fatal inability among large sections of the population to master basic arithmetic. For instance, incredible as it may sound, a huge proportion of my better educated peers do not seem to grasp the infallible, simple economic law of solvency: 'spend less than you earn'. Five short words of wisdom which, if followed, would guarantee you would never run into financial trouble again. Ever! In these pages I aim to encourage a frame of mind that will point you in exactly that direction. In this crazy, mixed-up world it's so easy to form a convincing argument in your own head to spend money on just about anything – especially when you have so much help in this regard from outside, vested interests. This book then is an antidote; the other side of that coin, arguing as it does, a logical reason for *not* spending money on things you had previously convinced yourself were unavoidable. Might I remind you that money has only been in circulation for the latter, small proportion of human existence. The human animal roamed and encroached upon almost every corner of the earth, growing in stature and number for millennia before first bartering and then the earliest forms of currency came into use – a simple reminder, perhaps, that all spending is optional.

It occurred to me that most media commentary on personal financial matters was biased and fearful of being brutally honest with the public for fear of insulting them and thus losing their custom. Plus, we all love a scapegoat: someone or some circumstance other than our good selves is always to blame for any mess, financial or otherwise, which befalls us. Even though we are all human and therefore fallible, we seem to have become incapable of holding our hand up and saying: 'Shit! I fucked up!' And of course if you cannot admit to a mistake for fear of it being seen as a sign of weakness, then you are defenceless to stop yourself from repeating that same mistake over and over again, ironically rendering yourself ever weaker, financially and otherwise. In writing this book I set about attempting to cut through the crap; to call a spade a spade as I see it. Some of you dear readers are perhaps going to feel insulted as I try to dispense my tough love but please try not to take it personally – instead draw comfort from the fact that I insult myself as often as anyone else. There is also the not inconsiderable risk that I have rendered my book un-publishable by criticising most of the powers that be in this country. But, had I concerned myself with that I'd never have sat down and written it or, worse still, I'd have written some rubbish I didn't believe because I had learned that that's what publishers felt the 'market' wanted. Instead, I have written what I believe the market most certainly does not want but what many people floundering in financial confusion badly need. I decided I'd cross the publishing bridge when I came to it and hopefully, the fact that you are reading this now means that I got across safely.

Having strived to keep repetition to a minimum I am aware that, several drafts later, some still remains. This may not be a bad thing as it should increase the chances of an individual registering the advice and incorporating it into their lifestyle. Not all points will be relevant to all readers while other tips are, by my own admission, a tad extreme for some to swallow. The book is intended as a menu of options to choose from; how much of it you decide to implement will be dictated by your desire and motivation to curb your expenditure. Having said that, I would be disappointed if there was a single person in the country who couldn't find a tip in the book that would save them at least a few hundred euro over the course of a year with a minimal amount of effort or disruption to their lifestyle. So, if you are reading this in a bookshop and wondering whether you should buy it or not, don't waste your valuable time procrastinating a moment longer. Buy it immediately! While I have advised elsewhere in this tome not to buy books – to get them out of the library or in charity shops – there is always an exception to every rule and in this instance, *The Justified Tight Bastard's Guide to Life* is that exception. Within a week of purchase you will have saved many multiples of the cover price as a direct result of the nuggets of wisdom it holds. Therefore it shouldn't be viewed as an expense but rather as an investment to be dipped into at regular intervals. Apart from the direct savings to be made from specific advice, I would hope that punters reading my book will use it to kick-start their own imaginations; to begin looking afresh at where they are haemorrhaging money in their own lives and start finding solutions by applying independent, lateral thinking to the problem.

You may be wondering what qualifies me to write a book such as this. Do I have a degree in economics? Nope. Do I have a degree in anything? No, Sir. I can, for what it's worth, claim to have been debt free at the early age of forty one (despite buying houses at both ends of the property bubble) and to be able, at this young age, to pursue freely that which interests me in life regardless of whether or not it produces an income. Some of this happy state of affairs I accept can be attributed to good fortune but we are all at times on the receiving end of luck, both good and bad, it's what we do with it that counts. My only qualification then is experience itself, a little independent thought added to that life experience and a curmudgeonly attitude which refuses to accept the political and marketing spin applied to everything. This volume is not aimed at high flyers, investors, students of economics and so on (although I'm sure they too could find something of benefit within it); it is more for the ordinary Joe Soap who is genuinely struggling to keep on top of his every-day bills. Whether he is succeeding in his valiant struggle or not, this book is telling him that it shouldn't be such an endless battle; there is another way. And to the fella who is doing okay financially but only because he continues to clock in to his monotonous job day in and day out – which in the immortal words of Morrissey 'pays my way, but it corrodes my soul' – and can't see any other option, well I'm saying to him there is another option and I hope to help this guy clarify his priorities.

I do tend to use a hefty sprinkling of what might be considered black humour to illustrate many of my points (a little sugar to sweeten the medicine, so to speak) and I hope the reader will enjoy my sense of humour whilst still letting the serious message sink in. The book is not written as a joke and, if it appears so, it is because a joke is only ever funny when it contains the truth at its heart. I am quite serious when I claim that, regardless of your circumstances, you can make ends meet comfortably with just a few prudent but reasonable lifestyle changes. Of course I do realise that if everyone adopted my advice with the same enthusiasm as a neurotic Jack Russell greeting his owner's return there would be an economic meltdown the scale of which hasn't been seen since the last ice age. But I don't think we need fear – the likelihood of a single book such as this, which requires proactive engagement by the reader, penetrating the thick syrup-like inertia of public consciousness to any noticeable degree is miniscule, to say the least. This begs the question: why bother writing it at all then? Well, for one thing it was a very enjoyable, educational (I've learned how to spell a few big words) and worthwhile challenge on a personal level with the added bonus that the process of writing and researching pieces for the book has led to my being able to shave a couple of grand per annum off my already thrifty budget by implementing much of my own advice. On a wider note, it is my fervent hope that at least a handful of individuals who are up the proverbial shit creek without a paddle will, having read this book, find the motivation to revolt and seize their financial independence back from the parasitic colonists who have infested their minds. If I achieve that modest goal my efforts will have been richly rewarded.

Adhering to the golden rule: 'write about what you know' and being forty three, male and Irish, I have written the book from that perspective. As a result, my writing may at times be a little top heavy in areas such as motoring and food and a mite lacking on subjects such as infants, technology and expenses pertaining specifically to women. However, I believe that much of the advice is general enough to be applied to these areas of expenditure that I am not overly familiar with and, who knows, perhaps some thrifty mother out there might take up the challenge of writing 'The Justified Tight Bitch's Guide To Life' to compliment my offering!

The book can be read in either of two ways: it can be read in the normal way, cover to cover from beginning to end or alternatively, it can be dipped into at random – just reading whatever page falls open. Perhaps a number of readers will use it rather like one of those self-help or spiritual guides which have a thought for the day for you to read each morning and then ponder over in quiet moments throughout the day. In any case it matters little how you use it – read it upside down while standing on your head if it works for you – just so long as you find the resolve to implement some of the advice and turn the theory into hard cash savings.

In attempting to adopt some of my tips I would suggest 'challenging but fun' should be your mantra. Don't bite off the challenges which involve the greatest change to your lifestyle first. Crawl before you try to walk and walk before you run. Build your confidence by introducing some minor and routine cost-saving changes initially. Keep it light. Try to involve other members of your immediate family or circle, make an enjoyable game of it all but one with potentially rich rewards. You will inevitably incur setbacks along the way but use characters like Henry Ford as inspiration at these times of perceived failure or disillusionment. The guy who brought the motor car to the masses went bankrupt four (or was it five?) times before finally finding success. The point being: the number of aborted attempts fades into obscurity in the face of your final success. So all you have to do is make sure the final attempt at anything is successful. Myself, I would consider 'two steps forward and one step back' to be excellent progress in any endeavour. Bear in mind the guy who never made a mistake never made anything – and the guy who refused to admit his mistake good-naturedly, even to himself, became the very definition of bitterness.

Finally, it is my intention that even the reader who is quite comfortable financially and is not looking to make any particular changes to his life can enjoy this book as an entertaining Victor Meldrew-inspired social commentary on some of our perplexing modern day behaviours and beliefs. In a nutshell, I hope my book holds some food for thought or inspiration for animated debate for everyone, regardless of circumstance. For the hell of it, I also tried to pepper the text with occasional colourful turns of phrase or expressions which used to be common in our everyday language but have sadly become all too infrequent in modern conversation. I hope you enjoy!

SECTION ONE

Getting your House in Order

1. Anal Recording

As we embark upon the task of becoming fully fledged tight bastards we should begin with a little preparatory work by keeping a detailed, daily record of **ALL** our spending. And I do mean all. The purpose of this exercise is to discover exactly where all your money is going and since information is power, we will then be in a stronger position to tackle any wastage. Include every even seemingly insignificant purchase on your list – remember that bar of chocolate you bought on the way home from work or the newspaper you picked up for your mother but then refused payment for. For the purposes of this exercise every time you part with money for any reason it counts as a purchase. This may sound like an obvious statement but there are plenty of examples of situations where you might part with cash and not receive any tangible or quantifiable return, like the €20 you put in your nephew's birthday card last week (don't forget the card itself or the stamp), the euro you threw to the busker on Shop street in Galway or perhaps you're a mass-goer and you throw a couple of quid in the collection plate every Sunday. Anyway, you get the idea: these types of purchases are very easy to overlook because they usually involve very small amounts of money and there is no physical evidence of the transaction, not even a receipt. So you need to be diligent and anal in the keeping of this list. And don't forget those direct debits and online credit card transactions which again can be missed because you didn't physically handle cash.

You will need to keep this experiment going for a minimum of one month but six months to a year would be even more beneficial as not all spending occurs in a monthly cycle. The longer you continue keeping these records the more benefit will accrue. If you carry out this exercise honestly and meticulously I guarantee you will be surprised by where a significant amount of your income is going. Initially our objective is simply to record our spending habits and not to curtail them but you will find that just doing this simple exercise has the effect of concentrating the mind: you will become more aware of each purchase and thus automatically question its value more closely. Sometimes you will decide you don't need the product or you can get the same item for less around the corner. In fact, you will be amazed to discover that there are occasions when you don't even want the product or service you are about to purchase; you are merely acting out of habit! And so you will begin to save money without even trying.

2. Reformed and Informed with Reminders and Receipts

Imagine for a moment having badly leaking underground pipes supplying your domestic water needs. They still serve their purpose in that you still get water from your taps on demand when you require it but in such an unnecessarily wasteful manner that it is truly shocking. Or rather, it would be shocking if you realised the extent of your disregard for scarce resources. But of course all this leakage is taking place out of sight just below the surface and if, as is often the case, it has been going on unchecked for years you may not even be aware that there is a problem. Ignorance may be bliss but it certainly isn't cheap. Being disorganised is a bit like the leaky pipes scenario because although you still get things done you do so in a clumsy and inefficient manner which costs you dearly in time and money. For instance, if you are not diligent about keeping receipts there will be times when you are unable to return goods which are either faulty or which you've decided you don't require as you will have no proof of purchase. Equally you will not be able to cross check receipts from different shops as a reminder of where you picked up the best value on a certain product. If you go to the supermarket without checking what you need and writing it down before leaving the house you will arrive home with items you didn't need while having forgotten others which were urgently required. Similarly, if you go into town with a dozen errands to run but without a list made out beforehand, the strong likelihood is you are going to forget some important task thus necessitating a second trip which, had you been organised in the first instance, was completely avoidable.

Forgetting appointments or deadlines is expensive; believe me, I should know, I'd forget my own head if it wasn't tied on. So if you are anything like me it will pay handsome dividends to put more effort into planning. Thankfully, nowadays this task is made so much more convenient as we can save all our lists on our mobile phones and also set alarmed reminders for important 'things to do'. I still reckon I'll be late for my own funeral though as I'm unlikely to hear the alarm going off. Oh well, nothing is fool proof I suppose.

3. Introducing the new Minister for Finance

Just as Michael Noonan is charged with the unenviable task of balancing the books of Ireland Inc., you are Minister for Finance of your own fiefdom. You – together with your better half, if you have one – are responsible for the health or otherwise of your household income and expenditure balance sheet. You may be helped or hindered in this regard by your cabinet colleagues (other family members), so one of your first tasks should be to call a cabinet meeting to draw up a household budget. This budget needs to be as detailed as possible and the spending record you have been keeping will be of great assistance here. Having an extensive record of all income minus expenditure – regardless of whether you are in the red or black – puts you in a far stronger financial position than before because now you are well informed about your monetary health and as we all know, information is power. Presumably you now wish to proceed by widening the gap between income and expenditure in your own favour. As you endeavour to improve the balance sheet of your 'nation' by implementing tough new policies, it is important to keep your cabinet colleagues well briefed in advance of any changes and to encourage regular discussion and debate highlighting the merits of your plans. This is especially advisable in a coalition marriage where the two party leaders have ideologically divergent fiscal viewpoints. Finally, as head honcho for finance the buck stops with you: with great power comes great responsibility – so no excuses, get your house in order!

4. Going Up In Smoke

While the list of reasons for giving up smoking are obvious and so well documented that it may seem unnecessarily repetitive to regurgitate them here, the benefits of quitting are so significant and life-giving that, at the risk of boring you, I will repeat just some of them:

(a) You'll make €3,600 per year in direct savings (assuming you're a twenty a day man)
(b) You'll likely save yourself tens of thousands in prevented medical expenses
(c) Your insurance premiums can be drastically reduced
(d) You won't be damaging anyone else's health, like your wife's or children's, for example (nothing like a bit of emotional blackmail if all else fails)
(e) You'll be more attractive to the opposite sex with better skin, hair, teeth, breath, nails etc.

Anyway, the list is endless. I could write a whole book full of reasons to quit and people have already done exactly that so get hold of one of those books if you need to but even the few reasons I've mentioned above should be more than adequate motivation. If you seriously want or need to save money then this has to be your number one priority. Look, I know it's an addiction that's difficult to break (isn't every habit), but get whatever help you need: self-help books, nicotine patches, hypnosis, meditation, counselling – whatever works for you. Leave no stone unturned in your quest. Make quitting your new addiction. Just do it. There is no more obvious, timeless or beneficial way to make such substantial savings; it's the ultimate 'no-brainer'. A couple of final points for those who still claim they'd love to give up smoking but can't – and I know this probably includes every smoker over the age of 25:

1. Every smoker who ever successfully quit (there are many millions of members of this club, incidentally) once believed the same thing with just as much conviction as you do now.

2. There is no such thing as 'can't'. When people say 'can't' you'll find what they mean is 'won't'. If you could tot up all the direct and indirect costs of smoking such as lost earnings and medications necessitated through smoking related illness; lost productivity in the work place due to interruptions for 'fag breaks'; increased risk of fire in your home; penal insurance premiums; damage to clothing and furniture from burn marks and so on and so on you would likely discover that your smoking habit is, over a lifetime, costing you more than €10,000 per annum at today's rates. That's more than the cost of your mortgage for many of you. Surely you have to agree that this is too high a price to pay for a single, simple habit which you would rather not have in the first place. And that is without factoring in the value of the ten years or so of life which you can expect to be deprived of if you don't quit.

5. Soft in the Head

Carbonated drinks or 'Soft drinks' as they are usually known are anything but 'soft'. In fact you'd want to be soft in the head to pay out good money for this shit! To illustrate my point I have listed below the ingredients as printed on the labels of the three most popular brands sold in Ireland:

Coca-Cola: Carbonated water, Sugar, Colour (caramel E150d), Phosphoric acid, natural flavourings including caffeine. Lucozade: Carbonated water, Glucose syrup (25%), Citric acid, Lactic acid flavouring, Preservatives (potassium sorbate, sodium bisulphite), Caffeine (0.012%), Antioxidant (ascorbic acid), Colour (sunset yellow) sunset yellow may have an adverse effect on activity and attention in children. Red-Bull: Water, Sucrose, Glucose, Acidity Regulator (Sodium Citrates, Magnesium Carbonate), Carbon Dioxide, Acidifier Citric acid, Taurine (0.4%), Caffeine (0.03%), Glucuronolactone, Inositol, Vitamins (Niacin, Pantothenic acid, B6, B12), Flavourings, Colours (Caramel, Riboflavin)

It isn't a pretty picture is it? Christ, if they are prepared to admit on the label that their own product 'may have an adverse effect on activity and attention in children', can we even begin to imagine the horror of what the reality might be? Now I'm not a laboratory chemist but you'd have to be a couple of sandwiches short of a picnic not to realise that these beauties are not good news for your health. If you're still not convinced you should Google a random selection of the listed ingredients and see what comes up. I did and it was a bit of an eye opener. Take phosphoric acid, for example. Apparently this little gem is used as a rust remover and can also be found in such products as detergents, fertilisers and industrial cleaners. I could go on and on, but I won't; you get the gist of what I'm suggesting; this crap is seriously damaging to your health so you shouldn't drink it even if you got it for free (because prevention is cheaper than cure), let alone shelling out hard earned money for it. Carbonated soft drinks should rightfully be called fizzy, sugary water with a dash of rust remover.

6. Liquidising your Assets

Alcohol! Where do I even begin with the reasons to stay away from this troublemaker? The problems associated with alcohol abuse in this country are legendary so this point doesn't need elaborating on. But in case you've just woken from a coma and haven't seen a newspaper in the last fifty years, alcohol is implicated in pretty much every kind of physical, psychological, emotional and social ill you could care to think of. The consumption of alcoholic drink is a major contributor to everything from our road accidents, suicide figures, domestic violence, unwanted pregnancies; patients with heart problems, cancers, liver cirrhosis, you name it, clogging up an already overburdened national health service.

The road safety adverts tell us that even one drink impairs your ability to drive safely and responsibly. That being the case, it's logical to assume it impairs your ability to do just about everything else as well. Not to mention the fact that it is ridiculously expensive. It also costs indirectly in so many other ways. On a typical booze-fuelled night on the tear you'll quite likely shell out for taxis and fast food that you otherwise would not need or want. Are you one of those who, while under the influence, buys drinks for fellas that you wouldn't cross the road to talk to the next day? If you're a smoker – which of course any reader of this book has no business being – you will go through the fags like there's no tomorrow while inebriated. Did I mention lost workdays due to hangovers? So look, it's another no-brainer; you are already out of your mind if you're getting out of your mind on drink week in week out. With the possible exception of the odd glass of cheap red at home for medicinal purposes, forget alcohol. You don't need it; there are plenty of less harmful ways to get a natural high. Now I do appreciate that anyone reading this who knows me personally will be laughing merrily to themselves at my hypocrisy. Hey what can I say: 'there's none so pure as a (semi) reformed whore'. At least readers can be reassured that my advice here is coming from a well of deep, personal knowledge.

Having said all that it must be acknowledged that alcohol has had a number of positives going for it, not least of which is the fact that it has been helping ugly people have sex since about 4500BC, but while propagation of the species may have been a good excuse for wine bibbing in the past, there are plenty of less expensive and less damaging ways to paint a more complementary image of yourself to the fairer sex nowadays, if you are 'no oil painting' as they say. There are dating websites and innumerable social media outlets to name just a couple. Beauty may well be in the eye of the 'beer holder' but what's the point if you can't recall any of it the next day?

7. Caffeine Fix

It's very trendy at the moment to bash tea and coffee drinking on health grounds. There seems to be conflicting evidence as to the good or ill of partaking of these beverages. Anyway, for our purposes here, we don't need to wade through all the contradictory evidences to figure out if my daily cuppa is slowly poisoning me. Suffice to say that even for a tight bastard a tea bag or a spoon of coffee doesn't cost much, so I think it's a luxury we can stretch to. Now, that's all good and well as long as you stick to getting your fix at home. The problem arises when you go into a café or pick up a take away coffee.

Can somebody please explain to me in the name of all that's holy, how can something which costs five cents to brew at home suddenly cost €3 or more in a coffee shop? That's like a 6,000% mark up or something! And don't give me all that waffle about labour costs and rent and blah de blah. Most businesses operate on anything from a 10% to 50% margin with slower selling goods attracting the higher margins. It's not like coffee is a slow seller either. The only product in the whole world that we're guzzling more of is oil. Yes Sirree Bob, oil and coffee; that's what's powering all our engines these days.

Bad value and all as the café is at least you get a bit of comfort in there and you can fantasize about your waitress, naughty little Magda from Warsaw while you sip your frothy little frapochinio or whatever it's called. But what really wrecks my bulb is the explosion in the popularity of this 'coffee-to-go' lark. I mean, I just don't get it! You pay €2 for an Americano to go (I know where I'd like every feckin' Americano to go) and then you have to immediately leave the premises and go back out into the wind and rain to drink it. How the hell can that be relaxing or enjoyable? Or maybe you pull into a motorway service station for a caffeine fix on a long journey. Back on the road there you are doing eighty, about to enjoy a piping hot drink – which comes in a flimsy paper cup by the way because the extortionate price doesn't stretch to a decent container – most likely with a twirl in your other hand because, like you know, it was 'on offer' with the coffee. Now picture the position of any male driver – yes they're always male, why? Because women always have time to stop for a chat with their coffee! Anyway there you are coffee in one hand, twirl in the other and guess where it's all going to land? Yep. All over your white chinos and cream leather seats! Once again, my advice is: don't bother; a bleedin' money lender's rates begin to look attractive next to a caffeine pusher's mark up. A little delayed gratification is a wonderful thing. Wait until you get home, put the feet up and enjoy a virtually free, self-satisfied cuppa. You can of course enjoy completely healthy, organic 'tea' for nothing – bar the price of boiling the kettle – if you gather your own leaves of dandelion, mint, elderberry and so on for a wildly refreshing cup of decaf.

8. Free to Go

If you really are a chronic caffeine addict of a calibre to compete with yours truly and you insist that sometimes you just can't hang in there for your fix 'til you get home you still shouldn't pay €1.50 to €2.50 for a takeaway tea or coffee. Make sure you keep a few teabags or small jar of coffee, whichever is your particular poison, stashed in the glove box or elsewhere. Then, when you feel the urge you can just pull into a service station or other shop, fill a takeaway cup with hot water and ask at the counter what you owe them for it. More often than not they will let you off without charging you anything. Sometimes you might have to pay a nominal charge of between twenty and fifty cents but either way you'll make a decent saving. If for example you buy only one take away hot drink per day, on average, putting this tip into action should save you €550 per year at a very conservative estimate.

9. Feeling Fruity

What could possibly be wrong with buying something as harmless as a fruit juice or smoothie? Granted, having a juice with your lunch would be a big improvement on washing it down with a pint or a coke but even here a lot of the brands you buy are laced with sugar and other crap. Even if you opt for a brand with no additives the jury is out as to the benefits or otherwise. Some theories suggest that because the juice of the fruit is where the sugar is heavily concentrated, coupled with the fact that a typical fruit juice drink will contain numerous pieces of fruit, this renders even natural fruit juice yet another sugar sweetened drink. You also miss out on the soluble fibre (slows down the body's absorption of sugar) contained in fruit when you only drink the juice. My conclusion then is to forget the juice, just eat an apple instead; it'll be a lot better for your body, your pocket and the planet (no packaging to worry about). Incidentally, that last point reminds me you'll also cut down on refuse charges.

10. The Milky Way

Infants and young children clearly require milk in their formative years but like our primate cousins and all other mammals for that matter, there comes a point at which we are supposed to be weaned. We humans are the only animals which continue to drink milk into adulthood and even old age. Come to think of it we're the only ones which drink the milk of an animal species other than our own, too. Out of about 4,600 mammal species on earth we are the only ones indulging in these two practices. Let's suppose a survey were conducted with 4,600 participants. There was only one question with only two possible answers X or Y. What if you were the only participant to think Y was correct? Add to this the fact that you were the only participant whose opinion had been influenced by vested interests (Corporations and Governments). I think it would be safe to assume that you were wrong with a capital W. So whether you're an adult horse, hyena, hamster or homosapien, sorry, but you should be weaned by now. You should only be drinking water at this stage.

11. Plant Milks

What the feck are plant milks? You might well ask! There's no such thing. If it doesn't come from an animal's tits then it isn't milk. What I am referring to here are products such as Rice, Soya and Almond milks to name a few. Calling these products milk is just a clever marketing ploy, capitalising as it does on the suspect public perception of milk as a wholesome, healthy and nutritious drink. These drinks aren't perhaps any harm to your health, provided they don't contain any of the usual crap like salt, sugar, preservatives etc. But it's a bit ridiculous to be paying good money for them.

I went for a little excursion around the supermarket aisles to take a look at some of these products. They generally come in 1litre cartons and cost between €2 and €3. One soya milk product I looked at contained only soya and water, so far so good, but the soya content was only 3.5%, meaning – as any ten year old will tell you – that it was 96.5% water. Now if I took some white paint and some black paint, mixed them at a ratio of 96.5 parts black to 3.5 parts white and then painted my house with the result what would I get? Well I'm no genius and I'm no bloody painter either but I can categorically tell you I wouldn't end up with a white feckin' house that's for sure. I would probably end up with a house which was the darkest shade of grey and looked black to the naked eye. So the soya product in our example should be called 'water with a hint of soya flavouring'. At €2.40 a pop that's a pretty bloody expensive hint. I use this company as an example because their product was the most ethical and honest I could find. They didn't add any crap to their product and they gave us the full percentage compliment of ingredients on the pack. This is extremely rare in the marketplace. They are to be commended as they've given you all the facts, so it's not their fault if you still want to throw your money away. Look, if you really feel you must have these products in your diet buy the raw material, blend them all together and enjoy. You will get a hell of a lot of soya or rice for €2.40 after all. An added bonus I discovered when I made my own 'almond milk' was the self-satisfied feeling I got. It's a bit like the superior feeling you get eating a fish you've caught yourself or if you were ever in the boy scouts and had to light a fire without matches, that kind of thing. My guess is it appeals to some dormant hunter/gatherer instinct deep within.

12. Water is Life

By process of elimination then we are left with only one drink which it makes any sense to consume: Water. Besides, 80% to 99% of the content of all liquid consumed is made up of water anyway. Of course you can spend just as much money on water these days as on anything else. When I was a wee ankle biter the mere suggestion of selling water would have resulted in your being carted off to the looney bin. Such is the power and ingenuity of the marketing moguls that we no longer bat an eyelid. In fact, our way of thinking on this issue has been completely reversed and you'll now get many a raised eyebrow for drinking this stuff straight from your tap. I have to admit to a begrudging admiration of our corporate governors for this achievement. My point is simple as always: buying bottled water was ridiculous thirty years ago and it's still just as ridiculous today. Now I know the Health Police out there will jump down my throat, giving me chapter and verse on the contaminants to be found in tap water, some of which, chlorine and fluoride for instance, are added deliberately and rubberstamped by our puppet politicians. Their arguments can be very good and well worth hearing but buying this stuff bottled won't save you from the contaminants; it'll likely only add a few more as the chemicals leak from the plastic bottle it comes in straight into the water. One estimate I've read puts our consumption of plastic bottled water at 200 billion worldwide, annually. Jesus Christ above! Enough already; go out and get a good water filtration system if you must but stop buying water. You'll save your pocket and the planet big time.

So there you have it in a nutshell. Any money you spend on beverages of any kind is completely unnecessary and probably harmful to you and the environment into the bargain. I do realise of course that if you are in the longstanding habit of drinking anything but water every day, you have become addicted to whatever your particular poison is. Thus your body and mind crave it and if you remove it all in one fell swoop every cell in your body will rebel with a ferocity not seen since Genghis Khan was on the war path. The trick is one step at a time; steady as she goes. Remember it is not natural for you to prefer soft drinks or any other drink to water. You only prefer it because of years of conditioning and training. You, with the help of the marketing and advertising gurus, have brainwashed or fooled your body and mind into thinking you prefer this sugary shit. You can retrain yourself to prefer water to other drinks. This reversal process is estimated to take as little as six weeks. It's the very same principal as training physically to get fit, except now we are training psychologically and emotionally. So, as with physical exercise, it is difficult at first to establish a routine and to change old habits but it does get easier as you go along, then one day you will discover that buying a bottle of coke holds no attraction for you and isn't worth the price or effort of bothering. If it helps, initially you can add a slice of lemon, lime or some mint leaves to your water for a bit of added flavour.

13. Bring a Packed Lunch

Pack your lunch for work instead of eating out. The benefits of this advice are obviously even greater when applied to family days out. Hell, just get into the habit of packing your grub and bringing it with you wherever you're going. Again forming this little habit can save you thousands per annum. Let's look at an example: say you work on average four days a week for fifty weeks a year and you normally eat out, costing, let's say, a conservative round figure of a tenner a time. By dusting off the old lunch box you will have clawed back €2,000 or as near as makes no difference in just one year. Also you have the not insignificant advantage of knowing and being in control of exactly what you are eating thereby giving you potential further savings in health benefits for the future.

14. Ye Can't Beat a Good Brekkie

It is often said that breakfast is the most important meal of the day. It's true, so don't skip it in the morning rush to get out the door. A good hearty feed of porridge or muesli with generous helpings of fruit and nuts will give you the energy to conquer your metaphorical daily Everest. In fact it's not widely acknowledged, but porridge was the secret weapon we used against the Brits to win the war of independence. If they had introduced us a little earlier to their sugary processed morning cereals we'd still be under the cosh. In fact if you compare the demise of the British Empire with the rise of a certain English corporation (beginning with K) who mass produce processed, additive-laced breakfasts, you'll find the two running in tandem, no word of a lie. Now that which can bring the world's greatest colonial power to its knees can't be much good for you or me so stick to a good wholesome breakfast and you'll be ready for anything. You can even skip the midday refuelling if you forget to bring the lunchbox; you'll have enough in the tank to tide you over 'til evening.

15. Develop an Adventurous Palette

You've probably heard the chef's maxim 'Eat what's in season'. Well, I've adapted that to 'Eat what's on offer' – the two will often be one and the same anyway. Instead of being boring and zombie-like, buying the same foodstuffs week in week out, make a decision to base your shopping around the special deals in store. One silver lining in the current dark cloud of recessionary Ireland is that there are plenty of special offers out there competing for your euro. So if pineapples are 'going for a song' this week include them in your fruit choices and if it's pears next week then let them be your preferred option. Apply the same principle to your meat and veg and so on. Initially you will be arriving home with what the family considers some weird food items but make a game of it; be creative and adventurous. Experiment with some new dishes that would astonish Jamie Oliver himself. The added bonus here is that you will end up with a more varied diet which should be healthier – and besides, they do say variety is the spice of life!

16. Don't go Shopping on an Empty Stomach

It has been well documented that the hungrier you are when you go shopping the more you will buy. Shopping on an empty stomach will cause you to suffer from 'the eyes are bigger than the stomach' syndrome so have a good feed before you leave the house. If this is not possible at least throw back a pint of water to fool the body and mind temporarily into thinking it is full.

17. Fast Days

There is a growing school of thought in the scientific community that having one or two fast days per week is beneficial to your health. The science behind this notion is not fully understood yet and research is on-going. You can Google away to your heart's content to find out about scientific work being done in this area, but here's the lay man's logic. It makes perfect sense to me that we as a species should have developed in such a way as to benefit from days of abstinence from food. I mean, when the caveman went off in search of food I presume it was a bit of a hit and miss affair as to whether or not he brought home the bacon so to speak; as a result I think it's safe to assume that intermittent fast days were a naturally occurring part of his lifestyle. Our bodies then should have developed to take account of this situation and still today be adapted to benefit from this cycle. Isn't that brilliant then in its simplicity; we can cut out eating on one or two days per week and benefit our health while saving money at the same time.

21

Now of course it goes without saying but I'll say it anyway, you have to use the bit of common sense God gave ya with this and all other advice. If you are underweight already it mightn't be the smartest move in the world to go fasting or, if you are on medication, you might want to have a chat with the auld Doc first. Actually, an interesting article I read recently states that during the great 1930's depression in America, to add to their woes the people were afflicted by severe drought resulting in unintended fasting being forced upon large sections of the population. Now anybody would think that during such hardship life expectancy would drop, but no, it actually increased by as much as six years! Now, there's a little food for thought for you, as you stuff your face for the fifth time today. Certainly the idea of fasting has traditionally been important to many of the major world religions. We may have thrown the baby out with the bathwater, as usual, when we rebelled against the church. Whatever you think about 'God' it seems the church had a few medically sound beliefs, what with fish on Fridays and fast days.

18. Stop Gobbling the Gob Stuff

Now I don't have a sweet tooth myself. I have, in fact, the full complement – a whole mouthful of sweet teeth. In other words I'm a bit too partial to the old chocolate and other confectionary that my old man liked to refer to under the suitable umbrella term of 'Gob stuff'. Added to this affliction is the fact that like that other great wit, Oscar Wilde, I can resist anything except temptation, leading me to a common modern day dilemma: how to curb my intake of 'Gob stuff'. Of course the simplest method is to make sure you don't have any in the house but, if like me you find that to be a tad extreme (after all, a little of what you fancy is a good motto), there is another little trick you can employ which I find helps cut down my intake. Keep the gob stuff out of easy reach, just like you might do with a child. Employ the same tactics against yourself. Certainly keep it out of sight for out of sight often means out of mind. But go a little step further than this. Gob stuff is usually kept with other foodstuffs in some kitchen press or other for handiness; our objective here however is the opposite of handiness; we want to make it somewhat inconvenient to reach for that chocolate chip cookie to go with your cuppa. So I suggest keeping your stash of nibbles upstairs in some drawer or at the back of some shelf which is hardest reached. That way if you have a desperate craving you can have your fix for the sake of world peace, but if you only have a mild urge presumably you won't bother until the desire reaches some critical volcanic level. Even if this plan only reduces your consumption levels by a small amount it's a step in the right direction. If nothing else it can drastically reduce the amount of crap your bottomless pit teenagers go through each week, especially if you make sure your supply is strictly rationed by keeping it under lock and key in that upstairs hideaway. Even if the plan doesn't work as intended you'll be burning off the excess calories with all that running up and down the stairs.

19. Check your Receipt

Remember, before you leave any shop double check your receipt. I have noticed from personal experience that   .

supermarkets and other retail outlets make errors at the till with alarming regularity and interestingly enough, almost always in their own favour. You are especially vulnerable to this problem when you have discounted items in your shopping (which you will always have from now on of course). Sometimes the shop has not changed their system to take account of the new pricing. So scrutinise your receipt before walking away from the counter.

20. Check your Change

You should of course always check your change immediately after any financial transaction, not just because of the obvious possibility that the shop assistant, being human, may have made a mistake at your expense but also for any foreign bodies in there. There are numerous coins around the world which are similar in appearance to our own euro currency and they almost always have a far lesser face value. The most commonly occurring of these is the British penny, which is superficially similar to our five cent piece, but has only 25% to 30% of the value. Now if you get caught out with a penny instead of a five cent piece that wouldn't make or break even a Cavan man's day, but there are some other coins which turn up in Irish tills masquerading in particular as €2 coins. These include, but are not limited to, the Philippine 10 Peso coin, the Egyptian Pound (value 12c-13c approx.), the Mexican 5 Peso (value approx. 28c), Turkish 1 New Lira (value approx. 50c, this one is apparently out of official circulation since 2008) and last but not least the 10 Thai Baht (value approx. 22c-25c). Some of these, particularly the last one mentioned are uncannily like the €2 coin, even being accepted in vending machines as €2. You have been warned; cast a cold eye over your coins.

21. Forget Brand and Customer Loyalty

The multinational corporations and the major supermarket chains they supply serve only one master: the shareholder. With no morals or ethics whatsoever, they exist for one reason and one reason only: profit. In an ideal world we would have nothing to do with them but they seem to have become a necessary evil. Do not listen to any of the claptrap they come out with about being part of the community, wanting to serve you, creating local jobs, supporting this and that, blah de blah: it's all just clever marketing. Their sole aim is to part you from as much of your hard earned cash as possible. Therefore your goal when dealing with them is to go into battle like David facing his Goliath and extract the goods you require from the monolith whilst parting with as little cash as possible. Treat it as you would a game of chess. Employ cunning and careful consideration; know that you are dealing with a very intelligent and sophisticated (albeit ethically bankrupt) enemy who is out to trip you up at every turn. You should be concerned with only three things when purchasing any food item:

(A) What are the ingredients? In other words when you cut through all the marketing bull, what's in it? What am I actually buying?

(B) What price is it? Is it the best value for money available or can I get an equivalent product cheaper elsewhere?

(C) Will it actually be eaten or is it likely to be left to rot in the bottom of the fridge and then dumped?

22. Off Their Trolley

When walking through shopping centre car parks keep a keen eye peeled for abandoned trolleys. Closer inspection may reveal a euro coin has been left in it and if you return it to the trolley bay you can legitimately claim it as your reward. I'm not sure why people leave these euro coins behind when shopping, perhaps they are in a mad rush or maybe they're just lazy sods, who knows? Ours is not to ask but just to wonder why, eh! Regardless, their reason is not important; all you need to know is that these coins are there very occasionally for the taking.

23. Shop Around

Don't do your entire shopping under one roof. No one supermarket is cheapest on every product, supplies the best quality in every area or has all the best special offers in a given week. In other words the term *super*market is a misnomer. There is no such thing. Their first deceit is in the very name they go by. Check out all the major (and minor) players and extract the best value from each. Having said that, if you are not doing a sizeable portion of your shopping in Lidl or Aldi you are spending far more every week than you need to on groceries.

24. Be Prepared

This is the scout's motto and a wise maxim they chose too. Your kitchen cupboards and freezer should suggest to a casual visitor who looks in them that you are expecting a 1940's style emergency to be declared all over again any day now. In other words, you should be extremely well stocked up with dry and tinned foods that won't go off for years such as tinned fish and beans as well as brown rice and pasta. In the freezer you should have a supply of frozen meat, veg and homemade wholemeal bread. This way you erase any risk of having to make unnecessary or unexpected trips to the shops with the attendant expenses and temptations which go with same. You will always have plenty of supplies to tide you over until you are ready to stock up again at a time and day of your choosing. You can consider this to be one tiny step towards your emancipation; reclaiming your time, finances and indeed life back from 'The Machine'.

25. Getting Caught Short

If, despite your best efforts, you find of a cold and wintery evening that you have run out of some essential item or other while preparing the dinner, begrudgingly you may decide a visit to the nearest (expensive) corner shop (a place you now normally avoid like the plague), is warranted. Don't be too hard on yourself; it happens to the most diligent of us. Only ensure to bring little more than the amount of money needed for that specific purchase, thus saving yourself the temptation of buying any unnecessary extras while you are there.

26. White is Shite

White bread, of the processed white sliced pan variety which sells by the truck load in every corner shop and supermarket in the land, has at best practically no nutritional content as pretty much all the vitamins, minerals and so on present in the original grains and other ingredients have been processed and bleached out of it. At worst it could be slowly poisoning you with all the chemicals and synthetic crap which has been added. Certainly the Swiss government are sufficiently concerned about its dangers to have levelled a tax on white bread with the money raised going to offset the cost of wholegrain breads to encourage a shift in that country's eating habits. If you are a regular consumer of those innocent looking fluffy white loafs I cannot stress strongly enough the value of doing a little research to reveal exactly what you and your family are bloating your guts with. Even the ingredients of so called healthy wholegrain breads deserve close scrutiny as many are little better than the white shite. The healthiest, tastiest and cheapest option is of course to bake your own thereby retaining full control and knowledge of what goes into it, while simultaneously saving a belly full of dough.

As research for this book I have just baked my first batch of brown bread (I have photos to prove it for those sceptics out there who knew the old me) and do you know what, it was a piece of cake! Now I must confess to having cheated slightly by using a packet of Aldi's brown bread mix (69c), but we all have to start somewhere, right? It turned out only mighty; edible even, if I do say so myself. The whole exercise was completely painless and hassle free, even for a total Muppet in the kitchen like me.

Now that I've got my first baking success under my belt (literally) and gained a bit of confidence sure there'll be no stopping me. I'll have to make the next one from scratch, eh! I was able to use some slightly sour milk which would otherwise have gone to the cat and my bread hitched a ride in the oven while another dish was cooking in there simultaneously so, the total cost of producing my 650grm loaf was 69c, a considerable saving on the €1.40 which is the cheapest price on the market for an equivalent product. There are further savings to be garnered here once I get the hang of it and besides what value can I put on the taste of the freshest piping hot brown bread straight from the oven, with butter melting on top, all washed down with a mug of Lidl's finest organic fair trade coffee (500grm, reduced from €5.99 to €3.99 for fair trade fortnight, so I stocked up). Now, that's what I call using me loaf – being a tight bastard isn't all sack cloth and ashes ye know!

27. Saving Organically

The idea of eating all organic food sounds great in theory, doesn't it? Who wouldn't want to sign up to this euphoric utopia? But all earthly utopias (as Karl Marx could testify if he graced us with his presence again) tend to come unstuck in the practical application. What image does the term 'organic' conjure up for you? Perhaps a rustic and ruddy, cheerful rural family living out their happy lives eating their home grown greens, veg and free range eggs? Well, something along those lines is the image that is peddled to us by those that like to charge twice or three times the price

– whilst almost never bothering with special offers – for their produce, just because it is labelled organic. You see, the term organic is equated with the words 'wholesome' and 'health-giving' to the point where, for most consumers, their vision is so blurred they can't tell the difference between them.

Organic in the agricultural sense means having been produced without the use of chemical pesticides or fertilisers. So, a buffalo living in the wild should be producing quality organic shite but you wouldn't want to eat it now, would you? Similarly, a rat living in some remote swamp would make for the finest of organic fare, but again I think we'd all pass. So organic is such a broad term that its use on food packaging renders it only slightly better than meaningless. It's the same trick that a lot of processed food producers like to use when they put the big banner headline across their product: 'No artificial additives'. This term has little beneficial meaning; it's just telling you that they've laced the food with all kinds of excessive amounts of cancer-causing and heart attack-inducing 'natural additives' like sugar and salt or worse. I mean to say, nicotine and cannabis are natural products and could be grown organically but that doesn't change the fact that they are lethal drugs. Unfortunately the old maxim, 'believe only half of what you see and none of what you hear', applies. The amounts of money and the vested interests at stake mean that you simply cannot believe what the marketing suggests you are being sold. For example, you will never ever see it stated on an organic chicken in the supermarket that it was processed in the same factory, using the same chemicals and bleach and so on as his even more unfortunate non-organic relatives which, in truth, is often the case. I strongly recommend Felicity Lawrence's book *'Not*

On The Label' if you want to learn more about real food production and supply standards. In the meantime if you want to eat what you understand by the term 'organic', I'm afraid you will have to produce it yourself. Besides why are people buying organic anyway? They hope it will help them to live longer healthier lives. Nothing wrong with that, but I'd say myself if we cut out the fags, alcohol, fizzy drinks and fudge cake we'd all be living to a hundred without having to bother our arse paying through the nose for supposedly life-giving, organic fare.

28. Living the Mean, Green Ethical Dream

In recent years it has become a very common marketing ploy to play on the customer's conscience by trying to suggest that he/she should purchase your product rather than the competition's because yours is more 'environmentally friendly'. Incredibly, this is cited as a reason even when trying to persuade you to buy a new car despite the one you have being in perfect working order! Now you don't have to have got an A1 in honours level Leaving Cert logic to realise what a load of disingenuous clap trap that is. The salesman will actually look you in the eye and with a with a straight face suggest that it is sound reasoning to scrap your perfectly working machine so that another, very similar one can be built in China and shipped half way around the world for you to purchase – and all in the honourable cause of saving the planet!

This reasoning is being used to sell us everything from detergents, holiday destinations and dry cleaning to dishwashers, dental treatments and doughnuts. Of course the unvarnished truth is that any product you care to purchase is by definition environmentally 'unfriendly' as they all require energy and finite sources to produce and distribute around the globe to the various markets. The straightforward, ethical and most environmentally sound thing to do regarding any product therefore is simply this: don't purchase it. How about that; it turns out that we tight bastards are also the saviours of planet earth, setting the good example for our less enlightened brethren to follow.

29. Eat Meat Sparingly

Now I'm no spokesman for the veggie brigade – it ain't natural – but neither is it natural to be putting away a whole cow every week. We are not carnivores and we are not herbivores. If we quickly refer back to that wise and unbiased advisor, 'Mother Nature' and our three hundred and fifty nearest and dearest relatives, 'The Primates' we easily conclude the obvious; we are omnivores and like most other animals in this category the bulk of our natural diet should be made up of non-meat items such as fruit, veg, seeds, nuts and so on. Meat, in other words, should play a part in our diet but a much smaller part than it currently does for the average punter. Red meat should be eaten even more sparingly, with the meat you do eat being biased in favour of fish (yes fish is meat because it sure as hell isn't a plant) and white meat. This is good news for the tight bastard because meat, particularly red meat such as steak, is probably the most expensive part of the weekly shop. I would suggest having two or three meat free days in the week. A bonus here for those of us not of a culinary disposition is that meat free dishes are generally easier and less time consuming to prepare and, after all, time is money.

30. Is Breast Best?

If you're an infant sucking on your mother's left one, breast is certainly best or, if you're ogling some beauty on a French beach it helps your viewing pleasure that she has a generous pair. But when it comes to chickens I'm not so sure; I'm a bit of a leg man myself. Seriously though, the Irish are obsessed with chicken breasts compared with lots of other countries where the thighs, legs and even wings are popular. Incidentally, have you ever wondered where all our processed chicken's feet go? Out to China where they are considered something of a delicacy served hot in soup dishes or as a bar snack to be washed down with a cold beer, that's where. Chicken breasts are scrumptious for sure but are they worth the premium you have to pay for them? The other cuts cost only a fraction of the price for the equivalent amount of meat. Try a little experimentation. The same suggestion applies to all meat products. Liver for example is cheap, nutritious and easy to cook. Ask your local butcher for advice about cheaper cuts of meat and how to prepare and cook them.

31. When Breast Really is Best

Now I am aware that I am a man; on top of that I am neither a nutritionist nor a paediatrician and as such, it's safe to assume I am not the world's authority on the pros and cons of breast feeding. I will just say however that from what we are told it is certainly the optimal choice from the infant's point of view. It will of course present the upwardly mobile adult with lots of challenges in today's still somewhat prudish society. Also I am assured that pre-weaned infants are not noted for their sensitivity to mothers tender bits so I won't claim breastfeeding to be a simple choice, but from a financial standpoint it makes sense dispensing as it does with the need for formula milk and bottle sterilisation. It also reduces considerably the plethora of paraphernalia you need to lug around when baby's in tow. The bond created between mother and child whilst breast feeding could not, I imagine, be overvalued either. Seeing as how I've never experienced the pain of a teething infant biting down hard on my swollen right nipple I'm not in a position to dictate to anyone which way they should go on this issue but any solution Mother Nature offers to a dilemma usually turns out to be the most practical, efficient, healthy and cost effective option. However I do give thanks for being born male when I reflect on such issues.

32. Solids Savings

Once the little nipple biter is on solids you can just feed the tiny tyke the leftovers from your own dinner, albeit blended of course. There's no need to be forking out for expensive branded baby foods that come with cute advertisements and colourful cartons featuring non-existent, perfect, airbrushed bambinos. Just remind yourself, people have been rearing infants successfully since long before cows or gates were heard of or catchy terms like 'infant formula' were coined – sounds like a maths equation, as if you had to be Pythagoras himself to feed a baby properly.

33. Disposable Savings

While we're on the subject of baby savings, I'll have to give a mention to the whole disposable -v- reusable nappy debate. Again, at the tender age of forty three, having never actually changed a nappy in my life, I am perhaps not in the best position to dispense advice here, but what the hell, I will anyway. It seems to me this conundrum can be restated simply as a time -v- money debate. Some people like to complicate things by throwing environmental issues into the mix as well but in truth, when it gets in the way of their convenience or pocket you'll find the vast majority of people couldn't give a crap about the environment. So what each individual needs to do is conduct a detailed cost benefit analysis of the issue to figure out if, for them, the extra costs of using disposables outweigh the time savings gained or vice versa. It is well worth taking some time over this and even implementing both options for a reasonable trial period to discover all the perks and pitfalls on both sides of the argument. Listening to other people's opinions is to be recommended but they will always be biased one way or the other, especially as this can be quite an emotive issue for many. I do realise I have somewhat oversimplified the decision being made and of course if you are a happy tree hugger you will no doubt factor that or any other pertinent points into the equation. Also it is sometimes forgotten in this debate that you don't have to come down squarely on one side over the other, you may well choose to have both varieties available for different times. Anyway the choice is yours, all I'm saying is there's a shitload of savings to be found here.

34. Baby's First Birthday

Will I let you in on a little secret? When your infant's first birthday comes around there's no need to bother with a party or a present. You see the thing is, he hasn't grasped the concept yet so he doesn't know it's his big day and therefore he won't be disappointed. Throw him a colourful cereal carton, he'll be just as happy and it'll keep him busy for hours. You'll probably get away with this next year as well, bless his little cotton socks! Naturally for the same reason, christening parties have absolutely nothing to do with the child and are all about expensive ego stoking and attention seeking for the parents, whilst providing an excuse for the extended family to pickle their livers in yet another alcoholic binge fest.

35. Raw Food

Some foods, such as carrots and onions for instance, can be just as enjoyable eaten raw as they are when cooked. Others like broccoli for example, whilst I wouldn't suggest eating them raw, can be cooked very sparingly. Prepared this way, you will benefit from the fact that these foods have retained more of their nutrients – much of which are lost in the cooking process – resulting in better value for money from the product. There will of course also be the resultant time saving with minimal preparation and washing up required and finally, further savings in reduced power supply costs.

36. For the Chop

It is a good trick to chop or grate foodstuffs into small pieces. This gives the impression that you've got more food on your plate than actually is the case thus reducing your overall consumption levels. For example, if you take a block of cheese and cut it into thick slices then you take another block of equal size and grate it into a pile on a second plate, which plate will appear to have more cheese? If you don't know try this experiment for yourself, it works.

37. Drink Up Your Veg

As vegetables lose quite a lot of their nutrient rich content in the cooking process don't throw the water you boiled them in down the drain. Allow it to cool and you will have a nutritious free drink packed with vitamins and minerals to have with your meal. A little experimentation will help to make these drinks somewhat tastier; for instance broccoli or cabbage juice on their own won't make for a very appetising drink but if you mix in a little sweetness in the form of say carrot or lemon juice it can be quite nice. An even simpler idea is to prepare the carrots and cabbage in the one pot in the first place. Everything new takes getting used to and if you ordinarily down a soft drink with your meal this suggestion will naturally appear revolting at first (and won't taste terribly appetising initially either), but I for one am convinced that there are very few drinks in the world more disgusting to your palette than that sugary, additive-laced crap they call coke. In a very short time you will retrain your taste buds and you will grow to enjoy these new nutrient rich beverages.

38. Cuban Wine Freeze

If you find yourself with an opened bottle of wine that has passed its desirable drinking point (this will vary greatly from individual to individual), pour the remainder into an ice cube tray and then freeze it. You can use it later to add a bit of extra flavour to sauces and casseroles.

39. One Will Do For 'Tea for Two'

If you are anything like my pre-thrifty self you will be in the habit of throwing two or more teabags in when making a pot of tea. This is unnecessary and done purely out of some long standing intergenerational habit. One tea bag will serve the very same purpose as two and if you like your tea a bit stronger, by just letting it stew a bit longer and maybe giving it a stir to extract a bit more flavour you will satisfactorily compensate for the lack of a second bag.

40. Optimal Boiling Amount

Only boil as much water as you are going to use. If you are only making one or two cups of tea, do not boil a full kettle of water. Yes I know I'm stating the obvious again but I guarantee you there are thousands out there who could benefit from this little nugget of uncommon sense.

41. Avoiding Food Wastage

It is estimated that the average household disposes of 30% of the food they buy, uneaten, costing them €1,000 per year. This is far too much. 10% is even too much. If you are one of these families you have huge scope for savings here. You should be aiming for 0% wastage. This I realise is an impossible target, but it should be our goal nonetheless. The first thing is to be careful about what you purchase in the first place; think about the week ahead whilst doing your shopping. What factors will affect the food you buy? For instance, will any family members be away this week therefore necessitating less food? Think about how you store your food at home. Can everything be found quite easily? No point in tucking something away so well that it'll not see the light of day for the next five years. Most important in all of this are the perishable items (almost 50% of salad leaves are thrown out uneaten). They should be seen at a glance when you open the fridge or press door. They should be almost jumping out at you shouting eat me, eat me! Ideally, if space allowed, things like fruit and veg would be kept refrigerated to extend their shelf life. Finally and most importantly, when thinking about preparing something to eat, have a thorough root around the kitchen, see what's in danger of being lost to the compost and base your meal choice around those ingredients. Develop this last point into an on-going habit and rest assured very little will go to waste.

42. 'Use by' Dates

While 'Use by' dates should not be ignored completely neither should they be a major factor when deciding to throw out uneaten food. If it looks, smells, feels and finally tastes alright then it probably is. Use your own judgement on this, always taking into account the type of product you're dealing with. A tin of beans, for example, may have a use by date a couple of years from the purchase date so if you find one at the back of your cupboard that's twelve months out of date, it'll be fine to eat. I'm currently working my way through a jar of Turmeric which was only recently rediscovered. It is ten years out of date and I have no ill effects to report. I also recently dusted off and devoured a jar of Thai green curry sauce I found hiding in the back of my press which was over a year out of date.

Obviously you would tread a bit more carefully with say the likes of eggs, although even with these I personally would chance eating them if they were a week past the date. Don't forget the powers that be are only too delighted to have you dump perfectly good food and then give them your hard earned money replacing it. A sceptic would think this was precisely the reason use by dates were introduced in the first place.

When buying perishables, make sure you select the item with the longest 'use by' date. You may have to do a little rummaging because these are usually stacked at the back of the shelf with shorter-dated stock to the fore. This will help with reducing that 30% food wastage figure as it will be less likely to go off before you get round to eating it. It is also advisable to remove plastic packaging from fruit and veg before storing. It will keep longer and is therefore more likely to be eaten rather than dumped.

43. Price your Products

Do you ever find yourself in a shop looking at an item you need to purchase but unsure whether the price is more or less than you paid for it the last time in another outlet? This can easily happen, particularly with those uncommon, occasional purchases. One way to reduce the incidence of this conundrum is to label your goods with their purchase price on the packaging as you put them away. This will help you commit prices to memory and even if you still can't recall a particular product price as you stand in the supermarket aisle scratching your solar panel, a quick phone call to her indoors will resolve the dilemma in two shakes of a lamb's tail.

44. You're for the Birds

If you go around spending hard earned cash on so called 'wild bird food' and then arriving home promptly scatter it around the garden for every crafty crow and vagrant of both furred and feathered variety to eat, I suggest you are for the birds yourself. Now I'm not saying you shouldn't feed our little feathered friends, by all means do. I enjoy watching their antics at feeding time myself, but there is no need whatsoever to buy food in especially for this purpose. We all have a certain amount of leftovers and food that goes off even after the dog and cat have had their fill which should suffice for the chirping mites. If you don't feel this is a sufficiently generous contribution you can always ask non bird loving family and friends to hold on to any stale cereal, rotten fruit and so on for you to take off their hands. This shouldn't be too much trouble, besides it'll cut down on their refuse charges too.

If you are really trying to emulate St Francis of Assisi you can take things a step further by propositioning some local greengrocers and food sellers of any kind to see if you can get a regular free supply of 'past it's sell by date' food. You never know, we live in such a throwaway society chances are some of it will even be fit for your own consumption. There's no reason to buy special feeders for the birds either, you can easily re-engineer other food containers for this purpose. I have a bean can swinging from my feeding station which allows small birds hop into it to feed whilst depriving magpies and the like from raiding its contents. Oh, by the way, if you are in the habit of feeding bread to the ducks and swans in the city park you shouldn't, it's probably the least nutritious food you could give them and damaging to their health. Why not bring along vegetable peelings and lettuce or other greens, chopped into small manageable pieces. They will also appreciate rice, peas or corn products which may be past their best. These foodstuffs will be far more nutritious for the birds and free for you to provide. Incidentally, you will have that priceless added benefit of feeling all superior and knowledgeable down at the local pond with your stash of natural food whilst all the other mammies and daddies are arriving with their toxic bags of poisonous white bread.

45. Fill your Freezer

As contradictory as it first sounds, a full fridge or freezer is easier on electricity than one which is empty or only half full, so fill them both up. If for any reason you can't fill them with food, perhaps you live alone, put in tubs of water to fill the excess space thereby reducing your electric bills.

If you don't already have one, invest in a freezer. This should not be seen as an unnecessary, expensive purchase but as an investment which will provide you with a steady regular return. Even if yours is only a small household of one or two people, the fridge-freezer in the kitchen may be adequate for the routine weekly supplies but now that you are reading this book you are going to need a separate freezer to take full advantage of all the bargains you will come across.

46. Buy in Bulk

Tread very carefully with this advice. It can be a great money saver but if you don't proceed with caution you could get burned. If you see an item which you normally buy selling at a generous discount, let's say half price, then you should consider buying in a bulk supply. But only buy what you are sure you can use. This is where use by dates can be a useful tool to gauge how long you've got to get through x amount of product. Let's say you normally go through one jar of sun dried tomatoes per week and they are on a 'buy one get one free' promotion this week and have eight months to their expiry date then mathematically speaking, you could afford to buy about thirty six jars and still have them all eaten inside their date. I would cut that back to thirty for safety. Beware though, this is a simplistic example regarding a product you always buy and have a fair idea how many you can get through. Obviously when dealing with less familiar products you can still take advantage, but only where the discount is large enough to justify the risk and even then only buy relatively small quantities.

If the items on offer are perishable we may still be able to bulk buy if they can be frozen. Even if it's something you don't normally freeze, like bread for example, it might still be an option. If there are non-perishable products which your household goes through a lot of, and you rarely if ever see them on offer, you should approach the manager offering to make a bulk purchase in return for a decent discount.

47. The Lone Ranger

If you live alone you can bulk buy long life items the same as anyone else but taking advantage of offers on more perishable goods will be trickier. It may be a good idea for the Lone Ranger to team up with Tonto and ride out to the supermarket together, pooling resources to take advantage of any bargains. In other words two single near neighbours can get together for the weekly shopping expedition, sharing transportation and splitting certain bulk purchases for their mutual gain. Take spuds for example, usually the most economical way to buy these is by the 10kg bag, but for a single person trying to get through this amount before they pass their best could present quite a challenge. This is where the single friend comes in. You split the cost and the spuds between you. This approach to your shopping can also have the effect of turning a boring weekly chore into a pleasant social outing.

48. The Recommended Amount

Use only a fraction of the manufacturers recommended amount of anything. From washing powder to mouthwash, you often have a guideline amount of product you are advised to use somewhere on the packaging. Quite a lot of you out there follow this advice unthinkingly like good little auto-morons. But hold on a minute, who is giving this advice? None other than the multinational manufacturer, and what have we discovered his sole purpose in life is? That's right, profit! This guy's advice is hardly what you would call impartial, is it? How better to maximise profits than to have people use twice the amount of product they need just because you 'advised' them to on the packaging. It's beautiful in its simplicity. So from now on you should experiment to see how much product you really need to do the job. I can assure you it is almost always less than half the 'recommended amount' and often a good deal less than that.

49. Watering down your Waste

Every liquid product you have in your house is probably at least 90% water, right? Everything from your washing up liquid to bottles of wine, household cleaners, mouthwash, cooking oils and so on. This being the case it can't do any harm to add another little drop of water yourself to all these products to bulk them up a bit and extend their lifespan. You will notice when you frequent the jacks of many bars and culinary establishments that this thrifty trick is already deployed successfully with their hand wash. You will register the 'liquid soap' in these premises as being a bit more watery than expected, the end result for you is unchanged, but the business has curbed its costs a little. So start liquidising your domestic assets, just a smidgen to begin. Slowly you can push the boat out to see how far you can go before noticing a deterioration in quality. This liquidation plan should help solidify your savings over time.

50. Bring a List

Before going out on a shopping trip check your kitchen to see what's actually needed, make a list and then when in the shops stick to it. Sounds obvious and it is, but a lot of people don't do it. This is understandable; it's harder than it sounds. First excuse is 'Oh I'm in a rush, I don't have time to write out a list', which of course is nonsense. Being prepared will save you time and energy not to mention lowering the stress barometer. Then there's the necessary willpower needed when behind enemy lines (that's the supermarket to those of you who skipped the earlier points in this volume). Everything about the shopping experience from the music they're playing to the packaging and positioning of the goods is designed to make you deviate from your list and spend more than you planned. Beat them at their game of psychological warfare. Step back from the swiss roll and return to your list.

51. Leftovers

A large producer of table salt was once quoted as saying he didn't make much money from the salt that customers consumed but rather he had become a multi-millionaire because of the salt left behind on their plates. The moral of the story here is of course to be careful about portion sizes. Don't let your eyes be bigger than your stomach. Prepare and cook only what you think can reasonably be eaten. If you do prepare more than is needed for one meal, no panic, just re-do it for the next meal. For me stir-frying is your only man here, you can stir-fry just about anything. Do all in your power to eat everything you have prepared no matter how many meals it takes to keep reducing that 30% wastage figure we mentioned earlier. Do not under any circumstances let any of your food end up in the bin destined for the tip head. If when all is said and done, you are left with food that is genuinely past fit for human consumption find some poor creature who will be glad of it. There must be a dog or cat somewhere that'll eat it? Or the birds? Crows don't turn their nose up at much in fairness! There's a pony up the road from us who is very glad of any vegetable peelings and so on that'll break the monotony of his usual fare.

52. Don't 'invest' in a Dishwasher

In theory they sound like manna from heaven and I wish to God they did what the name implied, even semi-efficiently. The idea is blissful: after the Sunday roast you bung everything in this machine and hey presto, all the dishes are sparkling clean! Unfortunately as most of you are aware, it doesn't quite work like that. Dishwashers seem to come in only one poorly thought out standard design and size which does not cater anything like adequately for the load after a half decent family meal. Every time you try to fill it with a load it's like trying to arm wrestle an octopus as you attempt to get the optimal use out of the inadequate space and design provided. You are left scratching your head wondering which pots and pans to prioritise and which you should just leave for hand washing. On top of this the wash cycle seems to go on for hours, leaving you worried about how much you've added to your next electric bill and guilty about how many polar bears deaths you're responsible for. Why it takes so long to wash a few dishes is a mystery to me. Added to all this – in the case of our machine at least – its cleaning abilities are roughly on a par with those of a ten year old. So you have to re-wash some of the dishes again plus you have to dry all of them. I will continue to dream of the day when someone will come up with a dishwasher which 'does exactly what it says on the tin'. In the meantime however I will not be replacing ours when it finally calves from lack of use. After all, as my old teacher, Joe May would wisely say: 'fool me once shame on you, fool me twice shame on me'.

53. No Need to Tumble Dry

It should be possible for most people to do without a tumble dryer. Once you are a little bit organised it's easy enough to have clothes washing, drying and ready to wear in a regular cycle without the aid of this machine. On a fine, breezy east-Galway day sure your clothes will dry nearly as quickly on the line and they'll feel and smell fresher too. Anyway, even on wet days, any time advantage accrued by use of the dryer will be lost in the extra ironing that will be needed for clothes dried in this way. Your clothes will also have a shorter lifespan as a result of the wear and tear from the tumble dryer. So unless you're holed up in a three room cottage in rain soaked Connemara with six or more urchins to clothe, save yourself the purchase price, service call out charges and the hefty electricity usage of these ice cap melters.

54. Don't Apply the Insurance

When buying domestic appliances you will no doubt be offered an insurance package to go with the product, for a sizeable extra fee of course. Do not be tempted. At best it will represent very poor value for money, at worst you will be paying for guarantees which you already have under current EU consumer law. Remember, all electrical appliances should come with at least a one year guarantee as standard (some come with more) so be sure to query this point in the haggling process. It is worth noting here that Lidl and Aldi generally offer a three year guarantee on their weekly promotional products which include, but are by no means limited to, electrical appliances. Any manufacturer of an expensive appliance such as a washing machine should be happy to guarantee it for several years at no extra charge, after all if he has any faith in the quality of his own merchandise he won't expect such a guarantee to cost him a penny now, will he?

This practice of offering insurance as an extra add-on with your appliance purchase is a typical example of the fried rice syndrome. At least it is an avoidable one, so steer clear. You might in some circumstances be able to turn this underhanded alliance between retailers and insurers to your advantage – an over eager commission-based sales man may be willing to offer you a discount on your purchase in return for you signing up to the insurance plan. If so you can agree but make sure there is a cooling off period with the contract so that once you have got the goods safely home at the reduced price you can contact the relevant party to inform them that, on mature reflection, you do not need the insurance after all and would like to cancel it for a full refund. Insurers by the way are legally obliged to provide this cooling off period for their products.

55. Insure a Reduced Premium

House and car insurance are, I have to begrudgingly accept, if you own such assets, unavoidable – at least if you value peace of mind. Apart from the usual haggling and shopping around there are a number of other measures worth considering when taking out insurance. Firstly, make sure you get quotes with a higher voluntary excess to see if this will reduce your premium. With car insurance you will, contrary to layman's logic, generally get a cheaper quote if you include your partner on the policy, regardless of whether she ever drives the vehicle or not. Also don't make the mistake of insuring your home for its market value; it should instead be covered for the rebuild cost which will be a lower figure (check the website www.scsi.ie for information on working out the figure for this).

56. Up the Pole

In the unfortunate event that you have to call out a repair or maintenance man for some domestic eventuality, you will of course shop around and get numerous quotes – and of course haggle to get the initial quote reduced. That is all good and to be applauded but make sure you include a couple of quotes from Polish nationals (and other foreign nationals if possible). Regretfully I have to say that on balance, you are likely to get a cheaper quote and have a more satisfactory outcome when employing a Polish tradesman or handyman for these small jobs. You can get a Polish/English dictionary if it helps. Regardless of who you finally choose for any job, even if it's your best drinking buddy, Barney or the brother-in-law who has lived across the road from you for the past twenty years, under no circumstances whatsoever should you pay in full before the work has been completed to your satisfaction. Employers do not pay employees at the start of the working week for obvious reasons.

57. Empty all the Contents

This point ties in nicely with a previous one about leftovers, in fact, you could accuse me of making the same point twice but it is in a different context and so could be overlooked. When you have squeezed with all your might on that toothpaste or moisturiser tube and cannot extract any more whatsoever, there is still plenty in there. Cut open the tube to get the very last of the product out.

58. Reduced to Clear

Certain supermarkets and others have a section in the shop for goods that are reduced to clear, in other words this is their last attempt to sell them before they are dumped to make way for new stock. These goods 'use by' date is about to expire and sometimes they're not worth bothering with but often the products are fine and can, albeit rarely, carry reductions of up to 90%. I've been known in the recent past to pick up a gateaux swiss roll for twelve cents or a bunch of grapes for fifteen cents. As with all things that sound too good to be true there is a catch. Discounts of that magnitude are quickly snapped up. You need to do a little homework to know when and where to pounce on these bargains. This is not a precise science, you will have to remain vigilant and conduct your own research in your local area.

59. Reduce the Frequency

Every time you go shopping you spend money and if we're honest, every time we go shopping most of us buy things we never intended to. We often buy things we never knew we needed; indeed most of us will have bought stuff we never knew existed at one point or another. We've already talked about some of the ways to combat this problem but you'd want to be a saint in shoe-leather traipsing around the aisles not to succumb to temptation occasionally.

A partial solution is simply to avoid putting ourselves in the way of temptation in the first place insofar as this is possible. If you are in the habit of going shopping weekly why not try pushing this out to every ten days or even fortnightly. This might create a few minor hic-cups towards the end of the two week period with regard to things like fresh fruit and veg but if you make optimal use of your refrigeration and freezer space, as well as being stocked up on tinned supplies like beans and fish, you'll hardly go hungry. Besides, what's rare is wonderful and you might actually find these trips relatively painless when they don't come around so often. You'll also claw back a few precious hours a month for yourself from this plan and which of us couldn't do with that? In addition, there will be the bonus savings on travel costs for most of you. So it's another no brainer; put it into action pronto – unless of course you enjoy dragging two screaming little ankle biters around Aldi on your afternoons off.

60. Sunday Shoppers

Putting the two words 'Sunday' and 'shopper' together should constitute a contradiction in terms. Once upon a time it did as all the shops were shut. I've said it before and I'll say it again, regardless of whether you're a card carrying atheist or not, religion did have its uses. Sundays should be a day for lie-ins and lovemaking; kicking a football about with the kids or your mates; putting your feet up with a nice cup of your favourite brew; falling asleep on the couch after a big feed of chicken in front of an old black and white movie, that sort of thing. If you're feeling energetic you could use it to paint the fence or mow the bloody grass. Maybe you're the real outdoors type, good for you, bring the family to the nearest beach or climb Croagh Patrick again for the day. But for the love and honour of God whatever you spend your Sundays doing, do not spend them sitting in traffic, fighting for a space in an underground urban car park or going shopping. If you truly are a sadist and this is your idea of a pleasant day out, you have six other days in the week, with late opening on some of those, to perform this irreverent ritual. Quit this practice and begin reaping the financial, matrimonial and psychological benefits immediately.

61. Northern Exposure

It's only a few short years ago since the euro almost reached parity with sterling, creating a mass exodus of bargain hunters from the republic to the north every weekend. These poor individuals who were just seeking a little respite from the never-ending upward spiral of boom-time prices were even labelled as 'unpatriotic' by some of their own politicians. Such ridiculous hysteria about a bit of weekend shopping seems hard to believe now that we've all come back down to earth with a bang.

At the moment there isn't enough of a difference in prices north and south of the border to create that kind of mass movement. Any savings you might make on certain products would be outweighed by the cost of the trip. Still, if you were to find yourself up north or close to it on some other business and with a little time to kill it could be worth your while checking out some of their shops for bargains. Some items are still quite considerably cheaper up there. Two such product types which spring to mind are paracetemol tablets (about thirty pence a packet in Asda) and condoms (one pound sterling a dozen). So, all you stud muffins out there, perhaps you should borrow a transit and take a day trip up north after all. Alternatively, in the run up to Christmas it might just be worth your while to do a little online detective work on cross-border price comparisons to see if it would be worth your while making a family day trip – after all a change is as good as a rest. A lot will depend of course on how far you have to travel, your tolerance level for long distance driving and what kind of items are on Santa's list this year.

62. Re-use

'Necessity is the mother of invention'. I was out in India one time, and be Jaysus I was amazed at the way in which everything was re-used and then re-used again. Everything got a second and third life before being discarded and even then an army of little urchins scoured the dumps to collect anything that was salvageable. They must have a hundred different uses for a plastic bottle. No need for 'Genuine Toyota Parts' out there I can tell ye! Anyway, luckily for us we here in the western world are never going to have the kind of poverty and therefore the incentive that those unfortunate souls have to re-use products. Still we could take a leaf out of their book; we could try to exercise a bit of imagination. Take a longer look at containers, bottles etc, before discarding them. At the very least you should certainly never have to buy a vase, lunchbox or a dog dish again. Come on and get those creative juices flowing. Think outside the box, so to speak.

63. A Catalogue of Uses

We are all familiar with the pervasive Argos catalogue; it seems to have replaced the old telephone directory as the required block book for every home. That's exactly what it is like, a block or brick. It is a very solid sturdy item, any number of which are available free from that kind retailer of the same name. If we put our thinking caps on I'm sure we could come up with lots of uses for such a product. I currently have nine of them stacked one on top of the other under a bed replacing a missing middle leg. In fact they can be used around the home as building blocks to give a lift to any household appliance, such as the TV, which may require it. Of course they can be attractively camouflaged for such purposes. I have also given one to our newly acquired puppy; she happily chews the corners of it which offers some respite to the household furniture until such time as she's properly trained. Anyway, you have the gist of this suggestion. Make a family game out of coming up with inventive uses for this freebie with a prize for the most imaginative. If you prove adept at finding uses for this ubiquitous brick you may want to horde away a supply for the future as it appears over the next few years Argos are inevitably heading down the digital route of doing business, so the colourful catalogues days are probably numbered.

64. Haggle

Haggle, haggle, haggle. And then, haggle some more. This used to be a time-honoured tradition here in Ireland but the practice had been eroding steadily over the past number of decades. Then came the Celtic Tiger era with people throwing money around like confetti, which finished off this fine art once and for all – or so it seemed. But seasons come and go in cycles and bust follows boom as surely as night follows day. We are in the midst of a recession at the moment, the like of which has not been seen since before the great famine (if you're to believe what I read in the paper). This means businesses are struggling out there. Competition is intense (apart from sectors where cosy little illegal price fixing arrangements are in place) and cash is king.

All of which creates the perfect fertile habitat for that endangered species, 'The Haggler', to make a dramatic recovery. Well, it is an ill wind that blows no good. So please, have a go. The asking price is by no means set in stone. Every time you are about to make a purchase, look for a discount. You have absolutely nothing to lose; it's not as if the seller will put the price up to punish you for asking. Also try to develop a bit of persistence and skill at this game. If you're not getting anywhere with the shop assistant, ask to deal with the manager. Finally, don't be afraid to call your opponents bluff by leaving without making a purchase (you can always come back later). I know not all of you have the balls of a brass monkey, some of you out there are a bit shy and will be a tad embarrassed at first, especially if you're a haggle virgin, but trust me, it gets easier. As with trying anything new you don't have to jump in at the deep end, you can start with baby steps and as you grow in confidence you can develop your skills. When looking at a child's bike recently, for which the asking price was €200, I got a discount of €25 and a free carrier thrown in. How did I do it? All I did was utter these seven short words – 'is that the best you can do?' That was all I said. Surely the most retiring among you can manage that as a starting point. There is a bonus here as well; there isn't anyone out there who doesn't love a bargain. It appears to be an innate instinct, so when you succeed in getting a decent discount you can bask for a while in the superior, self-satisfied afterglow it creates.

65. The Fried Rice Syndrome

What the hell is the fried rice syndrome, I here you ask. This is the practice many businesses have of quoting you a price for a product or service which bears no resemblance whatsoever to the actual price you will have to pay. This is because they have deliberately and disingenuously neglected to include various additional charges in the original quote. These extra add-ons to the cost can include, but are by no means limited to, things like VAT, service charges, labour costs, handling fees, acceptance fees, legal fees, set-up fees, commissions and so on and so on. These people are nothing if not inventive. I myself consider Ryanair to be the undisputed champions of this practice. I would even admit to a begrudging perverse admiration for their level of expertise in this regard.

But why do I call it the fried rice syndrome? The reason is simply because it was in a Chinese restaurant that I first came across this practice almost twenty five years ago. I noticed that the price quoted on the menu outside the door did not include fried rice. There was an extra charge for this which you did not discover until you were ensnared, that is to say until you were safely seated inside. Even then it was only mentioned in very small print at the back of the menu so you most likely did not notice the hidden charge until you were presented with the bill by which time you had already consumed the goods and had to cough up, so to speak. In essence, what this practice seeks to achieve is to deprive the customer of his right to make an informed decision when considering a purchase. The policy is unfortunately a successful one and therefore has become commonplace. What can be done about it? Our law makers could ban it but alas they won't because they indulge in the activity themselves with stealth taxes for example. So, as always, you're on your own. All you can do is be alert to the danger. When shopping around comparing the price of goods be sure to repeatedly emphasize that you want to be told the full and final price you will be required to pay including VAT and all other extras. If there are dubious sounding charges included don't be afraid to challenge them. You can have a lot of fun watching your opponent squirm as he tries to justify or explain the inclusion of an acceptance fee. I mean seriously, what's that all about? A charge for the privilege of accepting your business in the middle of a recession? I don't think so mate, I didn't come down in the last shower.

66. Bring your own Shopping Bags

This one is self-explanatory. We are all familiar at this stage with the plastic bag tax which has been so successful in its desired effect – reducing the use of plastic shopping bags by up to 90% – and so simple in its execution that you won't even get this tight bastard to bemoan its introduction. Besides, it's a voluntary tax and since we must have taxes these are the most desirable kind. You don't have to pay it; just remember to bring your own reusable bags with you to save the twenty two cent per bag levy. In fact you'll save more than that in all probability because I have noticed that when most supermarket cashiers are asked by a forgetful shopper for the twenty two cent bag they are conveniently out of stock and can only offer the poor captive shopper a more expensive version. At this point, with a week's supply of groceries on the conveyor belt and half a dozen impatient punters in line behind him, the unfortunate sucker has little choice but to accept. If as a novice tight bastard you do happen to find yourself in a supermarket without your own bags it is often possible to use some free empty cardboard boxes which they have in-store.

67. Loyalty Cards

I have very mixed feelings about these so called 'loyalty cards'. On the one hand I hate to pass up on a freebie but sadly I am all too aware that there is no such thing as a free lunch. The amount of knowledge the enemy garners from your transactions coupled with the personal information you supplied them with when you applied for the card is staggering. When they put all the details they gather from their card-holding customers together they have a formidable arsenal of info to use ever so subtly in their never-ending life mission of extracting as much cash as possible from gullible punters. The best compromise solution I can think of is to give false information when applying for your card and also to occasionally swap cards with friends and family, swapping back again later. Hopefully this will be enough to enrich the enemy's system with confusion while you still gain your modest discount. It is worth remembering too that these loyalty cards net you less than 1% return on your purchases. Is it really worth honestly handing over all that very personal information for such a pathetic return? It's a bit like turning informer, grassing on your own family to the enemy who wishes to swindle them; you become a modern day Judas except instead of thirty pieces of silver you receive thirty pieces of copper, which incidentally may only be traded with the empire from whose slimy paw it was extracted for such a high price in the first place. I think it's safe to say this is a classic example of a false economy.

68. Why Buy Newspapers

Once upon a time long, long ago buying the daily paper was a prudent and worthwhile investment of your few shillings as it provided good value recreation and was a scarce source of national and international news. That day however is long gone. In today's world of 24 hour TV news channels, smart phones, laptops, iPads and Google we have long since passed saturation point in terms of how much current affairs our poor old noggins can disseminate. You know Mother Nature is a cautious, slow-moving creature – something akin to a public sector employee – so our evolution can't possibly keep pace with our technological advances. On top of all this we have the inexorable rise of the free local paper which is funded exclusively from its advertising revenue. The Irish Independent could almost be added to the latter category as it is so widely available for free in outlets like Supermacs that, even if you happen to be a fan of its shareholders agenda which it passes off as unbiased impartial reporting, there's no reason to line their pockets for it. Then there are radios in every car, workplace and home with very good topical news items well covered on channels like RTE Radio 1. This is all a longwinded way of telling you that news comes free and is freely available. Besides 'tis a wise man that believes only half of what he sees and none of what he hears (reads).

Just a note on the tabloids in passing here; they often come in for unnecessary criticism being accused of sensationalising and exaggerating stories beyond belief. I think any negative image or confusion the public may have regarding these publications could be avoided if they were displayed in the correct section of the newsagents. They should of course be located with the other adult comics such as Viz to avoid customer confusion. If, after exhausting all the other sources of bad news – which is the only kind that sells – you still feel it's just the tonic in a recession, have you tried befriending a small farmer? That should satiate your appetite fairly lively.

69. The Financial Section

When you do find yourself with the feet up on a Sunday afternoon reading the auld gossip columns in the weekend supplements, be sure to scrutinise the financial section also; too many people discard this part of the paper unread, wrongly assuming it is only for the businessmen, shareholders and highfliers. They reason there is nothing of use or interest to the ordinary Joe in there. This is a costly mistake. The financial sections of newspapers are a great source of money saving tips for the common man. Particularly in the last few years since the recession took hold, such pertinent articles are a regular and popular feature. From now on the financial pages should be your first port of call. Perhaps you did take a peek inside 'the pink pages' in the past, but were put off by the language and jargon being used. You have my sympathy; some of these guys really do tie themselves up in knots in their determination to complicate a perfectly simple sentence. Nonetheless I advise you to try again with a little more perseverance; as with everything in life, you will get used to the terminology with practice and apart from the nuggets of monetary wisdom you pick up you will simultaneously widen your vocabulary.

70. Glossy Rags

Magazines are an even bigger waste of money than newspapers. They're all glossy pictures and no substance. In fact it appears to me they are little more than cover to cover advertising. Between the official adverts, which can take up a third or more of the magazine, you have a few articles peppered with product placement. This makes the articles you supposedly bought the mag for just a more devious form of advertising. Between all that and the tosh masquerading as information contained in most magazines you'd be as well off saving up all the annoying flyers that come through the average suburban letter box, stapling them together and hey presto you've got a free magazine of far superior quality I'd say to, *Hello* or *Loaded*.

71. Feck off with your Flyers

If you live in an urban setting, particularly if you reside in one of those sprawling suburban estates, you probably receive the equivalent of approximately two and a half mature oak trees through your letter box each week in the form of unsolicited flyers and the like. All this junk mail is trying to sell you goods and services that you were blissfully unaware even existed and so therefore you certainly didn't want to spend money on. Before that Chinese menu landed on your hall floor a king prawn kung poo with fried lice was the furthest thing from your mind, oh but now your evening won't be complete until you've devoured one; sure you can start the diet again tomorrow and anyway, don't you deserve a treat for surviving another Monday without getting the sack. Three hours and fifteen euro later you're belching n' farting like a beached whale on the sofa swearing 'never again' ('til the next time). Do yourself and the planet a big favour, put up a 'No Junk Mail Please' sign on your front door. It won't eliminate the problem as some Neanderthals can't feckin' read but it should go a long way towards reducing it. Meanwhile be sure to dump, unread, any flyers which still make it past your unequivocal signage.

While we're on the subject dump, unopened, any of those letters you get in the post addressed 'Dear Householder'. Believe me they contain nothing you want to waste your time reading and are surely attempting to part you from your cash in one way or another.

72. A Misguided Purchase

Now, TV Guides; there's one of the great mysteries of the modern era. What imbecile still buys these? Do they not know they can get a free TV guide with every second newspaper? And anyway the lists of programmes are all there on the feckin' telly for them. Just when you think you've reached the limits of idiotic consumer choice, before you get to the end of the magazine shelf, what do you see but several magazines devoted purely to the soaps. That's right, not one, but several. I don't get it? You either watch these soaps or you don't, right? If you are bored enough to be watching the soaps you know what's happening in them so you don't need a magazine to tell you and you certainly don't want to read in advance what's about to happen to your favourite soap characters in the coming weeks, ruining the story on you. If you don't watch them, you couldn't give a fiddler's what's going on in Albert feckin' Square or Carraigstown. Am I missing something here? Anyone? Answers on a postcard, please. Who in blazes is buying all these weekly TV Soap Magazines?

73. Elbow Grease

Ninety nine times out of a hundred there's no need for any washing up liquid when cleaning the dishes after your meals. Some piping hot water and a bit of elbow grease is all that is normally required to do a superb job in my experience. Besides, it's the only bit of exercise some of you are going to get all week, working up a sweat to get the grime off that frying pan. Now I did say 99% of the time; I would allow for an emergency supply hidden under the sink for the odd bugger of a roasting tray after you've accidently burnt a fat-filled duck to a cinder in it.

74. Ditch the Domestos

The same advice applies to Domestos or any other toilet bowl cleaner you happen to be using. Domestos is famous for its adverts claiming to kill 99% of all known germs. In other words it kills the ninety nine weaklings that wouldn't harm a fly and it is powerless against the one tough little bugger that can really do for you. Seriously though, it's all just marketing propaganda designed to terrify you into buying their product. It's not a desirable thing you know to eradicate all so-called germs indiscriminately. These organisms have been around for tens of thousands of years and for good reason in the first place. Besides, you're not going to be eating your dinner off the seat of the toilet any time soon. So relax, clean your Jacks with a toilet brush and a bit of soapy water if you must. If there's a slight lingering aroma opening the window should do the trick. If it looks and smells clean it's clean enough. Another point worth making here is that whatever little good these disinfectants do in getting rid of germs of the nasty variety will not nearly compensate for the harm the lethal chemicals contained in that innocent looking bottle can do. Is it really a good idea to be leaving poisonous substances sitting around your house within easy reach of all and sundry? I for one don't think so. On a lighter note all this talk of the loo reminds me of a joke, so here goes.

Q. What have a toilet bowl and the Starship Enterprise got in common?

A. They both circle Uranus looking for cling-ons.

75. Eating the Cleaners

Sometimes, but not often mind you, water and elbow grease alone will not do the trick for removing some stubborn stain or greasy grime. In this situation just ask yourself what did people use back in the day when dirt was dirt and Mr feckin' Muscle hadn't been heard of? The answer is staring you in the face when you open your food cupboards. Vinegar, lemon and baking soda among other common foodstuffs make cheap, non-toxic cleaning agents. Even coffee grounds which are handily somewhat abrasive can be used for cleaning greasy pans. Vinegar and lemon juice are mild acids and make great window and mirror cleaners (minus the smears some conventional products leave behind). You can use baking soda on a damp cloth instead of your usual cleaning product. If you want to give the oven a good cleaning scatter some bicarbonate of soda (baking soda) around its interior while it is still warm from use, leave it for an hour or so and then simply wipe clean. These and hundreds of other equally useful cleaning tips can be found on the internet or in various books on living cheaply, some of which I have listed later. So, praise the lord, you'll never have to fork out for another bottle of Mr Sheeny Shine again.

76. A Breath of Fresh Air

Do not buy air fresheners of any description for your home, office or car. They are a complete waste of money and worse than that the chemicals they contain can cause all kinds of irritations such as sore throats and eyes or itchy skin (which you will spend more money on medicating). Should you feel your home or other space frequented by you is in need of a little fresh air, did you know there is a wonderful, free, natural and effective air freshener available to all? It's called a window. You just turn the handle to open it and all this beautiful fresh air comes flooding in. If you are lucky it may even come accompanied by soothing sounds of melodic birdsong. If this action does not solve your odour problem then an artificial air freshener won't help either, at best it will only disguise the problem temporarily and make life difficult for yourself as you try to discover the source of your trouble.

77. Reusable Repellent

Fly sprays, or to give them their trendy title, insect repellents, are another useless and potentially harmful product. These are just aerosol canisters of chemicals which unbelievably we are advised to spray wantonly around our kitchen – filling the air we breathe and coating surfaces which we intend to prepare food on and eat from – in order to rid our home of that dangerous intruder, the bluebottle. Seriously lads, can we not think of a better way to dispatch this miniscule menace? Once again the tried and tested solution is right there at hand, the auld reliable Sunday Times (which you didn't buy of course, but borrowed from your neighbour on Monday). Just roll it up and swat the pest, dispatching the poor creature swiftly and humanely. If you are lucky your nemesis may turn out to be a tricky energetic little blighter affording you a free workout better than you'd get from an hour on a state of the art cross trainer.

78. Let out your Inner Artist

Instead of buying mass produced framed prints to decorate your home why not tap into your inner artist and have a go at producing your own unique works of art which will have meaning and emotion in them for both you and your family. If you've never put brush to canvas, fear not, no experience is necessary to create a work of art a hundred times more meaningful than anything Debenhams home wares can sell you.

Anyone can create a colourful abstract work with a loose wrist, a variety of paints, a brush and a canvas or sheet of paper. Alternatively you could have a go at creating a colourful collage, just save up those free Sunday supplement magazines and cut out any picture which catches your attention. When you've got a hundred or so try your hand at telling a story in images on a pre-selected base then frame it and give it pride of place in your home. If your story or message isn't immediately clear to viewers so much the better, it'll make for a great conversation piece. Many people display framed photographs around their home which is a fine idea but don't just limit yourself to family portraits. Try your hand at snapping landscapes, cityscapes, animals and so on. There is no excuse not to in this digital age; you can literally take thousands of pictures, dismissing them all and improving your technique without it costing you a dime, until you eventually capture a few worthy of your walls. Finally don't forget the works of art your five year old brings home from school. These should definitely not be dumped, even after the obligatory fortnight on the fridge. They will be worth their weight in nostalgia in years to come.

79. Sofa so Good

Okay, so the old sofa looks a bit knackered, the dining room table is past its best and one of the beds upstairs has a wonky leg. What are you going to do? It'll cost a fortune to replace that lot. It doesn't have to though; take another look. Is the damage just superficial? Is the sofa still solid but a little tatty around the edges due to the terrible twins' overactive imaginations – which invariably turn the couch into a pirate ship in turbulent seas, a racing car, and a wrestling ring at regular intervals. Well in that case there's no point in getting a new one, you just have to disguise the damage for the benefit of the upturned nose brigade. Get yourself a nice pretty throw and hey presto, problem solved. This also works if you've changed the colour scheme of the room leaving the sofa now sticking out like a sore thumb. Naturally, the same principle applies to the kitchen table which has become a bit scratched and stained from all the feeding frenzies your large litter have had around it. A nice attractive table cloth and you're sorted. After all what the eye doesn't see the heart won't feel. If some of your household furniture really is beyond being salvaged with these superficial solutions you can still pick up decent furniture for free on the freecycle website and others. Household items like these are the most commonly offered goods on these sites. Of course you can't expect what people are giving away for free to be new or in pristine condition but once it is structurally sound it can be attractively camouflaged with minor effort and expense. You'll be amazed at what you can achieve with a few nice cushion covers and a bright, extra large duvet covering the bed.

80. Waiting Day

If you find yourself with nothing in the fridge only the light bulb, the cupboards as bare as a baboon's arse and you're short a few cent for the price of a tin of beans to tide you over on waiting day (of course this can never happen to you again now that you've discovered this book), it might be worth your while to have a rummage down the back and sides of the sofa to see if you can't retrieve a few long lost coppers. You never know, you could get lucky and find an old crumpled fiver down there – be careful you don't get bitten though! Other places to check are old coat pockets or any drawers or cubby holes full of knick knacks which never normally let in the light of day. Remember if you find any old Irish coins they are still legal tender and can be exchanged for euro at the central bank. Even if you don't find any money you'll be so engrossed with all the other bits and bobs you come across that you'll forget your tummy rumbles entirely.

81. Wear an Extra Layer

Before turning on or up the heat in your home consider throwing on an extra layer of clothing. This could be a cost free, partial solution to those energy bills especially on those in-between Autumn or Spring days when you're not quite warm enough to be comfortable and yet not quite cold enough to justify a roaring fire. A thermal underlayer is a great first line of defence against an Irish winter. Also it is worth noting that most of your body heat is lost through your head and your feet so remember, a woolly hat can be worn indoors as well as out and don't be the idiot going around the house in your bare feet while at the same time turning up the thermostat.

82. Do a Warm Up!

Everyone knows that exercise keeps you fit and far from the doctors surgery but you know the benefits don't stop there. It keeps you warm too. So, if you feel a shiver down your spine but you think it's a tad early in the day to put on the central heating, get that blood flowing with a couple of energetic jogs up and down the stairs followed by a dozen press ups. Even better if you get out the hoover and do a spring clean. That'll kill two birds with the one stone.

83. Sealed in Savings

A relatively cheap and hassle free way to make savings on your heating costs is to apply draught strips to your windows and draught excluders to the external doors of the house. You should also insert inflated chimney balloons up any chimneys not in use to prevent heat loss. Taking these one-off, low cost measures (probably less than €100 in total) will pay for themselves in jig time.

84. Timely Timer Review

Setting the heat to come on with the use of a timer is mighty convenient but when did you last review the settings? Perhaps it could be time for an adjustment. You may still need your central heating in March but is your timer still stuck at the high usage level you set it at in the depths of winter last January? Also a lot of individuals and families have the heat set to come on in the morning, say an hour before they rise. This means they get up to a slightly warmer house, which is handy, except on a typical work/school morning does everyone not lie in the cosy scratcher until the very last minute and then having left it just slightly late, the whole family runs around like crazed, headless chickens for about an hour before departing to their respective daily destinations? Leaving behind a lovely snug, albeit empty, house. Besides there is such energy burning in the morning's activity and haste, I imagine you should be creating all the heat you need from your own internal furnace to suffice for that brief bridge of time between leaving Blanket Street and heading out into the main thoroughfare. So if your house is one of this type, left mostly empty during the day, I would seriously question having the heating on in the mornings. It may just be a hangover habit from when times were good and fuel was cheap but you might well benefit substantially from a sober review now that we are feeling an economic chill and fuel prices are escalating like wildfire. Remember, turning your thermostat down by just one degree will knock 10% off your heating bill.

85. Immerse Yourself in Savings

Even the most cautious of tight wads can be tripped up in their diligence by the blasted immersion. How many times have you put the immersion on to heat the water only to discover hours later that it is still on and burning a hole in your pocket long after its requirement had been fulfilled? Your immersion should only be used for the summer months or when your central heating is not in use. Discover through trial testing the precise amount of time it needs to be on for the various required amounts of hot water. How much time is needed for your immersion to heat enough water for a shower? For a bath? Do you know? If not then find out because not knowing is costing you money. Treat your immersion like a kettle, an appliance to be switched off once the water is heated. If, like me, you've misplaced your memory, take whatever initial precautions are necessary to form the thrifty habit, use post-its or put a reminder in your phone. Kerching! You'll soon be quid's in.

86. A Half One is Your Fill

If you have an oil tank you will have noticed in almost stunned shock how the price of the black gold has sky-rocketed in the past few years. Apart from the obvious there is another negative consequence to this occurrence. The more expensive a much in demand product becomes the more incentive is created and the more lucrative a target it becomes for the slime ball thieves. Unfortunately for this reason the oil in your back garden tank is now ripe for pillaging by these parasites of humanity. Anecdotal evidence strongly suggests this practice is reaching epidemic levels. Apart from the normal security measures you should take regarding any of your property, it is strongly advisable now to only half fill your oil tank when you run low. At least that way should the worst happen you are exercising a bit of prudent damage limitation. Implementing this policy also means your tank is always relatively close to empty which should ensure you are far more cautious with your now scarcer resource, ensuring you use it only at times of greatest need. By the way early summer is generally the cheapest time to refill your oil tank. As you might expect, because of the laws of supply and demand, assuming the yanks are not mobilising to invade yet another oil rich nation and all other factors being equal, prices begin to rise in august continuing their upward trajectory throughout the winter.

Check out the website www.cheapestoil.ie before ordering to find your most competitive local supplier.

87. Firelighters

Time was when a firelighter was another name for a match. Then some smartarse put together little cubes of peat chippings doused in kerosene, he packaged them up and started calling them firelighters. He was no daw either this fella – they caught on like, 'em, wildfire. They even come with instructions on the box; in fact there's great amusement to be had from reading a pack of firelighters. Did you know they even advise us that in the event that we are not entirely satisfied with the product we should return it to the store where it was purchased! I'm not kidding! Would someone please tell me how in the name of Jerusalem I'm going to return the firelighter I just burned to a cinder in the grate? Seriously though, I am extremely worried for the Human Race if you're telling me we need instructions outlining what we should do with a product called firelighters. Anyway if you are still living in the stone age, lighting open fires where ninety per cent of the heat quite literally goes up in a puff of smoke and out the chimney, will you do yourself a small favour and think of the humble match as a concentrated (that's the magic word these days when a manufacturer wants to sell you less product for a higher price) firelighter. I'll even give you the instructions to get you started in case you've forgotten how it works. Scrunch up some old newspaper, add a few twigs, sticks, turf mould or other flammable material, strike your firelighter, add to your material, throw on your logs or turf or whatever you're having yourself and bobs your uncle; you've got a blazing fire. Needless to say you can dispense with those new-fangled, oversized, overpriced firelighters they call firelogs as well. They used to be called briquettes, the only difference being you now pay more for one than you used to give Bord Na Mona for a whole bale. Who would have believed it! You'd be entitled to change your name to Keith Barry – you've just turned a match, with the help of yesterday's paper and a few twigs, into a firelighter and a bale of briquettes.

88. The Original Bottled Water

You don't need an electric blanket! Apart from the electricity you're wasting, they're a bloody fire hazard as well not to mention the purchase price of the feckin' thing in the first instance. No, if you feel your auld scratcher needs warming up before you hop into it on those frosty nights when the temperature drops into the minus arena, ideally what you want is a naked, warm blooded, feisty female (or male, depending on your own particular tastes) who is hot to trot in there ahead of you. That should get your temperature rising. Even if you can't procure such a creature, fantasies are free so indulge yourself; even the thought of such a nymph should boost the Celsius figure by a degree or two. Seriously though, if you do need to defrost the old leaba of a winters evening revert back to the original bottled water. That's right, throw a good old fashioned hot water bottle in under the covers, or two even if you must, but for heaven's sake forget that ridiculous electricity burning blanket.

89. TV or not TV

If asked, many of us will wistfully say that we wish we could find more time to read and, as reading can be a cost free pastime, then why don't we? Because of the bloody telly, that's why! And for the younger generation you can throw in computer games and Facebook into the mix as well. So I suggest that you call a family meeting and agree one night a week when all the gadgets in the house get turned off for a few hours and you begin a new family tradition called 'reading night'. Everybody can read that book they've been meaning to get around to for the past two years, or just the Sunday papers which usually get thrown out only half read. You should all read in the same room ideally; there's great bonding in just being together without saying a word. If reading's not your thing just gather around the fire and chat, play cards or board games. These simple and free pastimes still offer as much pleasure as they always did. Apart from being more enjoyable, you will make considerable savings on electricity. Besides if you do this on an on-going basis, rest assured the psychological benefits will save at least one family member a fortune in the years ahead on the antidepressant medication and psychotherapy that they will not now need as a result. Another loved one will be diverted from thinking he has to go to the pub every other night just for a bit of companionship.

90. Cancel the TV Subscriptions

How did we ever survive with Bog One and Bog Two (RTE) in the good old days, eh? Look, you really don't need 836 channels or whatever ridiculous number you're getting with your TV package. There are only twenty four hours in any given day! Take away a third for sleep, a third for work, mealtimes, playtime with the kids, quality time talking with friends and family, reading time, outdoor pursuits and hobbies. Ok I think you get it. What time is left for telly? There shouldn't be more than a miniscule amount. Anyway TV is all advertising and propaganda. It's 'The Machine's' most successful method in the modern era of keeping the masses captive and subdued in a trance-like state during those dangerous hours of freedom the inmates have between work and sleep. Even if you are enjoying your robotic existence, haven't we all got computers these days? With the advent of Facebook, Twitter, Youtube and so on you need look no further if it's time wasting you're after. At the very least, if I can't convince you to switch from your beloved goggle box to the Google box will you please at least cancel your UPC or SKY deal and contact one of the many communications companies who will set you up with hassle and subscription free TV for a once off fee but with no on-going bills thereafter.

One final point, if you have a TV in the bedroom do yourself a favour and sell it. If you can't think of anything more entertaining to do in the bedroom you really need to have a serious chat with yourself. Also your arguments against agreeing to TV's for the kids rooms will be pretty pathetic when the time comes if you've got a forty inch plasma at the end of your own 'auld scratcher'. At an absolute maximum one to one should be the ratio of telly's to households.

91. Flix for Thicks

Netflix seems to be the latest consumer craze. It is of course just another form of TV subscription which for the reasons outlined previously seems to me to be superfluous to requirements. Would you not be better off out there actively pursuing your own life rather than paying to passively engage in other's lives which are not even real, but unrealistically fictitious? I've nothing against Netflix itself by the way, I signed up for a free month's trial of their service (for research purposes of course) and I enjoyed it just fine – it certainly beats renting films individually down at your local movie store. But it's just that I've only two eyes in me head, a few spare hours in any given week and fifty seven other channels to choose from! I need another TV channel like I need a feckin' ashtray on me motorbike.

92. It's a Stand-off

Never leave any electrical appliances on standby. If it's not in use it should be plugged out at source. Unbeknownst to many, electrical appliances on standby account for a not insignificant percentage of the average household bill. With energy prices only going skywards for the foreseeable future and the number of electrical gadgets in use multiplying like mice, this habit is becoming increasingly costly. Equally, the incentive to tackle the problem has never been greater. Determine to develop a habit of doing a sweep of the whole house at regular times to ensure all appliances not in use are fully disconnected from the electricity supply. A natural time to do this would seem to be before going to bed; make it part of the routine when locking up for the night. Perhaps another good time would be when leaving the house to go to work or for other extended periods, even if this is only a quick check of the most likely suspects. The added reward for your efforts will be increased peace of mind and a more restful night's sleep due to the decreased fire hazard in your home. Don't forget those easily overlooked battery operated gizmos as well. Turn them off fully. If in doubt remove the batteries to save running them down.

93. Upwardly Mobile

The ubiquitous mobile phone has, in its latest guises, rendered a whole host of formerly useful and practical products redundant. These include, but are not limited to calculators, watches, alarm clocks, radios, diaries, address books and dictaphones. On top of all these, for the average five eights at least, if you have a decent Smartphone it'll suffice for the annual family holiday snaps as well. Needless to say that antique, formerly known as 'the phone' and then 'the landline' is now past its use-by date as well. I do realise that the latest mobiles on the high street come with a hefty price tag attached and I'm sure you know by now that I wouldn't dream of suggesting you part with a three figure sum unnecessarily. A perfectly adequate phone for the purposes outlined above can be sourced in second hand or pawn shops for a fraction of the price. If that fails put the word out with friends and family, especially teenage members, because one of them is bound to be upgrading soon – especially if their birthday or Christmas is coming up. They might even pass on their (six month) 'old' phone to you for free.

94. Texting Times

Don't you just love the advent of the text message? Even though I'm a bit cumbersome with the auld thumb talk, they're perfect if you need to get a message to somebody you don't actually want to talk to; or you have to contact the sister-in-law but you can't face or afford the two hours of insincere and incomprehensible waffle which seems to come as an obligatory requirement whenever you phone her. But do you know where they really come into their own? As a replacement for greeting cards, that's where. No need anymore, on your little sisters birthday, to line Hallmark executives' pockets with the purchase of an overpriced piece of paper with a coloured envelope and a corny rhyme written by some Rasta in India who's never even met your sis! At €3.50 for the privilege (and that's if they've a sale on), not to mention having to go down to the post office in the rain and join the queue for the stamp. Hallelujah! Those days are gone. Now you can send young Molly a cheerful, heartfelt and personalised message from the comfort of your own armchair for free – or for as near free as makes no difference. That's not even the best of it! At Christmas, giving yourself a spinal injury lugging 300 cards down an icy side street can also be relegated to an endlessly repeated interactive video playing in the 'Hard Times' museum. One group text and bingo! You're done.

95. Pocket Sized Golden Pages

Because we are all walking around with smartarse phones in our pockets these days (or soon will be), there is no need for anyone to be ringing those expensive (about €2.40 a pop) directory enquiry services to access a number. Just Google the company you're looking for and get the number from their website. Better still; send them an email requesting a call back. If they want your business they should oblige. For personal numbers find your target on Facebook or other social media and ask them or their friends directly for the number you require. If you don't yet have internet access on your phone, not to worry, your friend there beside you does. Ask him to do the honours.

96. Go Conquer the Mobile Market

When it comes to the mobile phone networks market, the cheapest show in town is Go Conquer 48. For €10 a month at the time of writing if you sign up with this crowd you get limitless free calls and texts to all other mobile networks and you also get twenty minutes of free calls to national landline numbers into the bargain. If you need to surf the net while upwardly mobile you can twitter on endlessly for an additional €10. No other company comes close to this deal at the moment. When I signed up with them online (they are an online company and don't have a high street presence; this presumably is one reason they are so competitive) I was pleasantly surprised to discover their customer service was also the most efficient I had come across in the market place.

Confusingly enough, this company purports in its advertising to only being open to customers aged between 18 and 22 years. I'm not sure what sound business reason they could possibly have for limiting their customer base so drastically, perhaps it's just the old marketing trick of deliberately courting controversy in order to garner a bit of free publicity in the media. Regardless, you needn't take any notice of this mythical restriction. If like myself you are of a more distinguished vintage simply adjust your birth year when registering in order to become an angst and acne riddled eighteen year old once more. Of course this payment structure is brilliant in its simplicity too, you are not tied into any lengthy contracts, you are not constantly watching your credit (you don't have any as such). Oh, as for those 2am phone calls which you always regret the following morning, well unfortunately you will continue to make them but at least they won't have cost you €20 in credit.

There are various add-ons you can purchase as extras should you need to, such as international texts and calls or more landline minutes, but I love the fact that once you pay your €10 they won't swindle you out of any extra with deceitful hidden charges as all other mobile contracts do. For example if you use up your twenty minute landline allocation in the middle of a call you will be cut off and can't make any further landline calls that month unless you consciously decide to go to the 48 website to order more landline time. So hip hip hurray! No more nasty, unexpectedly high bills. So what's the catch? There has to be one, doesn't there? Unfortunately yes, there is a big but. Their network coverage is pretty crap! Still if you spend most of your days in the concrete jungle this fact shouldn't be more than a minor irritant. If on the other hand you are a spear chucker from the sticks you can circumvent this problem by keeping a second cheap phone which is on a ready to go payplan. Use this phone for receiving calls only so it costs little or nothing (perhaps put €5 credit in every six months or so for emergency) Meanwhile you can still use the 48 phone to make limitless calls as you should be able to pin point a couple of spots around the house where it will pick up a signal and work fine.

97. Remain Ready to Go

Unless you are a highflying business executive or otherwise spend an inordinate amount of time on the phone you should not sign up to any bill pay plan. The various bill pay deals are designed to catch you out. They sound wonderful with free smart phones thrown in and all sorts but I promise you, regardless of the phone company, they are lying to you. There will be numerous hidden catches they neglected to mention so you will end up paying substantially more than you expected. In a way it's your own fault because, in all fairness, who did you really expect was going to end up paying for that €400 phone they gave you for 'free'? If you're that gullible you almost deserve to be parted from your cash. Vodafone currently have an advert displayed in their shop fronts offering gullible passers by a free Tablet. You may laugh but the thing is thousands of sad saps will fall for this blatant bait. Also did you notice how the lengths of the contracts the phone companies tie you into are getting longer all the time? It used to be six months, then twelve – many of them are up to two years now. Where's it going to stop? Ten year phone contracts, anyone? Please believe me you don't want to give away the last vestige of freedom you have to these parasitic corporations. Oh and just wait 'til your two year contract is up and you want to switch to another network. It'll be like trying to get an Irish divorce. You'll have to give them a month's notice, in writing no doubt. There will be the dreaded 'unlocking code' which you need for your new provider but the old provider has all sorts of excuses why he can't give it to you. They'll bamboozle you with some new 'too good to refuse offer' that will most definitely not be 'what it says on the tin' and alas, by the time you comprehend their complicated deceit it'll be too late; you're already signed into a three year deal.

So stay on pre-pay or, if you are in a contract, return to prepay at the first available opportunity. It is much clearer to see what you're paying for and why this way. You also retain your freedom to shop around and jump ship immediately should a competitor introduce a better deal. I was tied into an eighteen month phone contract which was costing me on average €44 per month and since exiting that situation to go freelance, so to speak, my monthly mobile spend is approximately €11 on top of which I now spend longer on my phone as I have a less restrictive deal.

98. Phone Owners Code

More than 15,000 mobile phones – mostly smart models – were stolen last year. Actually it was probably a lot more than that as many stolen phones are labelled as lost because of a lack of evidence indicating a definite theft. City centres are the hotbed for this activity where marauding packs of low lives operate, working their way through cafes, bars and shopping centres like human locusts harvesting their crop. As with most parasites their usual targets are the most vulnerable, in this case, young women. This crime is particularly prevalent because the thieves can easily fence the goods to dodgy shop owners for a fast fifty quid (never mind that the phone may have cost the poor schmuck who's just been robbed €600) or shipped abroad in large quantities. The phone's SIM is then replaced and it is sold on but not before being used to ratchet up huge charges in foreign calls.

So can you identify yourself as a prime target, ripe for the picking, for this particular crime? If so, smart young fair city ladies, you have been warned. Please take all prudent precautions. Regardless of who you are, or what part of the country you live in, you should exercise caution and make sure to record and keep safe your phones 15 digit IMEI code number. This number is on the side of the box the phone comes in and is also on another label inside the phone, underneath the battery. You can also access it by dialling '*#06#'. In the unfortunate event of the phone being lost or stolen you should contact your service provider as quickly as possible, quote your IMEI to them and direct them to block your handset. This will ensure an element of damage limitation for yourself in the immediate term but perhaps equally importantly, if everyone reporting a stolen phone had this number to hand when reporting the theft of their phone (apparently only 15% currently do), it would reduce significantly the incentive for opportunistic toe rags to rob them in the first place. Remember smart phones deserve smart owners.

99. Keeping up with the Phones's

It seems to me that people change their minds less often than their mobiles these days. In the name of the modicum of reason still remaining to you, will you please resist the urge to 'upgrade' your phone if the one you have is in sound working order. I know the little bollox next door has just been showing off his new gadget which changes colour according to the weather or has some other equally indispensable application which your old Nokia doesn't have but exercise a little patience, you'll no sooner have got your upgrade when that feckin' pinch-faced ferret from number fourteen will have leapfrogged you and stolen the limelight with an even more impressive model which sings him a lullaby at night in a sexy, Latino accent. With the pace of modern technology this is one race you cannot win. You shouldn't even enter. In the meantime don't despair, your old Nokia will pop its clogs soon enough as nothing is made to last these days. When it does you can, with an air of self-congratulatory satisfaction, buy the smartest phone on the (second hand) market to complement its owners superior acumen.

This techno march seems to be relentless and it appears that nowadays time, tide *and* technology wait for no man. This technological 'progress' can leave the ordinary halfwit, such as myself, in a state of confusion and bafflement for much of his life. But it's an ill wind indeed that blows no good! Because of this constant advancement and updating of things like mobile phones, lap tops and so on, allied to the 'keep up with the Jones's' syndrome which so many people suffer from, it should be perfectly possible for someone from the same era as the T-Rex to pick up a decent second hand iPhone, iPad, laptop or whatever at a much reduced cost. If you are an internet or Facebook virgin you may be able to get an old computer for free which satisfies your apprentice needs adequately but which the techno whizz would not be caught dead using. Remember you can search online for these things on websites such as Freecycle, Gumtree, Done Deal and eBay to mention just a few and in the meantime you always have the use of a computer down at your local library, community centre or friend's house.

100. Gadgets for Guineas

Although, in theory at least, I am all for the technological strides humanity is making at a dizzying pace in this brave new century, I would warn against any of you being the first to rush out and buy any new technological gadget, be it the latest iPhone or Tablet or whatever new gizmo has just hit the shelves – regardless of how cool or super useful it promises to be. The reasons are twofold: firstly, you will pay a huge premium for the privilege and secondly, if you are among the first group of buyers you are the guinea pigs on whom the product is being tested. You will be the customer that will discover the product deficiencies, which will then be ironed out by the manufacturer, with the end result being the next round of customers being sold a cheaper and superior version of the product. Of course the third round of punters will make further savings still and so on.

101. Computed Savings

I am not the ideal person to speak on the subject of computers as anyone who knows me will testify to – particularly my long suffering partner. In fact I only started using one at all about six years ago. I didn't have an email address until 2009. I have had to be dragged kicking and screaming into the computer era and now that I am here I mostly stare, scratching my head in confusion when I sit in front of one. All that being said though, just in case there are any Neanderthals to outdo me still around who are not yet able to use a computer, it would be impossible for me to exaggerate how much you will benefit by taking that leap into the unknown and tackling this alien creature. I myself, in the short time since I entered this world, have met my partner on a social networking site; I found our Bichon Frise, 'Lily' – who is chewing my big toe under the desk as I type – online on DoneDeal.ie. I have rooms to rent advertised (for free) on Daft.ie as we speak and of course I would not realistically have sat down to write this book without my new technological aid. There will never be any need to pay for developing photos again either; you'll just store them all on the computer. The list goes on. Believe me I feel your apprehension. I too used every excuse imaginable to avoid the inevitable day when I would have to sign up for classes. I spent twenty years in denial, repeating my mantra: 'I have no use for them yokes'.

The truth is the advantages of having a laptop at your disposal are endless (and yes, I know I'm already out of date again, it's all iPads and what have you now). I know it's a cliché but they truly do open up a whole new world to you. I implore you to take the bull by the horns and become computer literate. You will need help of course and fortunately help is readily available. Luckily here is a case where we can sleep with the enemy; 'the machine', for its own ulterior motives, wants us all to be doing everything online and as a consequence there are lots of computer classes for beginners available. You should be able to do one for free, even get paid a little for it with some government training body. You can also enlist the help of friends and family, especially the younger variety, to troubleshoot the inevitable teething problems you will have and to offer essential advice with purchasing a suitable first laptop along with other initial setup issues. Bring an experienced computer nerd with you when you go shopping for your equipment as those predatory salesmen would smell your innocence from Mars. The initial set up costs of buying a laptop and getting connected may be expensive but do not look on it in that way. It is a sound investment which will pay generous dividends in the short, medium and long-term not alone financially but also socially, educationally and so on.

102. Good old Virtual Aunty Virus

There is absolutely no point in you paying for an internet anti-virus package as there are perfectly adequate free versions available online which will more than suffice for your purposes. I got caught out on this one myself in the beginning due to my naivety. Ignore the salesman's predictions of disaster for not paying €100 plus for some package or other, his only motivation is his commission. Again, get a clued-in friend or family member to set you up with this essential security measure.

103. Smart Broadband for Free

Many thousands of people are currently paying for broadband services unnecessarily by monthly contract or as an ad-on to their ready-to-go plan. This is typically costing them about €20 per month, give or take. If you have a smart phone you can probably cut out this monthly bill as apparently, virtually every modern Smartphone has a tool on it which allows your phone to act as a mobile broadband receiver itself via the network signal. This little known money saver can seemingly be utilised very simply on your iPhone or android device. There are of course a couple of small drawbacks to utilising this freebee. Firstly, if you need high speed broadband you won't get it using your phone and the mobile network and secondly, mobile networks – stingy buggers that they are – don't like you doing this class of thing at all at all and are trying to clamp down on it. But luckily for you, the much maligned punter, in this case it is very difficult for them to detect people using this tethering application except in the case of the heaviest of users, so it's up to the public to police themselves for the most part on this one (for now at least), which basically means you'll have to decide if your conscience will allow you to deny big business €20 of your hard earned cash each month. Hmm, that's a tough one! I'll have to think about it.

104. Cripes! Time to Turn to Skype

Particularly if you ever make international calls it *is* time to subscribe to Skype. Skype is a device which allows users to communicate with others by voice using a microphone and a webcam for video connections from their laptop. It can also be used for instant messaging over the internet and video conferencing and so on. Nominal rates are charged to call mobiles and landlines via Skype but the real beauty of this service is that Skype to Skype calls are free. Yes that's right, I said free! So, if you are still paying for international calls to your aunt Betty in Boston; your daughter Irene in Italy or Sr. Philomena in the Philippines, now's the time to get with the programme and sign up. Obviously you have to make sure the people you intend calling have signed up too. This service has been out there for about ten years. How much money have you spent on international calls in that time? Don't repeat this wastage throughout the next decade. Get connected today.

105. Short Circuit the Laundry

Most adult's clothes that you'd find in the average laundry basket these days are not visibly dirty at all. Often, all we're really doing when we bung them in the wash is freshening them up a little, maybe getting rid of that slight whiff of sweat which has accrued after a hard day's toil in the office. Fair enough, by all means wash them, but there's no need to boil the bejaysus out of them for an hour and a half at 60 degrees. These clothes only need the shortest cycle available on your machine and no more than a 30 degree setting to come out smelling of roses. While we're on the subject it's not the best idea in the world to be putting a load on last thing at night before you hit the hay since this means when the wash is done the machine will be sitting idly on standby for the next seven or eight hours. Start putting these power saving tips into action today and not only will you be quid's in, you'll also be responsible for saving half a dozen icebergs from melting before a year is out.

To benefit from a little more money laundering only use your washing for full loads and avoid using electrical appliances of any kind between the peak times of 5pm and 7pm.

106. Energy Monitors

I think every household could benefit from getting one of these gadgets. You basically just plug them in and they tell you how much electricity you are using at that moment. They are particularly useful if you feel your energy bills are very high but you are unsure which of your electrical appliances the guilty parties are. They should also help in motivating you to switch off appliances not in use, as you will now be able to calculate in concrete terms the cost of not doing so. You can get energy monitors in the shops but you should first try phoning your electricity supplier and having a good old moan about your bills being much higher than you think they ought to be. Ask them if they're sure they are not making some mistake with the bills and so on which of course they will assure you is not the case. Anyway, when you've set the scene enough and convinced them you're at your wits end with despair and they are at the point where they are still trying to be polite but are sick to the back teeth of you and desperately wish you would just go jump off a cliff, you can mention that you heard about these yokes called energy monitors. There's a good chance they'll agree to send you out one for free just to get you off the bloody line. Failing that, they should still prove worth the purchase price.

107. Jumping Energy Ships is Great Gas

If you are one of the 60% of electricity or natural gas customers who has never switched providers you almost certainly should because it is a very simple process and will save you money. Once upon a time there was only the ESB, now known as Electric Ireland, to supply your electricity. They had a monopoly and so the punters hands were tied; unless you wanted to cook on the open fire and read by candlelight you were stuck with them. That day thankfully, is gone. There are now several providers in the gas and electricity marketplace vying for your business. Some or all of them usually have special discounted rates which they offer to new customers for a limited period of perhaps a year or so. You should treat your energy suppliers in the same way as your annual car and home insurance renewal and once yearly, shop around all the providers looking for the cheapest quote. Make sure you take into account both the standing charges and per unit usage charges as well as any minimum contract rules. There is a great website called bonkers.ie which gives you free, impartial up-to-date advice on the cheapest gas and electricity provider for your individual usage level and property type. They also help demystify the whole switching process for those of us that are not mathematicians. Go on, switch today; it will take a matter of minutes and save you at a guess €100 plus per annum. If somebody offered you €100 for a half an hour's work you'd jump at it, right? Well treat it like that, after all a euro saved is worth more than a euro earned.

108. Wrecking your Bulb

Go around your house and garden with a notebook and pencil to take a census of the light bulb population. How many 'light points' are there? How many rooms are there? A friend of mine took this little test recently after moaning to me that his electricity bill was sky high and he couldn't understand how. He discovered he had fifty seven light bulbs to his ten roomed dwelling. That was just inside the house, in the garden and shed there were twenty six more lights! I kid you not and I hasten to add it wasn't even Christmas or anything. You might think, so what, as long as you don't turn them on they're doing no harm. But the problem is sometimes one switch to light a room activates four or five light bulbs when clearly one would be perfectly adequate. A lot of people went mad during the boom putting in sensor lights, downlights, uplights, spotlights, chandeliers and who knows what else. Now, in this era of austerity, it may be an opportune time to review some of our bulbous excesses. One bulb to a room is plenty. The next time you get an electrician in for some other job ask him to give you a quote for revising some of your more elaborate lighting arrangements. In the meantime (or if you can't afford the sparks quote) remove any bulbs which are surplus to requirements to cut power costs.

109. The Lights are on, but Nobody's Home

Are you one of those plonkers who, not content with putting a few lights on the old Christmas tree, has taken the whole Christmas decoration thing outside into the garden? Is your humble abode lit up like Las Vegas for the whole month of December and half of January as well because like, you went to so much trouble putting them up it'd be a shame to let Christmas end on time? Never mind the ridiculous energy bills you're ringing in the new year with; or the major ice berg and the rare penguin species you single-handedly exterminate each festive season, have you any idea how many near fatal accidents have been caused by the distraction to poor unsuspecting motorists from your monstrous eyesore? Please give our over-exposed senses and your bank balance a break next Christmas and leave those 3,000 multi-coloured bulbs in the feckin' attic; after all, nobody likes a show-off, least of all the Irish.

110. Pay Utilities Directly

You should pay all your utility bills by direct debit. There is usually a surcharge of a couple of euro per bill for not doing so and it also saves you the hassle of wasting your time in bank or post office queues waiting to pay them. Furthermore, it eliminates the risk of bills being long fingered or overlooked thus avoiding any risk of being cut off and facing hefty reconnection charges as a consequence. This last point will of course only be valid if you are diligent about maintaining a healthy current account balance.

111. Post No Bills

Check the small print on your utility bills to see if you are paying a surcharge for receiving your bill in the post. In most cases you are. This excess can be anything from sixty six cents to €4 per bill, in my experience. Contact your utility providers if this charge does apply and arrange to have your bills delivered to you by email instead of snail mail to knock these fees on the head.

112. Share Your Rubbish

If for some reason – perhaps you live alone – you never have your bins more than half full by collection day, try to discover whether there is a near neighbour in a similar situation. If so perhaps you could both agree to share the one set of bins and halve your refuse collection charges.

113. Cash for Clutter

If you have a lot of clutter taking up space in your shed, attic or elsewhere around your house remember, space is money, so set aside some time to go through it all and separate it into four piles. The first pile will consist of items you may reasonably expect to use in the future, so these items can be kept (a note of caution here: you need to be strict and honest in your appraisal of every item – otherwise everything will end up in this pile negating the point of the whole exercise). It would be wise to have a second opinion from within your household on this first group. The second pile will consist of items that are genuinely rubbish and which you can't imagine yourself or another getting further use from; this crap is for the refuse men. The third pile consists of items which would be useful to someone else but not you and has very limited saleable value. These products should be given away, if not to friends and family then you could try advertising them for free on websites such as freecycle.com The fourth pile is made up of goods which seemed like a good idea at the time, have a reasonable value and are still in good working order but in all honesty you are not the person who will ever put them to any use. These items are for selling. You can try advertising them on websites such as eBay or Gumtree. Failing that, do it the old fashioned way at a car boot sale; either way they've got to be worth a few quid. In the aftermath of the Celtic Tiger the country's cubby holes must be full of stuff people bought on impulse during those disposable days and which would now make a useful, second-hand bargain for the right person. So clear out that clutter; it's a win-win situation for all concerned.

A word of warning though, empty space such as that which you have just proudly created has a way of filling up again with more useless crap so be vigilant lest all your hard work be in vain. To avoid this scenario you could operate a strict *one item in, one item out* policy. What this means simply is that whenever you purchase a new product for the home you resolve to get rid of another product. This will stop the slow but sure accumulation of crap from infesting your life like something out of a Stephen King novel. In addition, it will encourage you to pause for thought before each new purchase.

114. Batteries not included

And here's another thing, the vast majority of those small electrical or battery operated gadgets which you didn't know existed – let alone wanted until you saw them advertised some place – are useful only as dust catchers and are taking up shelf space leading you, the poor bewildered consumer, to thinking that your problem is a lack of space. So there you are, ringing handymen to come and put in more shelves and cabinets when all you needed was a junk clearout. You know the type of ridiculous product I'm talking about. Has modern man really regressed to the point where he can't operate a toothbrush without the aid of a battery?

How many kitchen presses are overflowing with cobweb coated juicers, blenders, sandwich toasters, coffee bean grinders, electric carving knives, fruit peelers and smoothie makers? The list goes on and on. Fair enough if you're throwing lavish parties which get featured in *Hello* magazine every second week but seriously, for the rest of us, get a grip! I kid you not when I tell you that a mate of mine got an electric shoe polisher for Christmas one year! I'm not a fan of drug pushing, legal or otherwise, but if you are going around buying your loved ones feckin' electric shoe polishers you need to be on some very strong medication indeed. Then there are the back massagers, foot spas and the like. Now don't get me wrong, I'm all for a bit of pampering but you and the missus should be giving those massages to one another in the bedroom. After all the human touch is going to beat a bloody machine every time on this score, but of course I forgot, what are ye doing in the bedroom instead? Ye're watching 'Stars up their Holes' or some equally moronic rubbish on your big screen TV.

115. Water Wastage

Of course it was never a good idea to waste water but be honest, nobody really gave a toss as long as it was being supplied free of charge. Nothing supplied freely is ever valued very highly, even when that product is water and the source of life itself. The most valuable commodity in existence yet we didn't give a rat's arse as long as it kept flowing. It's just one of the not so admirable universal truths of human nature. If you give anybody something for nothing they will abuse it. Anyway, our endless tap of free water is about to be turned off any day now with the introduction of domestic water charges.

Now I'm just as allergic to taxes as the next fella (and probably more so) but it's a service which, like all services, costs money to provide and as somebody's got to pay for it then it might as well be the guy who's actually using it for a change. How's that for a novel idea? Still, it's going to be a pain in the arse receiving yet another utility bill to add to our collection. However now is the time to start developing some thrifty habits around our H20 consumption to cushion the blow. One simple and often suggested idea is to put a brick in your toilet cistern so as to use less water with each flush, this can save 3000 litres per year. Alternatively you can pee against a bush and avoid the flush altogether. Showering uses considerably less water than taking a bath (forty litre saving). You can also save by reusing 'grey water' – water already used for another purpose such as dishwashing – for hydrating plants and the like. What about the endless supply of water falling from Irish skies? Set up a simple water butt to harvest some of this. Once again the possibilities are almost endless, you can Google these and many more water saving ideas but begin by becoming conscious of your water usage and then take it from there.

116. No Vision

How the hell can I be passing Xtravision stores on the high street with their doors still open for business (I realise some are earmarked for closure as we speak)? Once upon a time in the land of videos and two channel TV yes, they had a place but surely that day is long gone. I suppose they have diversified into games as well as sweets, ice cream and other rubbish for eating in front of the goggle box but even so, a cursory glance inside reveals most of the shelf space taken up with films. Who in their right mind is paying good money to rent these things out? I mean the effort that's required should be enough to put you off, never mind the expense. I am genuinely confused. Why would anyone bother getting up out of their nice comfy armchair of a wet winter evening to go downtown to rent a movie and then have to go through the same hassle again tomorrow night to return it? Hasn't everyone got at least 101 channels now with all kinds of new-fangled recording facilities, on top of which there's the internet for downloading films if you really must. Seriously, get a life, lads. If you are honestly telling me there isn't anything worth watching on the telly, I can buy that, God knows they do put a lot of tosh on there but in that case light the fire, put on the woolly socks and pyjamas and put the feet up with a good book. Alternatively retire with partner for fun and games to the bedroom.

SECTION 2

A Healthy Perspective on Personal Care and Relationships

1. Universal Law of Attraction

Now admittedly this piece of advice is going to seem a little flaky to some of you but my experience suggests there is something to it and anyway, even if I'm wrong, you certainly won't be out of pocket for having tried it out. Many people (scientists included) around the world believe in what they call the universal law of attraction. This law simply states that 'like attracts like'. Physical examples of this can be proven with simple experiments, such as in the case of two magnets being drawn together. There are differences of opinion about how far you can take this rule. Some – a growing number, it seems – believe that this law applies to everything in the universe, even your thoughts. If this were true it would be all but impossible to comprehend the significance of that.

Imagine if you could draw positive events into your life solely through your thoughts. Some claim that's exactly what you have been doing your whole life, whether knowingly or not. You have attracted everything that has happened to you into your life. I am firmly sitting on the fence on this one if asked whether I believe in it or not but I reckon it can't be any harm to practice thinking positive thoughts in any event; push out the negative, self-defeating rhetoric and replace it with the power of positive thinking. What harm can that do? It can only be beneficial. Ask the Universe, God, Your Guardian Angel, The Wind or whoever you believe in to send you whatever it is you desire. Then, and this is the difficult bit, act as though your request is being processed and is already on the way, it's just a matter of time before it manifests physically in your world.

The secret to this concept is *belief*, we are told. You have to earnestly believe in your own power to manifest your dreams. This is no easy task for a natural sceptic such as my good self but I would also claim an open mind which allows that anything is possible so, if you are anything like me, you can begin with less than absolute fate in the process but become a method actor and you can fake it 'til you make it. Act as if you believe and see where the journey takes you. If you are interested in learning more about this concept, I should direct you to those with more knowledge of the subject than myself. There are plenty of them out there but a good place to begin would be with Esther and Jerry Hicks book 'Ask and it is Given' or another famous book in this vein is 'The Secret' by Rhonda Byrne. I just mention these two titles because I found them on my own bookshelf but there are many others as this idea is as old as civilisation itself. Check out your local library and look for titles in the spirituality section.

2. Healthy Self-esteem

Low self-esteem and sheer boredom are the main driving forces behind most illogical spending. They are probably the single most expensive attributes you can ill afford to possess. You know the kind of behaviour that seems to make no sense from a pragmatic sensible viewpoint. Take the guy who goes binge drinking every Saturday evening, spending upwards on

€100 – to say nothing of the eventual resultant medical expenses – just to feel sick as a dog all day Sunday and won't be capable of firing on all cylinders until at least Tuesday. If this guy earns €500 for a five day week it means one day is also taken up with working to earn the money for his session. So at a minimum he has given over three of his seven days in the week in pursuit of eight or ten hours drinking which he only has a hazy recollection of afterwards. As a one-off you'd say, what about it, don't die wondering, eh! But he does this religiously, every week. This chap is not an alcoholic either, he is otherwise a sensible fellow, loves his mammy, holds down a steady job, probably has a girlfriend. He himself – on the rare occasions he reflects on his behaviour – knows there is something inherently insane in it but somehow lacks the motivation to change anything. How do I know this? I was that Muppet. We're not just bashing drinkers here either. The same insanity manifests itself in a myriad of different ways: take smoking for example; or putting yourself in debt to the tune of €25,000 to buy a new car when you only drive 10,000 miles a year and the car you've got is in perfect working order; or what's known as retail therapy – buying a shit load of clothes every other week that you know in your heart of hearts you will rarely if ever wear. Anyway the list of behaviours is endless and diverse, but the root cause is the same: a lack of purpose and meaning in one's life. So unfortunately, while becoming fully aware that your expensive distraction makes no sense is an essential first step, it is not enough. If you want something to change you must change something.

Ideally, if you don't already have one you should find a job which interests and stimulates you and which you believe provides usefulness to others. If this is not immediately possible, at the very least you need to find a pastime – inexpensive of course – which satisfies these same human needs. Also keep good company; surround yourself insofar as possible with positive, encouraging individuals. Doing this will immediately alleviate the boredom and will gradually contribute to those intangible but invaluable feelings of healthy self-esteem and purposefulness in life. All this is easier said than done, believe me I know, but the considerable effort and initial fear of stepping outside your comfort zone will be richly rewarded. This goes way beyond aiming for a healthy bank balance. We are talking here about the difference between choosing a life or a mere existence. In the western world today, for all my criticisms of it, the choice truly is your own. So no excuses – the road to hell is paved with them.

3. Look You in the Eye

Look yourself in the eye (you'll need a mirror for this, unless you're some kind of circus freak) and ask yourself to be brutally honest in answering the following question. Are you one of those individuals that spend money you haven't got, on things you don't want, trying to impress people you don't like? Be truthful now! There's only yourself in the room, no one else will hear. If the answer is yes, congratulations! Not many would have had the balls to admit to the truth of that statement – even to themselves in an empty room. I can assure you however that there are many tens of thousands in that same crowded boat with you who are in denial. The good news is you've done the hard part in admitting to your insanity. The second bit is easier. Quit this madness immediately.

4. Soap

This must surely be the most underrated, versatile, long lasting and cheap little household product. Shower gel for instance is just a new fangled name for liquidised soap which comes in a fancy-assed, environmentally unfriendly plastic bottle. Even the cheapest generic brands cost multiples the price and don't last half as long as a good old fashioned bar of soap. There's likely to be a lot more harmful chemicals and other shit in the gel also. Now you know, there's no need to buy shower gel again. It is a great example of a product being brought out that serves no new, useful purpose for the end user but with endless creative marketing, exhaustive brainwashing – oops! Sorry, I mean advertising – and a bit of celebrity endorsement, hey presto you have a bewildering number of brands of a product that can be found in every home but that nobody was looking for and worse still, had no need of, in the first place. It's brilliant really. You'd have to stand back in admiration as the whole population is hoodwinked. Not us though! It's back to the humble soap bar for the tight bastard.

5. More Soap

Liquid soap also comes disguised as 'hand wash'. In fact I am quite convinced that there is no difference whatsoever between your bottle of hand wash and your shower gel, save for the name of the product and the fact that the former comes with a cute little pump action dispenser attached. So again, for the same reasons as above, dispense with the dispenser. Take your next step towards saving the planet and throw another bar of soap on the kitchen and bathroom sinks instead.

6. Even more Soap

It's becoming obvious that I'm a big fan of the soaps but there is another very commonly used product which the humble bar should replace and that is shaving foam, cream, gel or whatever the hell they're calling it these days. I have used nothing but soap, a decent disposable blade and hot water with which to shave for donkey's years. I can attest that almost without fail I benefit from a smooth, incident free, enjoyable experience. On those rare occasions when I have nicked myself it has been because I was missing the latter ingredient, namely hot water.

7. Still more Soap

Did you ever wonder how lately some cosmetic companies have managed to combine shower gel and shampoo in one bottle to get an edge over their rivals? It must have been very difficult and expensive for them to discover and harness the technology to combine these two very different products and present them as one purely for the convenience of you their valued customer. Actually no, if you look again at the ingredients on the labels of these two 'different' products you will notice – despite the fact that they seem to be written in the unintelligible language of some yet to be discovered alien race – that whatever the ingredients might be, they seem to be remarkably similar in both bottles. I can only conclude by extension of my preceding arguments that your average bottle of shampoo is yet another version of a bar of soap. So you really don't need it, especially if you keep your hair short.

8. Hair today, Gone tomorrow

To eliminate hair care costs altogether you could just shave all your hair off. Speaking as a guy, which is of course all I can do because I am one, you wouldn't even look out of place taking this seemingly drastic action. It's quite fashionable nowadays for fellas to go for this look. Sometimes the tactic is employed by men that are – how shall we put it sensitively – 'em, becoming follicly challenged, as a pre-emptive defence. Clever enough really: disguise your imminent baldness within even more baldness. Certainly it is a simpler, sensible and most importantly free solution if this is an issue you find yourself unduly concerned about, far better than ending up paying ridiculous amounts of money for hair transplant treatments or buying a plethora of products promising to stem the unstoppable outgoing hair tide.

While we are on the subject, guys going grey, I just want to say dyeing your hair jet black when you are forty five looks a tad ridiculous – now we not only know you are going grey we also know you're paranoid about it. Is it really worth the slagging you'll get from your mates? Go grey gracefully I say. Seriously, if you've got any hair left at all above a certain age who gives a hoot what colour it is? Rejoice and be glad. I appreciate all this advice is not so easy to put into practice for women, society placing so many more unreasonable demands on the fairer sex. A woman shaving her hair off is unlikely to be left in peace to do what she will with her own tresses. Unless she has the looks of a twenty year old Sinead O'Connor (who pulled this stunt off with remarkable success, even managing to improve her looks by losing her locks), she will come in for severe criticism, mostly from her fellow females, whilst at the same time eliciting endless looks and expressions of sympathy from well-meaning strangers believing her to be suffering from the big C.

Such a pity so many of us feel we have to conform to some invisible standard of behaviour we can neither define nor understand. I really don't have the answer for ladies out there who are fed up to the back teeth of feeling coerced into spending a small fortune on expensive hair products and salons. The Taliban's treatment of women would seem lenient in comparison to the fate western women mete out to their own friends and family if they fail to conform to societal norms – which by the way are difficult to keep up with as the goalposts keep moving. This is becoming an increasing problem in today's mono-cultural, globalised world. The independently minded individual has been labelled 'an eccentric' and become as rare as a corncrake, which is in serious danger of extinction. For what it's worth I have to admit I find it a bit of a turn on when I meet a woman who is giving 'The Machine' the metaphorical two fingers by going grey with style and panache. In that one act is demonstrated (in a quiet understated way) for all who would see, the very attractive qualities of independence, determination, bravery, intelligence, thoughtfulness, psychological strength and emotional health – to name but a few.

9. Shaving Costs

You could cut out shaving expenses entirely simply by growing a beard and why not if you like beards, although you might want to run that one by the missus first, – after all, our objective here is to curb expenditure and divorce is pretty damned expensive! Still, we can cut the cost of shaving (sorry). We've already seen we don't require shaving cream in a previous point so that just leaves the blade we use. Gillette is the Rolls Royce of razors. You will be wasting your time looking any further. This doesn't mean they are not rip off merchants, they are, but what can you do – their product is so superior to any of their competition it still makes economic sense to purchase it. The basic Gillette Fusion blade is as near perfect a product for its job as you are ever likely to encounter. There's no need to go to the expense of upgrading to the newer gimmicky replacements which involve messing about with buying batteries and all sorts.

Also, as always, don't take a bit of heed of the advice on the packet to dispose of your blade after every few shaves. These blades last for months and months, this is what makes them more economical than the cheap, plastic disposables which really are past it after a couple of shaves. Electric or battery operated bladeless shavers sound and look great in the adverts but they just don't work properly; if they did disposable blades would have died out like the dinosaurs. So get yourself a Gillette Fusion and a bar of soap, I say. If you feel the initial cost of this product is a bit prohibitive start dropping the hints for Christmas or your birthday, it'll be a nice novelty to get a useful present for a change. It just goes to show, even though the advice to avoid brand name products is absolutely solid 97.5% of the time, there is an exception to every rule.

10. Moisturiser

I've got great news for you. You don't need moisturizer. Now that you are following the wisdom contained within these prophetic pages, you've given up drinking alcohol excessively and smoking. In fact you only drink pure, beautifully filtered water. Fatty, sugary, salty processed foods are a thing of the past too. In other words your skin is getting all the moisture it needs naturally and at the same time less of the modern day crap that drains said moisture from it. You see, in case you hadn't realised, the definition of 'to moisturize' is 'to make less dry'; that's it, nothing else. That is the only purpose moisturiser serves. This is what the cosmetic companies are making billions out of each year. It's genius really. You needn't take my word for it either. I got that definition from no less an authority than The Oxford Dictionary. It goes on to add: 'especially the skin by use of a cosmetic moisturiser'. Isn't that mighty! You have dispensed with the need for expensive branded moisturisers as a beneficial by-product of following some of the other earlier tips given. Just to hammer home the point then, no moisturiser – no matter how expensive or what miraculous claims are made for it via celebrity endorsement – is designed, by definition, to do anything more for you than can be got from good old fashioned water and healthy eating.

11. No Sweat

Another nonsensical product to be found in many bathrooms the length and breadth of the developed world are antiperspirant sprays; puts a new perspective on our understanding of the word 'developed'. Anyway the name of this product clearly explains to the half thinking semi intelligent would-be consumer why they shouldn't use it but for those of you who fall below that low standard of consciousness let me elaborate in a way that your last few remaining brain cells can comprehend.

This item, as the name clearly states, prevents perspiration. Now hands up, who among you thinks it is a good idea to aim an aerosol can full of chemicals directly at your naked defenceless body and spray it at such a close range that you can breathe it all in as well as soak up the poison through every pore of your skin? And for what purpose, exactly? To prevent the body from carrying out it's necessary function of sweating. Sweating is essential to prevent your body from overheating and also to keep your body's largest organ, your skin, actively healthy. So please don't be throwing away good money for the dubious purpose of fucking with Mother Nature's perfect rhythms; you will eventually pay a high price for such folly. Deodorants aren't much better, I picked up an aerosol deodorant idly in a shop the other day and it warned me on the side in bold print 'Abuse of this product can kill instantly'. Holy shit! How in the hell is your ordinary half-wit consumer supposed to know where the invisible borderline lies between use and abuse here? I was tempted to call the bomb squad to tell them I'd discovered a batch of suspicious looking canisters in aisle twelve in Tullamore's Tesco, but decided it more prudent, on balance, to return this dangerous product to its shelf and walk away quickly. I'd advise all of you dear readers to do likewise. Incidentally sweat, contrary to popular belief, does not actually have any smell; rather the slight whiff which we are obsessed with eradicating is caused by the skin and hair follicles not being properly clean. So we're back to the unbeatable simple bar of soap again and a good auld scrubber if you must.

12. Breath Fresheners

Naturally a waste of time, money and potentially dangerous, all these products can ever do is temporarily cover up your bad breath and I doubt many of them can even do that effectively. They certainly can't cure bad breath. The smell of your breath good, bad or indifferent is of course the result of whatever you have been ingesting into your body. Repugnant breath is one of the marvellous ways your body has of speaking to you. It is to be welcomed for what it is; namely an early warning from your body that you've been shoving the wrong fuel into it. You need to cut out the fags, alcohol, Indian takeaways or whatever crap your ingesting that's causing the problem. If you just spray over the problem with some chemical or other you'll disguise the issue and lull yourself into a false sense of security, believing the matter has been dealt with and needs no further consideration. The difficulties associated with your diet will continue causing more serious conditions down the line (but don't worry, the pharmaceuticals will have a drug for those too). So if you want to eradicate bad breath there is only one solution, find the offending food or drink item(s) and cut them from your diet.

13. Day by Day Decay

Tooth decay would, when you first reflect upon it, seem to be an entirely negative and depressing image to conjure up. In fact you might decide it is such a depressing prospect that not alone are you going to defy this naturally occurring phenomenon with brushing, flossing and mouthwash gargling but are also prepared to put yourself through uncomfortable and expensive professional cleaning and teeth whitening processes to erase any hint of it. Fair enough if you have buckets of money and that's what you wish to spend it on.

There is however another way to view this subject which has a strangely positive aspect to it. You could decide to use that minute or so every morning and night as you brush your teeth and are confronted at close quarters with undeniable signs of decay as an opportunity to reflect on the fleeting nature and decay of life itself. Provided you don't overdo it this can be a very empowering practice. All of us are on a gradual one way journey in life, never sure if the next stop is ours. Personally I believe regular fleeting reminders of this fact, such as a momentary glimpse of a yellowing molar, can serve to focus our attention on that which is important in life and detract us from the meaningless (almost all products). Changing our outlook like this also reminds us that when life seems all uphill there is a positive aspect to almost every circumstance, you just have to look anew with fresh eyes.

14. Cheap Scent Makes Sense

Apparently, in a blind testing of two perfumes recently, the cheaper product was preferred by a whopping majority of almost 90% – and the testers were knowledgeable perfume experts. What makes for a perfume expert I wonder? I suppose a famous French honker akin to the one belonging to the ever-expanding Gerard Depardieu would be an advantage, but I digress. Anyway, one expert described the cheap scent as "a timeless classic with fresh citrus and floral notes, and an alluring, exotic, oriental accord". I bet you are wondering what two perfumes were used in this test. Ok, I'll put you out of your misery. The cheaper and much preferred product was Lidl's, Suddenly Madame Glamour retailing at a heavenly €3.49, whilst the more expensive brand-name product was none other than heavyweight Chanel's Mademoiselle coming in at a dizzying €89.00. So, for Chanel's perfume products, punters are forking out at a ratio of €3.50 for the product in the bottle to every €85.50 paid for the name on the label. Put another way, you can buy twenty five bottles of the superior product or one bottle of the inferior quality one for the same money. Decisions! Decisions!

Now I realise that with Valentine's Day fast approaching as I write, there will be a temptation for some guys out there to do a legger down to Lidl, pronto. But producing the cheapest of cheap parfum de toilette as a pressy on Feb fourteenth is not going to get you your leg over, regardless of what it says about your financial acumen – much more likely it'll end up in a cast! So hold up big boy, how do we get around this horny, sorry I mean thorny problem? You're just going to have to keep your eyes peeled for empty Chanel or other brand-name perfume bottles and figure out how to transfer the contents of said cheap stuff into the fancy ass bottles. Alternatively, you could carry out the blind scent test on your better half (in store, of course) to demonstrate to her which is the better quality product. You can then try explaining that your only motivation was to buy the superior item as nothing but the best is good enough for your beau and it is just a happy coincidence that it is also ridiculously cheap.

15. Testing Retailer's Patience and Perfume

If you find your bathroom bottle of smellies is empty don't rush out spending €50 on its replacement. You know well it is only a matter of (a short) time before one of your nearest and dearest buys you another one. We all buy this stuff as presents for other people because we're too unimaginative or lazy to look for something they actually want. So hang in there, all good (and boring) presents come to those who wait.

In the meantime you can pop into the cosmetics section of your local department store or pharmacist on your way to work each morning to 'test' their fragrances, so you can still arrive into work each day clean as a whistle and smelly as ever, impressing Miss Higginbottom the temp no end, not alone with your aroma but also, after a couple of weeks, with your extensive knowledge of the various colognes on the market.

16. Paper Tissues

Turn your nose up at paper tissues. If you have a cold you'll go through them like nobody's business. It's cheaper and less hassle to use the old fashioned hankies. It can even be free if you can cut your own from some clean and soft suitable clothing or other material that's past its original usefulness. Keep a watchful eye out and always be thinking outside the (Kleenex) box.

17. Give the Gift of Time

No, I don't mean buying herself a watch or bringing home an antique grandfather clock for the hallway (although I always wanted one of these for no good reason I can think of). What I'm talking about here is giving the kids – and anyone else you're fond of come to that – the most precious gift possible, regardless of means. Time. Isn't it wonderful to know that at least up until the terrible teens all your kids really want from you is your time. You can buy them all the latest expensive PlayStations, Xbox's, iPhones or whatever new-fangled nonsense is out for the Christmas market this year but it's all as nothing next to spending time with them. As always, the beauty is in the simplicity; it doesn't matter what you do with them, kick ball in the garden, watch a Disney movie, go fishing, read them a story, play board games, whatever you all fancy. It doesn't have to cost a penny; the time itself is the key. So this coming year tell the little people you're keeping the Christmas and birthday presents simple. Watch any initial disappointment disappear when you inform them that you have several fun-filled family days planned instead.

To be honest the same advice applies to your adult friends and family as well. Tell them you've been overcome by a flash of enlightenment; suggest trading the useless bi-annual gifts for more time together. If they are friends worth having they will immediately recognise your wisdom and begin worshipping you as the reincarnation of some ancient Guru or other. As for those impossible teenagers, they're the easiest of the lot to satisfy. They don't even want your time – unless you count the time it takes for you to stand quietly on the stairs whilst they grunt at you in passing before hiding behind the locked door of their bedroom. When, one morning, they suddenly start behaving in an eerily pleasant manner, they are in effect giving you ample warning to have your excuses ready for the impending expensive demand. When you refuse said demand, they are secretly delighted (although of course they can never show it) because now they have fresh ammunition with which to berate you to their 1,245 friends on Facebook. No, all the adolescents need from you is to know you're there for them despite their behaviour. Apart from saving everyone a bucket-load of cash this plan is going to eliminate that annual intolerable tsunami of feelings you experience in the run up to Christmas every year as you run around like a headless turkey trying to find the impossible, ten perfect presents for your nearest and dearest, again. First you have the stress of the hunt for the unattainable and then the wave of depression as you realise on Christmas morning, from the perplexed facial expressions as the unwrapping begins, that you have inevitably failed once more. Those days are over. It's all laughter and relaxation from now on for your month of December and a stress free January into the bargain with no more mad credit card bills to deal with.

18. Free Flower Power

Do you know what's even more romantic than arriving home with an unexpected expensive bouquet of flowers for the missus? Arriving home with a bunch of wild flowers which you've picked enroute, that's what! You see the fairer sex, being less shallow than us men, are impressed most not by the amount of money spent, but by the thought, effort and imagination of your actions. This being the case it is plain to any casual observer that the guy who picked the free flowers put in exactly that – a little thought and effort, whereas the other robot with the shop-bought bouquet demonstrated a complete lack of originality. It's such a brilliantly unfair world sometimes isn't it? The tight git wins hands down again.

19. The Mamas and Papas

Forget mother's, father's, grandparent's and any other ridiculous special days recently dreamt up by the greeting card industry. I loved my Mammy as much as the next Irishman, and sure Grandparents are great but I wouldn't be caught dead getting them a card and a bunch of flowers on some Sunday preordained by some nerdy marketing whizz. When you arrive over to yer granny's on that much publicised Sabbath with the aforementioned €30 interflora offering and she calls you a soft eejit, she's not covering up her true feelings as grannies often do. She bloody well means it! Grannies come from a more pragmatic era and can think of a thousand and one better things to spend thirty quid on. So she's trying to offer you a bit of sanity in the nicest way she knows how. Now if you brought her over for a nice cuppa tea, a fruit scone and a bit of a chin wag she'd be made up entirely. Look we all have a birthday, that's enough of an opportunity for anyone so inclined to lavish you with love and gifts and if they miss that opportunity they can make it up to you at Christmas. Twice a year to be pampered is enough for anyone.

20. Robotic Romeos

While we're on the subject of romance and special occasions, you know what's the biggest con job in the calendar? Valentine's Day. Now don't get me wrong, I'm as romantic as the next guy but nobody is going to tell me when I should or should not be romantic towards my lover, thank you very much. Last time I checked that was a private matter between myself and herself. But no, every February 14th, robot like, every male in the country is expected to buy a card, chocolates and flowers in that order and at twice the normal price. He must then deliver same to the missus upon arrival home from work, whereupon he will surprise her (just like he did last year and the year before) by telling her to get ready – he has a table booked for a *spontaneous* romantic meal out! Even if you haven't got a bloody partner you're expected to treat your mother and later go on a singles' night out so that you'll be ready for next year! For heaven's sake lads, could you be less romantic if you tried? Being romantic to a prescription formula, concocted by an inhumane corporate machine, alongside a billion others around the globe behaving identically?

Here's what I suggest: treat your lover to a genuine romantic surprise involving a little thought and creativity (but not necessarily expense) on any day other than bloody February 14th. At the end of the date explain your new found conscientious objections to St Valentine's but reassure her that you are looking forward to sharing many more special occasions with her in the future, just not on that pre prescribed date. Trust me fellas you'll reap the benefits in more ways than one. In the extremely unlikely event that this plan backfires and you get the old red card consider yourself even more fortunate. You've just had a very, very lucky escape indeed.

21. Hollow Shells

Easter eggs must represent the worst value possible when buying chocolate; worse even than Christmas selection boxes. Gram for gram you pay a hell of a premium just because it comes in an oval shape and is nestled inside an oversized colourful cardboard box. But how do we get around this problem? Kids love the idea of their Easter chocolate fix and even a tight bastard can't deny the little tykes. Wait though; what are kids if not greedy little self-absorbed monsters? Could we not use this universal trait to our advantage with a little well presented bribery? In the run up to Easter waste no opportunity to point out to them how little chocolate there actually is in their favourite egg before finally suggesting that you could get them twice the amount of chocolate in the form of their favourite bars should they so wish. The trick is of course to make them think it was their own clever idea in the first place. No need to mention to them the fact that even though they are getting twice the amount of goods it's only costing you half the money.

Of course if you are in the habit of buying eggs for nephews and neighbours at Easter then your head is as hollow as the bloody eggs themselves. Have you not noticed that there is an obesity epidemic and a general health care crisis in the country at the moment? Still, if you will persist against my sane advice you should at least wait until the Easter Monday bank holiday to call around because all the goodies will be on offer at half price by then so you can pick them up on your way over.

22. Self Selection

Christmas selection boxes are another golden opportunity for the confectionary industry to part the dim-witted from their dough but the solution is even simpler than our egg problem earlier in the year. You just buy the chocolate bars individually, picking up whichever ones you see on exceptional special offer in the months leading up to Christmas; then you package them up in some plastic using a bit of fancy coloured paper with some ribbon tied into a decorative bow and Bobs your uncle! You have a selection 'box' that'll do the finest. Not alone that but you have a one-off designer selection bag which can be filled to the fussiest of individual tastes. You never know where the idea could take you, family and friends might take a shine to them and start ordering a few from ya. Many's a cottage industry started from such humble beginnings.

23. DIY Christmas

The next time you are looking for something fun to do with the kids you could do a lot worse than making a few Christmas (or Halloween or birthday party) decorations with them instead of buying expensive ones in the shops. All you need is a bit of colourful paper – maybe crepe or even just cut up a few old colourful magazines – and a bit of glue perhaps. Don't worry your head about the lack of artistic ability, the more idiotic your creations are the more fun the kids will have laughing at you. There is nothing, and I do mean nothing, children enjoy more than watching an adult make an idiot of themselves and besides, you might surprise yourself and unleash your inner artist. While we're on the DIY Christmas topic, if you have a corner of a garden going to waste and you are one of those people who like to have the real Christmas tree as opposed to the artificial one, why not plan ahead and plant a few for the Christmases to come.

It'll feel a bit more special and personal if you've grown it yourself – as well as saving you a few quid of course. What about making a Christmas log for the table? Just bore a hole in your log, pop in a candle, tack on a bit of holly and tinsel and finish off with a bit of snow or silver spray. There's nothing to it, even I can do it with me ten thumbs. In fact the young fella made a fine few shillings selling our log creations around the locality last year.

24. Present me with Cash

Why in the name of Allah, can somebody explain to me, are gift vouchers such a popular present? I mean I get the bit about them being a lazy sod's idea of giving you a present without having to bother getting up off his hole to look for a proper gift (which, heaven forbid might require a bit of thought and effort). But if that is the objective why not just give cash instead? This requires even less effort on the part of the giver and provides the recipient with endless choice as to where and what to spend it on. On top of this gift vouchers can go out of date if forgotten about or mislaid for a longish period or the shop they were bought from may close down. These risks can easily be eliminated by giving cash instead. Also you have no bargaining power when purchasing a gift voucher. You can't haggle with the shopkeeper to give you a €25 voucher for €20 – well you can but it won't get you anywhere. Seriously though, there is no point in giving me a book token worth fifty quid when I'm broke and my oil tank is empty. What am I gonna do, burn the books to keep warm? In conclusion then, just so we're clear: gift vouchers serve no useful purpose, so please don't bother with them. Even if your brother is a roaring alcoholic and you don't want to give him cash 'cos he'll only drink it, even then don't give him a voucher; he'll only flog it for well below its face value and drink it anyway.

25. Presents in the Post

If you happen to receive any unsolicited goods in your mail, such as Christmas cards from some charity which you never ordered, what should you do? Keep them but don't pay for them, I say. You should not have to pay for something you didn't want or ask for. Equally it is not your responsibility to send back unsolicited goods, wasting your time and money doing so. No, the simplest thing to do is thank the universe for the generous offering, enjoy your free gift and leave it at that. To do anything else is only to encourage the company involved and others to continue this dubious practice. If this seems a rather harsh position to adopt, especially where a charitable organisation is concerned, I would respectfully point out that any group which can afford to send out thousands of packaged goods in this way begins to look more like a well oiled large business operation and less like a charity in nature. Besides, just as with a bold child, sometimes you have to be cruel to be kind to point out to them the error of their ways.

26. The Wedding Summons

Is there anything more likely to put you in a bad mood for the week than a bloody wedding invitation? It's worse than a feckin' summons and it'll end up costing you a hell of a lot more too. You have to get your good suit dry cleaned; the missus has to buy a new rig out – whatever's wrong with the one she wore to that christening six weeks ago is incomprehensible to the male brain – and marks and sparks won't do either, it'll have to be from some fancy ass boutique, probably necessitating a weekend campaign traipsing up to the big smoke and trawling through every rag shop in the place. You'll have blisters in places you didn't know ye had places. Then there'll be the hair do, beauty treatments and the divil knows what. On the big day itself, which is on a Thursday because the happy couple got a cheaper deal midweek with the hotel (sod the 300 guests who've lost two days wages because they couldn't have a Saturday wedding like everyone else), you'll have to travel across the country on byroads that the sat-nav doesn't even recognise before finally ending up in a quaint little church halfway between Ballygonowhere and Ballygobackwards. How the hell did they find this place, you'll wonder? It's not like anyone at the wedding even lives in the same province. Of course the hotel has the only accommodation for miles around and mysteriously when you checked online their prices on the wedding night were three times the rate for any other bloody night of the year.

Then there's the present – well I say 'present'. Nobody bothers with old fashioned presents like a nice toaster anymore, so what I really mean is the fee; that unspoken yet curiously known to everyone minimum amount which must be included in the card so the grateful couple can clearly see what value you've put on them. It is of course a two tier fee system, the larger payment being required if you are attending the full event as opposed to the afters. If you ask me they've got that arseways; you should get a discount for having to go through the torture of the full day. Normally you're a very sober and sensible fellow but the stress of the whole thing has got to you so you've snuck off to the public bar where you're eventually found downing pints and chasers at €10 a pop – cheap too you're thinking by the time you've thrown back the fifth one. Did I mention you're back on the fags too by this stage? To cut a long story short before the night is out you've made a complete tit of yourself, you wake up with the mother of all hangovers, the wife's not talking to you, in fact your only friend for the next fortnight is gonna be the dog. You're confused as hell, what's all the fuss about? It's not like we're even related to these people.

It's simply not fair or reasonable of people to put a small army of guests through this torture and outrageous expense just because they want to do something daft like promising that they'll love one another for the next fifty years. Fair enough, they're entitled to any absurdity they like but does it have to cost twenty grand and why the hell should you and I pick up the tab? The thing you want to do is have a good plausible excuse for not going, one which can be utilised whenever these wedding or other formal family invitations arrive. You need to lay the foundations of your plan long before the annoying event is looming; perhaps you could develop a vague illness like say depression, which can lay you low at any time and the symptoms of which are hard for anyone, even your second cousin Nigel, who's a doctor, to contradict. Alternatively it could just be that you're holiday or business travel arrangements, which you've already booked, sadly clash with the impending nuptials. What a shame, eh! Whatever you do don't even consider that next nightmare invitation. You could have a forthnight on the Costa del Sol with herself for the same money. One final word of warning though: when your own inevitable turn comes around you can't reasonably expect people to do for you what you're unwilling to do for them, so throw a welly wedding instead.

27. Welly Weddings

What the hell is a welly wedding you're wondering? Well basically, a welly wedding is one where you dispense with all the formality and most of the expense. You get yourself the use of a field, preferably with access to a decent road, maybe even beside your own house if you live in the countryside, stick up a bit of a makeshift marquee and perhaps a couple of spare tents. Get a big blazing fire going. Inform all the guests on your homemade computer-generated invitations that there's no need for a present, their presence is present enough, but ask them to bring their own booze, food and accommodation (tent). Also encourage everyone to come armed with a musical instrument and a willingness to attempt a song or other party piece of their own choosing. You'll need to get hold of a shaman or a druid to replace the priest for the ceremony. People can dress however they wish, some may want to get dolled up and why not? But because this event is happening in an Irish field one item of attire all those attending should be wearing is a good old pair of wellies, hence the name. Now that the scene is set the gathering can settle in for a night of craic that can go on 'til first light and beyond. No need to worry about licensing hours, bar extensions or any of that nonsense. You'll have yourselves a shindig that'd be the envy of the Beverly hillbillies themselves. The cousins will be talking about it for years, long after they've forgotten the details of their own big day. Of course your marital vows won't have any legal status which is an added bonus; now there won't be any room for complacency or taking one another for granted so your union should beat the odds and stand the test of time. Plus in the unlikely event that the thoughtful and imaginative pair who would come up with such a setting for their union should ever part, the need for the most traumatic (never mind expensive) avoidable life event it is possible to experience, yes divorce, will have been dispensed with in advance.

28. Communicating and Confirming your Insanity

I read with horror recently that the average family spend on first unholy communion in 2011 was €1,000. Lads, this is certifiable lunacy! Has nobody told ye about the down turn which has many more years to run in the same direction yet? There is thankfully some small sign of sanity reappearing amongst the population as it seems the average spend in 2012 was down by 25% to €744 per child (god help ye if ye had twins). Still there is a hell of a lot more scope for further savings. These figures do not include the average individual cash gift of approximately €36 given to each child by friends and relatives, bringing the national total handed out to these seven-year-olds to €20 million.

It was estimated in a survey in early 2012 that over €100 million would be spent on communions and confirmations in total this year. The breakdown of this year's €744 figure is as follows: €179 on outfit and accessories – which will be worn only once, for a few hours and then left to the moths in the back of the wardrobe; €176 on clothing for the rest of the family – what the hell do they need new clothes for? It's not their big day! Are they trying to steal the limelight from the poor child?; €303 on food and drink – for the adults to party and get pissed on while the child soaks it all up huddled in a corner bored senseless; €86 on entertainment – for bouncy castles and trampolines upon which the little angels can attempt to break a limb, making their big day really memorable with a visit to A & E. Seriously, it's time to get a grip on reality folks. These communion children are seven or eight years of age, they don't need you to spend up to €1,000 to ruin their big day!

Here's what you do for your child on their communion day: get a cheap but trendy second hand outfit online or in a shop or alternatively, a still good-as-new 'only worn once' hand-me-down from friends or family (remember to store it carefully for the siblings following behind). After the ceremony, take a few pictures of little Johnny picking his nose in his finery for posterity and then bring him off to the cinema or the zoo and even Supermacs if you must, for a treat. On the way home his new found wealth will be burning a hole in his pocket so stop off at the toy shop to let him loose with €100 or so (open a bank account with the rest to start the savings habit), then it's off home to spend a family evening together having great fun behaving like big kids playing with the new toys. Total cost to you about €150, special memories and enjoyment for child: immeasurable.

Honestly, I know I'm repeating myself here, but it's all about time spent with the child, not money.

29. A Bite-Sized Contribution

Do not give your kids pocket money for doing sweet F.A. What message do you think that gives them? I'm all for youngsters having a small income early on and learning how to handle money wisely, so by all means give them a few quid but make sure they do a few simple age-appropriate chores for you in return. Of course you can't stop some people, such as well-meaning aunts and uncles turning up out of the blue and giving the child €20 when it's not even their birthday or Christmas or anything, and why would you want to, sure a fool and their money are easily parted. They might as well waste their hard earned dosh on your little nipper as anyone else's. One way or another kids these days come into a lot of cash so it's important that they learn the value of it. They shouldn't be allowed to spend it all on the latest Xbox game or fancy iPhone. These things are all well and good but you should also introduce the idea of them contributing to some of the household expenditures which they are the beneficiary of. Now I'm not saying they should be paying a share of the electric bill but they could commit a token gesture towards the cost of their school tour or, if they are really pressing you for something like a new bike there is no reason they can't help by putting a little something from their ever expanding piggy bank towards the cost. Also if your little darling has their heart set on something for his/her birthday or Christmas which you consider to be outside your (or Santa's) budget, explain this honestly and suggest that they contribute a portion of the cost. If they are unwilling, the little imp didn't want the thing too badly in the first place, did he?

30. Gone to the Dogs

Pets can be a wonderful addition to the family but they can also be a bloody expensive addition. Ok so you could get a goldfish, they're pretty cheap to run but you kind of get what you pay for on that one, don't ya? They're not big on interaction are they? No, I'd say if you're determined to have a pet you're as well off to stick to the auld reliable, that's right, a dog. There's a reason why they're known as man's best friend after all. Even though they can be costly to keep, you could consider one to be extremely good value for money – worth its weight in gold in fact if the little pooch can put your broody partner off starting a family for a few years. Maybe if you're lucky and you get a real nightmare of a dog, you know, one that destroys everything in sight, you might put her off wanting kids altogether. Now that would be a stroke of good fortune because we all know what a great big financial black hole kids are, don't we? Failing that, at least when deciding what type of pooch to get, be sure to make it a female puppy. Don't be tempted to go to the pound either to pick up a free mutt. Believe me it's not worth it; that flea pit is probably going to have mange and numerous psychiatric issues, he'll cost you a fortune in vet fees and you know what that rabid profession are like for fleecing you! They're worse than doctors the whole lot of them, at least there's an enquiry if a doctor gives you a lethal injection in error. I never heard of a tribunal investigating the unexpected demise of Lily the Labrador. No, sometimes you have to throw out a sprat to catch a salmon; get yourself a nice, pure-bred puppy, registered with the Kennel Club, the works, and make sure it's a female. That way if the hungry tyke is going to try eating you out of house and home at least you can breed from her and she'll be earning her keep. Best off to stick to a small breed as well just in case the plan goes horribly wrong and you can't breed her because she's barren or something. Knowing my luck she'd turn out to be a lesbian. Anyway, God forbid but if that does happen at least with the toy breeds you're exercising a bit of damage limitation and unlike Adolf the Alsatian, she's not likely to be devouring T-bone steaks for breakfast.

31. Pimp your Poodle

Oh suit yourself then, if you're going to be all posh and you have a strong objection to the regular arrival of a small army of puppies shitting and pissing all over your gaff, not to mention the hassle of minding them, have it your own way. Scrap the puppy production idea. Assuming however that you still want a canine companion it remains a good idea to purchase a pedigree. Get yourself a male pure-bred of your choice and then when he comes of age you can advertise his services as a stud dog. Fido can earn his keep, running around enjoying himself with frisky frauleines. This is seriously easy money. You, in your new role as pedigree pimp can potentially earn several hundred euro per performance depending on breed, demand and quality of your hound. As for the dog, you'll hear no complaint out of him; he'll be happy as a cock in a hen house. You can even afford to throw him a couple of lamb chops to put the icing on the cake to his working day.

32. Boning the Butcher

You might remember I mentioned in an earlier point that you should seek the advice of your local butcher about cheap cuts of meat. Well while you're there, getting all friendly-like, don't forget to proposition him for a few free juicy bones for Bruno at home.

33. Forget the Vet

Vet fees are quite simply astronomical! Impossible for me at any rate to comprehend the prices they charge for seemingly routine, simple procedures. Admittedly, they are sometimes a 'necessary evil' but for minor issues with your pet, steer clear. Seek first the free advice from the people in your local pet stores who often prove to be just as knowledgeable as any vet. They will of course also have a vested interest in making a sale but at least the 'consultation' will come free and what's more, the mark up on any product they do advise you to purchase is almost certain to be a minor fraction of that which the 'professional practice' applies. The jury, as far as I am concerned, is also out on things like inoculations and booster doses. How many people even enquire as to what exactly they are protecting their dog from let alone what level of risk existed in the first place or how much risk still remains even when injections are administered! What about the side effects of these drugs? I'm not going to tell anyone what they should do where their pet is concerned because it can be quite an emotive issue – I am aware that the dog can be considered to be one of the family. But it is precisely because it is an emotive decision that you are at risk of a type of emotional extortion when parting with large sums of money in these circumstances. When your dog is on the vet's table and he is telling you – with the tone of authority which medical practitioners always employ – that a certain (expensive) course of action is necessary, it is very difficult for even the most independent-minded, strong-willed individual to disagree or to even ask for time to digest the information.

So, as always, the advice is to be prepared. Information is power. Don't forget to apply the general advice to your unique circumstances, to see if it fits. For instance, it may generally be advisable to have your dog immunised against certain contagious diseases which are most often picked up from other carrier dogs but if your pampered pooch spends almost all it's time indoors, rarely coming into contact with others of his ilk, perhaps the risk you are protecting him from is negligible to begin with. Get into the habit of always performing a cost/benefit analysis before any major outlay. A second opinion never goes astray either, assuming you can acquire it free of charge.

34. Go for Gore-Tex

When shopping for your next pair of brogues, go for Gore-Tex or other waterproof footwear. This is Ireland after all. Worse still where I'm sitting, here, in the west of Ireland where the only difference between summer and winter is that the rain is warmer in the summer. Even after shopping around, waiting for the sales and haggling they may cost a bit extra but they will be absolutely worth it beyond a shadow of a doubt. You will get years out of them, no exaggeration. If Gore-Tex shoes were an animal, they'd be a Turtle. All this talk about shoes and the rain reminds me of a story, back in the pre-Socratic era; 1994 to be precise, I was looking for a good pair of shoes. I thought I had found just that and I bought a pair in Dunnes Stores costing £30 in old money, I suppose with inflation and the currency change that'd be €80 to €90 in today's money. Anyway, to get to the point my new shoes fell apart after only two months. I brought them back to the shop and when I got no satisfaction at customer services I asked to speak to the manager. Well do you know what he said to me? He said I shouldn't have been wearing them in the wet. Now bear in mind this was early February in Ireland. 'For fucks sake' says I, 'how in the name of jaysus could I avoid wearing shoes in wet conditions?' If I wanted a pair of slippers for wearing around the house, that's what I would have bought. Back then wearing waterproof usually meant a pair of wellies but luckily today we have lots of choice and styles available to us. So no excuses, forget Dunnes not-so-cheap crap. Get yourself a decent pair of clogs. You'll save a packet in the long run.

35. Walking Billboards

Did you ever think there is something arse-about-face ways when it comes to people paying a serious premium for the so called privilege of wearing 'branded' clothing? I mean to say if I walk down the street with Adidas or Abercrombie emblazoned across my chest I'm advertising that company's wares, am I not? So why the bloody hell are they not paying me for the advertising space that is my body instead of me paying them, hand over fist? Any other medium a company uses to advertise their goods through whether it be TV, websites, newspapers or billboards they pay a small fortune for. Ever more unusual locations are being used as advertising space such as public toilets, petrol pump forecourts, taxis and even private motor vehicles. Good luck to them I say because they are paying for the space but you've got to ask what is wrong with the masses – particularly the youthful variety – when they are not only willing to advertise Tommy feckin' Hilfiger for free but are prepared to shell out €50 on a flimsy t-shirt for the honour. Seriously, cop on lads! You're not a walking billboard and if you are you should contact JC Decaux, sign up and start getting paid for it. Otherwise get yourself down to Penneys or a second hand charity shop and buy yourself a €2 top. If you're worried that you won't be original enough or that a €2 plain Penneys t-shirt doesn't express your creativity and individuality, I'm sure you can splatter it with a little colourful fabric paint and hey presto you have a unique, one-off work of art to strut around in. No longer are you a slave to fashion; oh no! Now you are a fashionista; a leader.

I know the Conscience Police out there are going to raise a righteous eyebrow at me now and ask how is it, do I think, that budget retailers can offload t-shirts at €2 a pop and still make a profit? The answer of course is obvious, because they're made in a sweat shop in India where the workers are treated like sub-human shit. Unfortunately it's in the same factory or the one across the road that the €50 item is made. Look around, where's Fruit of the Loom and the rest of the textile industry we once had in Ireland and other western countries gone? They've gone east my friend and all for the same reason. So if you want to assuage your guilty conscience, lobby your MEP or better still join Amnesty International; the annual membership will cost you less than the price of a pair of Brown Thomas boxers.

36. Human Peacocks

If God wanted you to have skin more colourful than a New York gay pride march he'd have made sure you were born with the full complement of courting, male peacock tail feathers growing out of your arse. But he didn't, did he? What's that telling you then? Well it could mean you're not after all 'God's gift', that you're not his proudest creation and he'd prefer if you would just keep a low profile, thanks. Who knows? But it should certainly be telling you not to go mutilating your body with tattoos. It just isn't natural or healthy. It should be obvious to the dimmest Neanderthal among us that we are not meant to absorb ink into our bodies through any orifice! It's just one of those things, you know, like putting your hand into a fire will result in serious pain – you don't have to be told. So why am I telling you? Because everywhere I look these days I seem to see idiots covered in what some call 'body art'. God preserve us, but body art used to mean a nice painting of a nude female. Seriously fellas – and it is mostly fellas that cover themselves with ink, women tend to be sparing at least in its application – why would you want to spend good money inflicting pain on yourself and seriously diminishing your chances of landing that job you applied for last week. And if I haven't given you enough reasons to steer clear of the inky artist's studio, let me just remind you that a tattoo is like a bad marriage; it's for life. You *will* regret it, sooner or later. It will be the first thing you see each morning and the last at night, beginning and ending every day with this not-so-gentle reminder of your foolish youthful whim. When at last you have finally had enough of the mental torture, like the hasty marriage it too will be expensive and bloody painful to erase.

So if you are feeling a strong urge to reincarnate the last of the Mohicans then knock yourself out – get the haircut and dye it all the colours of the rainbow if you want, it's only hair after all, it'll grow out. And if you need a few tattoos to complete the image, fine, you're only young once, I suppose, but for Christ's sake get the temporary, removable variety because by the time your hair is respectable enough to call round to your gran again you'll have outgrown the tattoo novelty as well.

37. Men in Black

If you are anything like me and prone to slobbering coffee down the front of your top or, if again like yours truly, an observant individual could hazard a fair guess at what you just had for lunch with a quick study of your shirt, then it is time to join the men in black. In other words save yourself a lot of laundry loads, replacement clothes buying, frustration and expense by wearing dark clothing. Accept it, you are a messy git and you're unlikely to change any time soon. No sweat, just ditch the light coloured clothing and hey presto, problem solved!

38. Tight Genes

I recommend living in navy blue denim jeans. They are universally fashionable, comfortable, hard wearing and cheap – or at least as cheap as you want them to be; they go with every conceivable kind of outfit or footwear you care to match them with and you can easily get several days wear out of them, maybe even a week at a stretch, before you have to wash them. If all that wasn't enough, because they are the single most popular item of clothing in the western world, you should have no problem finding a decent pair in good nick down at your local second hand shops. Also, if you only have one type of pants in your wardrobe it's one less thing to procrastinate over in the morning.

39. Scan and Scram

There is a recent clever phenomenon which is developing amongst savvy shoppers which has been dubbed 'scan and scram'. Catchy jargon aside, what this phrase refers to is simply the practice of browsing the high street shops looking for the goods you want, trying on clothes in store and so on in the usual way but you don't purchase in town. You note down the pertinent details of the items you like and then you check online to find the same item cheaper. The online price can often beat the high street price by a reasonable margin due to very much reduced overhead costs and the fact that retailers are eager to incentivise us away from the expensive traditional shopping model. With today's technology you can often compare and contrast prices on your phone whilst still in the shop. Look out for the tumble weed coming to a town centre near you soon.

40. Switch to Swishing

Swishing is a new phrase coined by one Lucy O'Shea and her work colleagues back in 2000 when they wanted to curtail their consumption levels without curbing a healthy appetite for 'retail therapy'. But it's not a new idea, just the repackaging, rebranding and reorganisation of an old practice which has been with us for as long as people have worn clothes. Basically swishing is the term given to the practice of a group of people (always women I'm willing to bet) organising a get together to swap clothes, shoes and other accessories. Everybody turns up with some item or items of clothing they are willing to donate. You must donate something to participate and you are then free to browse and choose any items donated by others which catch your eye. No money changes hands unless it is organised as a charity event in which case there may be a nominal entry fee or voluntary donation involved. Swishing is rather like a jumble sale it seems to me except you turn up with some half decent gear you no longer wear in lieu of hard cash.

The idea has become quite popular around the world, helped along of course by the necessary celebrity endorsement seal of approval. There are now a number of swishing websites in operation and the goods being 'swished' have extended to include books, furniture and more. I haven't as yet indulged in this art form myself but it sounds like all good ideas: brilliant in its simplicity. You basically swap your old clutter for some new clobber without any money changing hands. What's not to like?

41. Undercover Investigations

In a recent survey I read on the intriguing subject of how often people change their underwear, here are the results: once a day 79%; twice a day 8%; more than twice a day 1% (who are these people!); once every two days 6%; once every three or four days 3%; once a week 1% and the commando brigade 2%. What can the tight arse learn from these statistics? Well most of us by definition are in the 79% grouping and if you are in a romantic relationship and are happy in it, I suggest you should remain firmly in that category. But what if you secretly wish to extricate yourself from said union? Well lads I imagine there is no surer guarantee of success in that objective than to join the 1% 'once a week' category. You'll be single again before you can say Tommy Hilfiger designer Y fronts and reaping the financial savings of the singleton. This is of course provided you don't spend your newfound freedom in the pub every night looking for a new romantic entanglement. If you are already single and change your jocks every day whose gonna know if you push it out to once every two days? You'll save on laundry and wear and tear costs.

According to these statistics 12% of the population have already adopted this or an even more restrictive knicker turnover policy. 2% of the population have taken the ultimate step and removed all brief expenditure from their budgets, that's 100,000 bravehearts throughout the land, throwing caution to the wind in the event of an untimely visit to A&E. Are you courageous enough to join this elite clan? Finally what of the 1% or 50,000 souls changing their smalls more than twice a day? These poor creatures must be leaking profusely from every orifice. My strong advice to this category is to forget the underwear altogether and invest in a few nappies, reusable ones, naturally. Anyway, it's pause for thought; the savings may be brief and go unnoticed but they won't be negligible.

42. Killer Heels

I've just read about how yer one, Carol Vorderman, has broken her nose having smacked into a wall after a nasty tumble down a flight of stairs. Just goes to prove it's not the fall that does the damage but the sudden stop at the end. Seriously though, the culprit in this case is the same one which has caused one third of the female population to fall and injure themselves while wearing them. That's right, those killer heels have struck again. High heels are the great equaliser of women everywhere; they raise up, then level all comers regardless of social standing. Easy knowing it was a bloke who invented them. Girls look, I know a nice pair of stilettos can really make an outfit, leaving women green with envy and otherwise perfect gentlemen frothing at the bit with desire but it just isn't worth the cost. I'm not talking here about the rip off price tag either.

The higher long term price of those added couple of inches begins with relatively minor physical ailments of the foot such as calluses, corns and bunions. However, the more attached you are to the gravity defying unnatural posture which these mini stilts force you to adopt (resulting in you bending your spine and contorting every part of your body from your toes right up to your neck), the more likely you are to eventually suffer anything from sciatica, a painful condition where nerves become trapped; osteoarthritis, due to sustained pressure on the knees to ankle sprains and more general back, neck and shoulder pain. These I assure you are just a sample selection of the potential problems in store for you if you continue to choose fashion over function. By the way there are greater risks still to teenagers who begin wearing heels before their bodies have fully developed; thwarting the process and causing, amongst other things, permanent hip problems. Now I'm just a guy and sure what do I know but it seems to me the wearing of these ridiculous fashion statements results in many women in their prime suffering the kind of conditions they should not reasonably have expected to deal with until their dotage. Is it really worth overlooking the myriad health risks for a momentary feat of elevated fashion? Incidentally, even this small payoff is often ruined anyway by a cumbersome wearer or the introduction of half a dozen double vodkas into the mix. If you are drinking alcohol you really should start with both feet firmly planted on the ground. Ask yourself if any man would put himself through this excruciating pain for some perceived and dubious payoff? Not on your Nelly.

The high heel should by rights be abandoned and chronicled in the same chapter of the history books as that other prehistoric symbol of women's subservience to men which masqueraded in its day as an indispensable fashion accessory; the chastity belt. No other current item of attire comes close to inflicting so much damage to your body, bank account, gait and even your ego. This is one of those rare occasions girls when you should take a leaf out of our book. Besides there are endless ways to look stylish without breaking the bank, undoing women's progress towards equality or ending up in A&E.

43. Pretty in Pink

It has been reported that men who wear flamboyant pink shirts to work as opposed to the more sombre traditional colours like blue or white earn on average €1,000 more per annum than their more conventional counterparts. I am aware that there could be many reasons for this which have little to do with shirt colour and more to say about the psychology of individuals who deliberately break the mould. Of course there is also the fact that any set of statistics should be digested with a healthy sprinkling of scepticism, but hey what if it's true? You could earn an extra grand a year just by changing your shirt? Well heck it's a long shot I know, but I for one am not going to risk losing out. From now on I'll be pretty in pink. After all this could go a long way towards explaining Mick Wallace's election as a T.D. – pink shirts were his secret electoral weapon. No need for policies or principals then, just wear pink and you're a shoe in.

44. A Watertight Investment

Can anyone understand, in a country like Ireland where it rains at least every other day, why will almost nobody invest in decent head to toe wind and waterproof clothing? Every 'soft' Irish day, in towns the length and breadth of the country you see people rushing to buy those lethal weapons known as umbrellas. Apart from the damage these yokes can do to your fellow-pedestrians optics as you hurtle along head down to your destination, they're just not equal to the task of defending you against an incoming Atlantic onslaught. Besides, if the weather doesn't do for your newly purchased brolly you know you're going to lose it at the first forgetful opportunity. The only person looking more ridiculous than the umbrella lady is the guy attempting to keep his bald patch dry with his copy of The Irish Times. Seriously lads, the clue to why that won't keep you dry is in the name, newspapers you see are made of em, paper and therefore are defenceless against a downpour. Then there are the hordes that clog up all the shop entrances when an unexpected short Irish sun shower arrives. There they stand with frustrated skyward looks and sighs, wasting twenty valuable minutes of their lunch break waiting for a hint of blue to reappear between the clouds before making a run for it.

I know we're an optimistic bunch at times but there's no point living in denial. Ireland is a wind and rain soaked little island bog sitting forlornly out in the Atlantic. Therefore if you happen to be one of its long-suffering inhabitants, isn't it time to face the truth? You need to invest in a decent arsenal of weatherproof clothing. This will unfortunately involve a little initial financial pain because decent gear of this sort doesn't come cheap but it will save you a small fortune over its lengthy lifetime in avoided medical expenses and lost workdays as you are now adequately protected from all those winter coughs and colds. You also happily no longer have to worry about what our esteemed judiciary consider fair compensation to a young mother for the loss of an eye. PS: This tip will be of no bloody use to you if you leave the gear at home, so have it handy, in the car or wherever for use in an emergency.

45. The Power of No!

Do you find it difficult, sometimes even impossible to refuse an invitation or a request for help? Do you think the word 'no' is a negative term? Do you regularly find yourself attending family or other social functions because of a sense of obligation even though you would prefer to be elsewhere? If you are nodding in familiar agreement at these suggestions then sadly, you are a 'yes' man (or woman). You are not alone however as this is a staggeringly common affliction. How do you think anybody succeeds in getting 200 people or more to attend their wedding? Surely you don't honestly believe even half of them actually want to be there? Or that they all really think this is the best possible use they could be putting their valuable time and money to? How do seven-year-old kids end up getting €2,000 or something ridiculous like that for their first unholy communion? You don't really think anybody except mammy and daddy gives a hoot about little Johnny and his bloody second sacrament, do you? Are you one of those people who sends birthday cards to a dozen different nieces and nephews with twenty quid in each, every year? Or worse still, you feel it necessary to drive half way across the country to delivery said penalty in person?

When you stand back and reflect – with the benefit of a modicum of emotional detachment – on all the occasions over the past year where you found yourself 'buying' into something you really had little or no interest in, it may seem as though the lunatics have taken over that asylum which is your judgement. Your inability to utter that simplest of short words 'no' is costing you a small fortune. Still all is not lost, now you are aware of the insanity you just need practice at getting comfortable with the sound of those two letters 'N' and 'O'. Put this plan into action for the smaller, more inconsequential invitations first; just to get used to it and to build confidence and resolve into your decisions. When you are next faced with an unexpected invitation or request from an acquaintance, politely tell them you will think about it; let them know or you have to check your diary, whatever. Buy yourself a bit of time and breathing space so that you can calmly assess, weighing up all the pros and cons, whether or not it is in <u>your</u> best interests to accept or reject their proposition. This also gives you a chance to articulately formulate your reasons should you decide to let them down. At first you may find it difficult to refuse a request face to face; it would be a good idea to get to the point where you can but in the meantime it is fine to communicate your decision by text. This will reduce the risk and pressure of being talked out of your decision and enable you to word your argument accurately without getting flustered.

If you have spent a lifetime avoiding the word no, your

peers will not like this change in you; people are by definition conservative in nature and their instinct will tell them there is something wrong with your new approach. So initially at least, many will be suspicious, perhaps even unaccepting; some will try their utmost to change your mind, to 'make you see sense'. Be patient with them. Those that are worthwhile members of your circle will eventually apply reason and intellect to the new circumstance, thus becoming accepting, perhaps even encouraging of the new, empowered you. As for the others you can gently let them go, feeling the relief as you lay down the burden of their 'friendship'. Remember the power of NO! Those two seemingly inconsequential little letters may hold the key to transforming your life, not to say anything of your finances.

46. Eat Healthily

This might not seem like the right place for this advice as, superficially, it would appear to be more expensive than filling yourself with the cheapest of the cheap, crap food. This excuse for not eating healthily is a crock of shit. Fruit, vegetables, brown rice, pasta, natural yogurt and lots of other basic but healthy foodstuffs can be bought for chicken feed and, prevention being cheaper than cure, eating healthily will prove to be a sound investment in the medium to long term. Besides, if you follow all the other nuggets of wisdom proffered here it shouldn't prove burdensome to keep a sound and balanced diet even if some healthy foodstuffs are a tad on the expensive side.

47. Stopping Pill-Popping

25% of Irish adults now take food supplements on a regular basis. The figure for Britain is 40%. For Americans in excess of 50% and growing is the worrying figure. This global market is now worth a whopping sixty four billion dollars annually. All this despite the fact that the safe food website (www.safefood.eu) states the obvious quite simply when it advises: 'Generally, you do not need to take food supplements if you are healthy and eat a normal balanced diet'. It goes on to tell us that in fact, 'Too much of certain supplements can be harmful and cause unwanted side effects'. So unless you have been advised by a medical practitioner to do so, cease this senseless practice of popping pointless pills. You know this book could just as easily have been called 'The Little Book of Uncommon Sense' because I am about to impart to you yet another glaringly obvious nugget of true wisdom. A varied diet of natural, healthy foods along with no more than a minimal amount of the unhealthy processed synthetic crap is all you need to live to a ripe, hearty old age longer than nature ever intended. So remember, the seven seas are for swimming, sailing and fishing and not for feckin' swallowing.

48. Put a Halt to Salt

Table salt is a product nobody should be buying and yet most households do. Granted, our bodies need a certain amount of this stuff but we are all getting too much salt already included in the ingredients of the food we buy. Irish men are consuming almost twice as much salt as is good for them and women about 40% more than the optimum. Cutting the salt from the shopping list may reduce your intake by up to 30%, saving you a few shillings in the short term whilst much more importantly reducing your risk of high blood pressure which is a major contributor to heart disease and stroke statistics. The good news is it takes just six weeks to retrain your palate when you stop eating this tasty poison of convenience. Well worth a little short term pain for a lengthy life time gain, wouldn't you say?

49. You're Sweet Enough

Unless it's for the purpose of baking some occasional homemade sweet treats, you don't need any sugar in the house either. Again, you get enough of this stuff already added to various food stuffs. If your morning muesli really does need sweetening try some chopped fruit or sultanas instead, also replace sugar and salt flavouring in your home baked bread with grated orange or lemon peel. It'll be a lot tastier and will save you from having to upsize all the clothes in your wardrobe next year as well.

50. Sleepwalking into the Lions Lair

If you find you can't sleep at night please, please, whatever you do don't reach for a sleeping tablet. Tablets and medication in general should be reserved for use only when you are in serious chronic pain or when you have a potentially life threatening illness. Do not get into the habit of popping pills every other bedtime just because you're having a restless night or you have a mild headache. These things are natural and normal; they are just gentle early warning signs that something is slightly amiss. Perhaps you need to reduce the stress in your day or cut down on your caffeine intake; whatever it is you will find that some slight change in lifestyle is the answer, not medication.

If all else fails and you still can't sleep at night don't lie there fretting about it, that's only sure to exacerbate the problem. Every problem looked at from a different viewpoint is an opportunity. If you can't sleep the quiet of the night is a wonderful chance to do things you want to do but can never seem to get around to doing in the hustle and bustle of daylight hours. Read, write poetry, meditate, do the ironing or whatever you fancy. Just do something pleasant and calming. Believe me your insomnia will soon be resolved. Perhaps your sleepless nights are being caused by something more serious like relationship problems or bullying in the workplace. These things are going to be trickier to resolve but again medication is not and should not be used as any part of the solution. In general if you include a bit of physical and intellectual activity in your day and you cut out the caffeine intake in the second half of it you are well on your way to a good nights slumber. If all else fails everyone knows you can't beat a bit of 'how's yer father' for sending us guys off to dreamland and even if it's only a bit of a DIY job it should do the trick. Remember, don't sweat the small stuff. Sleep tight and don't let the bed bugs bite!

51. Sleeping On the Job

My last point is similar in many ways to the guy who can't get Johnson to perform on one particular occasion. So the next time he's thinking about what happened last time and guess what? Poor old Johnson can't take the pressure so he dives for cover again and suddenly you're in a viscous circle. Next thing you know he's giving €50 to the doctor to tell him his plumbing don't work so good and that's it, he's being medicated for life with Viagra. Of course over time there are side effects to the 'stiffy in a jiffy' pill so off you go again to Dr Spock, hand over another €50, whereupon he will oblige by medicating the effects of your medication and so on and so on until the good Dr is driving an eighty grand Merc, the pharmaceutical company's annual profits would solve Irelands debt crisis overnight and you are popping your own weight in smarties every month. For heaven's sake lads there was no problem in the first place! It's an illusion created by modern society which in turn has been seized on by the multinationals.

This delusion perpetuates the myth that every desire, including artificially created desire, must be satiated instantaneously. So what if you couldn't get it up last night? You're not a bloody machine or a trained monkey that performs on demand. It's a perfectly normal part of ageing that all of our bodily functions slow down a bit as time creeps up on us. If erectile dysfunction (even the official term for this everyday normal occurrence sounds like a terminal disease) becomes a concern for you my advice is talk to the only other person who is affected, namely, your partner. Initially at least, leave the feckin' doctor, pharmacist and everyone else out of it – unless you're into open relationships. If you both decide you would like a bit more jiggy jiggy there is more than one way to skin a cat and popping a pill isn't one of them. If a pair of furry handcuffs, a blindfold and some massage oil doesn't get ya goin', throw in a full length mirror and some flimsy lingerie. If that still doesn't do the trick it's not the doctor you need but either a new missus or an undertaker.

52. HRT: How Ridiculous is that?

How did the very word menopause, let alone the transitory period it relates to, become so feared in our modern era? Just a generation or two ago it was often welcomed by women as a time of freedom; freedom from the fear and risks of pregnancy and the workload that went with it. All women experience the menopause at some stage (usually not too far either side of the 45 to 50 year age bracket) and have done for millennia. How is it then that this completely normal and naturally occurring phenomenon became something to strike fear into the hearts of all females (and quite a few males also let me tell you); something to be avoided at all costs and, getting to the crux of the problem, something to be medicated away with HRT (Hormone Replacement Therapy)? Once again the pharmaceuticals have done their (ground) work well. There is nothing like instilling the fear of God into your intended customer base before appearing, saviour-like, with the antidote to their perceived affliction. You'd have to admire them really, in the same sick sort of way you'd marvel at Nidge from Love/Hate. Look! The reality of what happens before, during and after menopause can be summed up succinctly with the words oestrogen withdrawal. So, not unlike the addict giving up his drug of choice by going 'cold turkey' who experiences symptoms such as cold sweats, hot flushes, anxiety, sleep deprivation, aches, pains and exhaustion, there is an uncomfortable and somewhat painful transitory period which a woman goes through during menopause. There is no painless way for a woman to avoid this time. Taking HRT for menopause is rather like replacing your heroin addiction with methadone. It is not a solution and only long fingers the day when you will have to experience the change anyway. As with all powerful medication there are side effects to bear in mind as well. For example studies have shown that women taking HRT have a higher risk of heart attacks, strokes and leg blood clots than those taking placebos. Now I know I have left myself open on this point to all kinds of ridicule as women everywhere scoff at the very idea of me commenting on an area I could know nothing about, after all I'm just a man! Ye don't go through this phase (God help us all, but I won't get into the male menopause) I here you say! This is absolutely true and a fair point and I am only commenting from a position of one remove from the issue. But if that's a reason for dismissing my argument I would point out that it is men (for the most part) also who are concocting your HRT potions and pills. Anyway, I just want to sow the seed of doubt in you. Stop, think and remember to question before medicating.

53. Prevention Is Cheaper Than Cure

I know I mentioned this earlier in passing, but the obvious 'elephant in the room' solution to curbing our ever-expanding medical bill waistlines is to practice prevention rather than cure. After all there's no use closing the barn door after the horse has bolted, is there? At this stage we are all aware of what is needed to give yourself an excellent chance of living to a ripe, healthy old age. You don't need a master's degree in medicine – in fact you could cover it all on a sheet of a child's copy book. For anyone who's just dropped in from outer space here's ten commandments, which if followed, will mean you won't be able to remember your doctors name should anyone ask:

i   Don't smoke
ii   Drink alcohol only very sparingly or not at all
iii Get plenty of exercise
iv   Eat a plentiful and wide variety of fruit and vegetables
v   Consume modest amounts of meat
vi   Include a high proportion of oily fish in your meat intake
vii Keep your caffeine consumption to minimal levels
viii Include a good selection of nuts and seeds in your shopping
ix   Reduce sugar, salt, confectionary and processed foods generally to a minor level
x   Keep stress to an appropriate level and maintain a healthy work life balance.

Follow these ten simple points and you're sorted. You'll be richer, healthier, smarter and happier and surely that's worth the initial effort required to make the necessary changes. The ten tips here can of course be increased and expanded on but this is not a medical journal. If you want to be Superman – and why wouldn't you? – I suggest you read a couple of Patrick Holford's books. He's better placed to offer you in-depth nutritional advice than this mere mortal. Just as an aside, if everyone in the country would follow those ten easy guidelines above the seemingly insurmountable problems of the HSE would, in part, be dealt with instantaneously, with the balance of the solution following on soon thereafter as the benefits to society begin to kick in. In turn, our overall financial woes would be very much reduced in not only direct but in a multitude of indirect ways also.

54. The Buck Stops with You

There is always someone else or some unfortunate circumstance to blame our misfortune on, isn't there? It's a national pastime here in Ireland, pissing and moaning, complaining about the Government, the weather, the EU. You feckin' name it; we're world class at moaning about it. I'm a dab hand meself, I'm sure you'll agree – and why wouldn't I be? Isn't it inbuilt in my DNA? If only complaining was an Olympic sport then you'd see the Irish stand up and take their rightful place among nations. It does serve a useful purpose though. Sometimes you just need to have a good moan to let off steam. Better out than in, as they say. Often it's a healthy sign of a democracy when we can openly criticise government policy to get a good old 'hot under the collar' debate going. In fact it is my fervent wish that with this very book I might do my tiny bit to spark some questioning and critical reflection as to where we're all headed and whether or not we want to go there.

Unfortunately, like a lot of good and healthy things in life, we have a tendency to take this attribute to an unhealthy extreme. It's all very well to complain about problems we see in the world in general and in our own lives in particular but *not* to the exclusion of taking concrete action to change that which we perceive to be dysfunctional or wrong in our lives. In short, the buck stops with you. Complaining is only useful in so far as it is used as a mechanism to kick start some change in yourself or another. You must take personal responsibility for your own actions or failure to act. You must take full responsibility for your own knowledge or your failure to hear or acquire the knowledge which will impact on your life. It isn't good enough to say 'I didn't know'. Yes, there are powerful forces at work which seek to keep you in ignorance and inertia for their own greedy interests. In fact they are too numerous to mention but thankfully it is also true, here in the western world, that never before in history did we as ordinary citizens have as much freedom in any area whether it be financial, geographic, informational or sexual. It is true to say that you can live your life pretty much any which way you choose once you're not harming anyone else. Granted, you might suffer a passing shadow of disapproval – a remnant leftover from more restrictive times – in the odd dirty look or ignorant comment for certain lifestyle choices you might make, but at least you won't be thrown in jail or have your name publicly blackened with a call from the pulpit for your ostracising.

The upshot of all this is: if you smoke and get lung cancer, you are responsible. Not the tobacco company or the government or anyone else you care to mention; just you, 100% responsible.

If you are obese, you are responsible. Yes there may be unfortunate circumstances in your past which led you, through no fault of your own, along the road to where you are today. But today you are obese and you alone have the power to change the situation. No one else has that level of control over you. With power comes responsibility, so it is up to you and only you to make the necessary changes. I would like to add a little caveat here regarding obese and overweight people being solely responsible for the position they find themselves in. I do acknowledge that in a minority of cases people carry excess weight through no fault of their own, perhaps because of side effects of medication and so on. However, I still stand by my remarks being true in the main.

If you are an alcoholic it will be your own fault when you get cirrhosis of the liver and die prematurely. No point in blaming Arthur Guinness, a guy who's been dead these past two hundred years or more. You are not so naïve as to think you can drink large quantities of alcohol without serious negative side effects. So certainly look for and accept help in your determination to change expensive and unhealthy habits but first accept that the sole responsibility rests with yourself. There will always be reprehensible companies and individuals you can use as scapegoats in order to divert attention from yourself and to avoid change but that will get you nowhere except a shortened, miserable, meaningless life of suffering and penury.

55. Physician Heal Thy Self

Take the medical profession certainly, but sparingly. If symptoms persist seek alternative advice. Remember please that the corporations now govern all so called western democracies and the most powerful of these are the pharmaceuticals; they dictate government policy either directly or indirectly and so they rule us. They hold a particularly strong grip on us Irish, so dependent are we upon them for the jobs they provide, particularly in these recessionary times. They have replaced the Catholic Church here which, in turn, had replaced our colonial masters. Unfortunately our elected government has never at any time had any meaningful power in our short history as a nominally independent state. There was you thinking we only just gave away our ninety odd years of independence to the Troika two years ago. I'm afraid it was all an illusion. It was never ours to give away in the first instance. What's all this got to do with me, I hear you ask. What can I do about it, says you. At first glance, not a whole bloody hell of a lot would seem to be the answer. But mountains are climbed with single steps. Once you have a grasp of the basic facts that's your base camp. Not a bad place to be if you want to climb a mountain.

So we know our dictators are a bunch of multinationals headed by the pharmaceutical brigade. What is any stock market listed company's only motivation? That's right: Profit! So what is the best way for any company to maximize profit? Sell more and more of its product, preferably at greater and greater profit margins! When you apply these basic universal economic truths to the pharmaceutical sector you are left with an undeniable sinister conclusion. How best for a supplier of medical products to maximize sales of his produce? Not by making you well when you are sick, that's for sure. If you get well you'll stop taking his product. No, the way for him to maximize profits is to convince you to begin taking medication as early on in your life as possible and to keep you taking it throughout your life in ever-increasing varieties and dosages. To put it another way, he has the ultimate vested interest in either arranging for you to become ill or falsely convincing you that you have become ill at the earliest opportunity in your life; to hook you onto his conveyor belt as a customer for the rest of your natural. If you are genuinely ill it is in no way in his interest to make you well again – there's little profit in that outcome. The only good thing that can be concluded about this sorry state of affairs is that at least it is not in his interest for you to die either. Alive but ill is the permanent condition he would like to hold you in throughout your lifetime.

Now I'm not saying your GP is a ruthless profit grabbing son of a bitch. I'm sure he absolutely is nothing of the kind, but neither was anything like every German citizen evil during the 1930's. Most of them I'm sure were decent, well meaning, hardworking individuals just as the medical profession here are today. But they still didn't do much as a collective to halt the dictators march towards world domination, did they? Powerful dictators have many ways, both subtle and overt, of making you comply with their objectives. If they have whole western governments in their pockets (and they do) then a few independent doctors and pharmacists won't present much of a challenge, however well-meaning or ethical they are.

So what can you the individual do about all this? Exercise the freedom we spoke about earlier to maximum effect, that's what. In the first instance, arm yourself with as much information as possible about what it involves to live a healthy lifestyle; we all know the basics but we can always learn more. Put that information into practice in your life. Keep well psychologically and physically so as to keep away from the pharmaceuticals clutches for as long as possible.

Prevention is better than cure. Do not seek medical attention immediately for minor complaints, they will be only too happy to dispense some drug or other unnecessarily for your ailment which had you just left well enough alone, just keeping an eye on it, would almost certainly have cleared itself up. The body is not given nearly enough credit for the healing powers it has, especially in your younger years. Remember, every drug, even ones bought over the counter without a prescription, has unwanted side effects; they may not be immediately apparent but they are always there, lurking and accumulating in the background. Exercise critical thinking with regard to your medical issue. Are their alternative or complimentary solutions? Is your complaint one that you can reasonably expect, however desirable, to solve with a drug? Maybe a person has a psychological or behavioural issue. Is popping a pill really going to solve the problem in this case? I personally don't think so, at least not without a lot of hard work and life changes on that person's part as well. In short, thread very, very carefully around the whole health industry. As I said they have their uses. If you are genuinely, seriously medically ill it is in their best interest and yours to treat you but remain alert and sceptical; you are sleeping with the enemy. Good luck, you will need it.

56. General Generic

If you do find yourself sitting in front of the good doctor and he is reaching for his prescription pad at least ask him to prescribe the generic equivalent of whatever pill or cream he is about to write out for you. For good or ill it will have the same effect because it has the same ingredients. The only difference will be the name on the box! Oh, and the price; that will be quite different as well – it'll probably be halved or better. Be warned though, the doc may not thank you for this request. Be wary of any reasoning he has for wanting to give you the brand name drug. He may be on a bigger margin for doing so or it might not be such an ulterior motive he has in fairness, it could just be he's a conservative old fogey who is just unthinkingly going through the motions. Whatever his arguments or motives be sure to compare and contrast the available products for yourself. Don't be at all nervous of politely but firmly questioning the doctor. The days of putting doctors on pedestals should be long gone. Don't be in any way embarrassed to let him know that cost is an issue for you and should be factored into his prescriptive powers. Even if you have a medical card this advice should still apply as money wasted on unnecessarily expensive drugs will result in direct cuts to vital services elsewhere in the health service. So, if you are a card carrying hypochondriac you will be indirectly responsible for the unnecessary extra suffering and premature deaths of others.

57. Our Dearly Beloved Aunty Biotic

I know a few of my little nuggets of wisdom are going to land me in the bad books with our esteemed medical profession, so just in case I come down with a critical illness any time soon, I thought it prudent to offer a little olive branch by way of a tip which the medical profession agrees with me on. In fact they spend quite a few quid every winter publicising this advice: antibiotics should have no role in the treatment of coughs, colds and flu. They simply don't work in curing or alleviating these ailments. The best advice is to simply stay warm, get plenty of rest, drink lots of fluids and try to eat as well as possible. If you follow this simple advice you shouldn't have to bother your poor overworked GP or Pharmacist at all as you'll be on the mend in jig time.

There is another serious problem with the common habit many people have of popping antibiotics with the onset of these symptoms. You see antibiotics are intended to be used to fight serious bacterial infections such as meningitis and others. If we continue the habit of swallowing these pills like smarties what happens is the bacteria, clever little buggers that they are – which are present in our bodies and all around us in the air – begin to develop immunity to the antibiotic's effect, thus rendering this medication useless when you really need it.

So remember, when you have the flu antibiotics won't do! Of course we could ask how the general public got into the habit of taking medication for an ailment which it can't cure in the first place. They didn't come up with and execute this longstanding idiotic practice without a lot of encouragement, to say the very least, from some trusted other party down through the years, did they? But enough said, I'm supposed to be behaving myself; no more ruffling my medical peer's feathers now.

58. Kiss your Hacks Goodbye

Sore throats are another minor irritant which people run far too eagerly down to the chemist to medicate away with minor drugs. In most cases a completely unnecessary waste of time and money. Personally I tend to just ignore minor physical irritants like these trusting my own body to resolve the issue satisfactorily and expediently. I'm rarely disappointed. However, if like a lot of Nancy's out there these days you have a zero pain threshold you can just gargle with a bit of salt in warm water next time you have a tickly throat and that should do the trick. Alternatively you could chew on a bit of chopped or crushed garlic if you have some lying around the house. Garlic should actually be a regular feature in your diet when you are well as it has long been renowned for its great preventative and curative properties for all kinds of complaints.

59. Nasal Salt

Did you know that salt is a traditional decongestant. Salt and warm water have been used since time immemorial to clear up a blocked nose. It's an ayurvedic medicine originating in ancient India which is as simple as it is old. You simply pour the salt water solution in one nostril and allow it to run out the other. A lot cheaper than forking out for Lemsip or other pharmaceutical products and most likely closer to hand when needed too. There are endless other cheap household food products which can be utilised to clear up minor medical irritants. Turmeric for instance is an inexpensive spice which has been credited with being everything from a cure for a chesty cough, depression and skin ailments such as psoriasis, to helping slow or prevent the development of numerous cancers. In fact it is said to be of benefit to every system in the body. I don't know how much truth there is to these lofty assertions but it's a tasty, economical and exotic compliment to many meals and certainly won't do you a bit of harm, so keep a jar handy. These are just a couple of everyday remedy suggestions to get you thinking in a different way about medicine. Many books have been written on this subject. Educate yourself and reserve the drugs for emergency use only.

60. The Minty Python

Once upon a time long, long ago before nonsensical inventions like Nicorette gum and patches, I knew a chain smoking bloke of many years standing who was known as 'The Chimney', such was his consumption of the blasted weed known as nicotine. Anyway one fine day, The Chimney decided it was time to quench the fire once and for all. No more ifs or butts, he said. And that was it. He never smoked again. How the hell did he do it, you might well wonder. Well, on the same principle as Nicorette but a hell of a lot cheaper and less damaging; every time he got a craving he replaced the cigarette with a Silvermint. Naturally enough he went through a difficult period of withdrawal for some time when he could be quite bad tempered with his nearest and dearest. This earned him the new nickname of 'The Minty Python' – after all they could hardly call him 'The Chimney' any longer could they? But he stuck to his guns and never smoked again. My point is you don't need these new-fangled pharmaceutical inventions if you want to quit. People were successfully quitting before these things were on the market and there was a hell of a lot less social pressure to do so back then too. Having the right motivation is the key to any successful major lifestyle change. Minty's motivation came from the fact that he had a young son just diagnosed with asthma. This was the real key to his success. His methodology was very much secondary. But of course all that being said if you are a smoker giving up should be your number one priority. How you do it is of far less importance.

61. The Killer Cure

The prevalence of prescribing antidepressants, benzodiazepines and sedatives has reached epidemic proportions in Ireland and elsewhere in the western world. Some alarming estimates put the use of antidepressants in the Irish population at as high as one in five. This seems too high even for a sceptic of the psychiatric profession such as myself to swallow but I have little doubt that it is where we are heading if our fixation with popping pills for every minor physical, psychological and emotional hiccup that life inevitably throws at us is not diverted to more holistic and less pharmacological 'cures'. I've just read that over the past five years the three above mentioned drug groups have an increased prescription rate to medical card holders of 25%. That statistic is alarming to anyone who genuinely cares about the health of our nation's population. Regardless of who you are, psychiatrist, doctor, layman, mental health patient, pharmaceutical company employee, politician or other if the increasing use of these medications is not a cause for alarm to you then you quite simply are not interested in the wellbeing of our population – and that is to say nothing about the health of the nation's finances which, as we all know are in an unholy mess.

Now I don't claim to have all the answers and I'm sure prescription drugs serve a useful purpose in patients with severe psychiatric problems, but we have all heard the stories of patients being diagnosed by psychiatrists as having severe mental health conditions such as manic depressive disorder within minutes of a first consultation. This is quite plainly wrong and a purely profit-oriented practice with no regard whatsoever for the human being in front of them. All I can advise anyone to do if they are already on these medications or considering taking them is arm yourself with as much information as possible. Seek the advice of as wide ranging a group of individuals and professions as humanly possible; consult with psychologists, nutritionists, psychotherapists, doctors, nurses, herbalists, spiritualists, energy work practitioners, homeopaths and fellow sufferers to name but a few. If it proves unreasonable to see members of all these professions by appointment at least find out what they have to say by consulting texts written under these headings by leading practitioners in each field. Ask questions incessantly of everyone you deal with in this regard, Demand to be treated as an equal, dismissing any individual who does not comply. Maintain a healthy scepticism but be open to intelligent persuasion.

Above all, remember that it is not reasonable to expect anyone to have a greater interest in your wellbeing, mental or otherwise, than yourself (with the possible exception of your mother). Therefore, the ultimate responsibility in the first instance and the power of recovery lies with you. If humanly possible do not hand over this responsibility to another, certainly not to someone who is benefiting financially from your condition (real or invented). That simply is not fair, reasonable or prudent behaviour because their impartiality (however subtly), has by definition been compromised, no matter how well intentioned they may be. As in all walks of life, be particularly distrustful of anyone who seeks to convince you through any means that they are absolutely certain of their own beliefs; this is fundamentalism and extremely dangerous to your wellbeing.

I will repeat my earlier assertion here: you should do all in your power, exploring every other avenue open to you before resorting to the medical profession. You are never going to cure an illness of the mind with a physical concoction of synthetic chemicals in the form of a tablet, in my view, and the best that can be hoped for from these products is that they form part of the solution, being used temporarily in extreme cases in order to give the patient a necessary initial crutch to lift them to a point where they can engage meaningfully in alternative therapies in search of a permanent solution without negative side effects. Take good care and thread cautiously if you are one of these invisible, walking wounded.

62. Blank Health Cheques

The great mantra of the moment in media and other circles is to advise us all to go to the doctor for regular health check-ups. Now I have long thought this to be a silly notion at best.

The idea of going to the doctor when you're feeling hale and hearty and forking out €50 or €60 for him to go poking around for symptoms which don't exist is just looking for trouble. With all due respect, the poor old doctor is trained to detect illnesses, he's not going to be happy until he's found something wrong with ya, however minor, and sent you off with a prescription for it. This being my strong belief I was delighted to read in the paper the other day that new Danish research published in the Cochrane library suggests there is no convincing evidence that general health checks are beneficial. I always knew them Danes were no daws. If you don't feel well or you happen to know your family is predisposed to a certain condition by all means get checked out. Otherwise do yourself a big favour; live a healthy lifestyle, be happy and stay the hell away from the doctor's surgery.

63. Moral Hazard

The cost of medical insurance has been skyrocketing in recent years with no sign of a slowdown in this trend anytime soon. But what can you do? You have to keep paying it, don't you? After all your health is your wealth. Perhaps, but did you know economists use a term known as 'moral hazard', which basically states that if you compensate people when bad things happen to them they may get careless. In other words you could be lulled into a false sense of security by paying a hefty annual premium to look after you in the event of ill health. You might unconsciously take your eye off the ball thinking, 'I've ticked that box, no need to worry about my habits, healthy or otherwise, sure I'm covered if there's any problem'. If this is the case, when you make those crippling medical insurance payments you may actually be unintentionally paying to increase your likelihood of getting sick. Crazy as it seems it could make sense, couldn't it? Hardly what you would call a sound value for money purchase in that case, is it? You can add to this scenario – given that everyone loves a bargain – that there will be a natural temptation to make a claim on your insurance even when there is nothing at all wrong with you. Bizarre as it sounds there will be people in robust good health clogging up doctors' waiting rooms looking for a return on their insurance investment.

There is a similar problem with the medical card system. If you give somebody something for free, especially if it is perceived to have a high value, they are naturally enough going to be very eager to use it, regardless of whether or not they will benefit. Now I'm not telling you all to cancel your medical insurance. I'm only suggesting you should consider it, taking into account all the pros and cons. It might be doubly beneficial to your pocket and your life expectancy if you were to cancel the premiums as this may provoke in you a sense of urgency to protect yourself in a more personal way. You could start by ditching the fast-food take away and the after dinner chocolate fudge cake. The crux of the problem is that no matter how exorbitant the sum you pay, you cannot incentivise some stranger – least of all a multinational insurance corporation – to care about your health more than you do yourself. In the event that you do make a claim for treatment from your insurer, they will naturally want to provide you with the cheapest option while you will of course want to opt for the best. It is also worth reminding ourselves here that if you do opt out of your policy you are not denying yourself treatment in the event of necessary medical intervention. If you turn up at a hospital in need of care you will still be attended to, regardless. Admittedly your stay may not be terribly pleasant as you wait some considerable time on a trolley in a corridor to be seen to but perhaps that's as it should be: we don't want you overly eager to repeat the experience, now do we?

64. A Daily Date with Death

It occurs to me that many of the woes of modern society are connected to our morbid obsession with avoiding death at all costs, which is quite ironic as it is the one thing none of us can avoid under any circumstance. It is the one quality which unites all of humanity the world over. Of course there are many ways to attempt to delay our ultimate date with death and that's all very good but our refusal to face this one certainty of our lives in a frank and honest way as a society (and perhaps for you as an individual), reduces our quality of life to an alarming degree. Let me ask you, if you knew you had only one more year to live would it change your priorities? I'll bet it would. I'd hazard a guess that it would change how you view the world and your place in it to an unrecognisable degree. Ok, let's shift the goalposts a little. What if you knew for sure that you had exactly ten good years left? Would that change anything for you? The fact of the matter is no matter what age you are reading this your time on earth is short, beautiful but brief.

What would you consider to be a good age? Here in Ireland at the present time, if you live to let's say eighty three, heck we'll call it eighty three years and four months to be precise, almost everyone would agree that was a fair innings, right? What this means is, if you are fortunate enough to survive illness and accident (and there is no guarantee that you will) to reach this better than average milestone, then you would have lived for 1000 months. If you are lucky then from birth, you get 1000 months on this earth to do what you will with before the final curtain is drawn. Now if you are let's say my age, that is forty two years and ten months old as I write, then the sad news is you and I have only 486 of our original 1000 months left. We may be lucky and get a little bonus time or unlucky and pop our clogs earlier but this is hair splitting. The point remains we all have precious little time here. We should use it wisely. Of course obsessing morosely upon death is not a wise use of your time but busying yourself like a beaver, never raising your ostrich head out of the sand to look around and assess your life and its priorities is equally wasteful. I would gently suggest a middle ground between these two extremes. Reflect on death every morning but only momentarily, just long enough to appreciate life and enjoy the day ahead in all its glory. What, you may reasonably ask is this little nugget – however well intentioned – doing in a book about saving money? Well I believe it's perfectly relevant as I'm convinced that if we could all keep in touch with our mortality without becoming obsessed by it, as a natural consequence our priorities would change hugely. Amongst other things I'm fairly certain our incessant consumption of expensive goods, services and indeed the earth's finite resources would be curbed considerably. So, reflect on death fleetingly at reasonably regular intervals in order to live fully and enjoy the happy by-product of a diminishing demand on your bank balance.

65. The Hundred Year Cheque

There's a death bed bonus pay-off too if you live the ultimate healthy lifestyle. Having followed all my sound advice up to this point you will now no doubt live to be at least a hundred at which time you will receive a cheque from the president – currently €2,540 I believe – for no reason other than to say: Well done, you crotchety auld bollox! You've defied all the laws of science and God, now please put this money towards you're funeral before shuffling off somewhere to expire.

66. Keep Only Good Company

Of course as I keep saying, prevention is better and cheaper than cure. If there was only one piece of advice I was allowed to give you to encapsulate almost everything in this volume I suppose it would have to be this: 'Keep only good company'. I intend that advice to be taken in its broadest possible meaning. In other words if you want to utilise all your assets including financial, physical, intellectual, social, emotional and so on to your own and society's maximum advantage then I suggest following this advice in every area of your life wherever and whenever humanly possible. Be extremely conscious always of what influences you subject yourself to. Who do you associate with and where? What newspapers or other material do you read? What TV programmes do you choose? What substances do you ingest into your body? Could your workplace be considered a good environment for you personally? If not it is not good company and you are unlikely to be content or very productive there. This keeping good company rule can extend with practice into every minute area of life. For example, you wouldn't normally think of the clothes you wear as company but for the purposes of this exercise you should; after all the clothes you wear can affect your mood and your mood in turn can affect every other part of your world. All this simply boils down to remaining alert to your surroundings and your feelings and trying to be aware of the connection between the two as often as you can.

If this is a new concept to you it will be difficult at first to remember. To help in this regard you can put reminders on your phone or elsewhere. Naturally the object here is to spot occasions when, according to your own honest opinion, you are not keeping good company, in other words you are not being true to yourself. Initially these occasions will be numerous and if you find otherwise I suspect you are not being entirely honest. Once a situation where you are not being true to yourself is acknowledged the next task is to consider how one might reasonably change the situation. This will not always be possible immediately, but with time, practice and patience you will notice the accumulation of positive little tweaks and changes to your life having an enormous beneficial impact. If everyone played this enjoyable and challenging game with themselves as an on-going daily exercise it is my strong suspicion that mental health issues in Ireland would almost disappear; there would in fact be a huge improvement in all health issues effecting the population. The benefits to the individual and society would not stop there of course; crime for instance would be greatly reduced. Anyway while we are dreaming of that utopia we can begin by being the change we want to see in society.

67. You're Write to Free Speech

Do you know what a great idea for saving money is? To write a book about saving money! In fact, to write a book about anything! You never know it might even be published and make you rich so you don't need to be a tight bastard anymore. But that's only the icing on the cake if it happens. Since I've started writing this rant I have spent endless cost-free happy hours typing away, getting all my frustrations about modern life out of my system. This worthy tome – like most other worthwhile writing – in all likelihood will never be published. Why won't it be published? Because book publishers being a savvy bunch would quickly realise that the public wouldn't buy it. And why wouldn't they? Because reading a book like this might result in having to take a critical look at one's own behaviour and we, the general public, do not like that class of thing at all. If we did that sure it'd open up a whole can of worms; we'd realise how idiotic some of our behaviour is and have to make difficult changes to improve our lives. We can't be doing with that! No, no – much better to keep the blindfolds on and continue to go around criticising everyone else. Besides, I have insulted almost everybody at some point in my little tirade which I suppose is not the best way to go about building up a fan base.

But whether I am published or not isn't the point. The point is that anyone can indulge in a little creative writing. All you need is a pen and paper or preferably a lap top. It's very therapeutic too – you can get all your frustrations, insecurities and fears out of your system in a safe environment. That's right. It's therapy for the tight bastard, called 'Tell it to the Computer'. After all the computer won't judge you; it will provide an impartial listening ear and offer you the chance to look back at exactly what you've said, reflect on it and analyse it. Brilliant, eh! So you can cancel those weekly fifty minute sessions with your therapist that cost you €70 a go. You've got free therapy right at your fingertips. Hey, I like the sound of that. I think I've just invented a new fad. It's called 'Fingertip Therapy'. Don't forget where you heard of it first when it catches on!

Writing can take many forms of course so there must be one to suit you. You might decide to simply keep a diary or the modern day equivalent, the ubiquitous blog. Maybe poetry or short stories are your thing? If there is a topical issue which really gets you hot under the collar you could start your tentative foray into the murky world of journalism with an irate letter to your local or national paper. The list of possibilities is long. Go on, give it a bash! There's nothing to lose and all to gain. After all, unless you're a vegetable you like to think, right? And what is writing except thinking in print so you are guaranteed to get something out of it. Plus, as suggested at the outset, as long as you've got your nose stuck in a laptop writing you're memoirs you will be blissfully forgetful of all those costly other things you need to be doing or buying. As a final point, don't be put off if you never learned to type properly and like me, operate at the speed of evolution, typing only with the index finger of each hand. Sure that's an added bonus, guaranteeing you a happy lifetime chipping away at the keyboard without any fear of running out of things to say. You will be operating at such a pace that your life line will expire first.

68. Cheap Friends

Nurture and cherish your good friends. Why? Because they are cheaper than a psychotherapist, that's why. Better yet, befriend a good therapist.

69. Practice Appreciation

A lot of the goods and services that we buy can be listed under the heading of retail therapy, in other words they are purchases which give us a boost, improving our mood or perhaps just supplying a momentary euphoric feeling. When looked at like this it begins to seem like a drug. In and of itself that's no harm, a lot of drugs, such as a glass of red wine, are very pleasurable, beneficial and can even add to our quality of life when taken in moderation. The problem arises however with overindulgence – when the bank statements arrive and the hangover kicks in. You look at your debts and while you can feel the pain you are hard pressed to recall the pleasure. We ask ourselves, how did we let this happen? In a nutshell, we arrived at this pitiful place because we spend too much time coveting the things in life which we don't have, creating an illusory fantasy about how life would be perfect if only we had X, Y or Z and not enough time appreciating the very many good things in life which we do have. I would suggest beginning each day by practicing the gentle art of appreciation for a few minutes. It really is a painless way to set you up for a more positive and contented day ahead. It helps you to separate the wheat from the chaff, to remember what's important and what's dispensable. Over time practicing appreciation of the myriad wonderful gifts we enjoy in life offers a protective layer, insuring us against the ceaseless onslaught of consumerism which we are bombarded with. It really empowers you to see through the crap; to identify the pointlessness or even risks of many purchases. Most of our desire comes not from genuine want but from comparing ourselves negatively to our peers. Turn this habit on its head and think instead of what you enjoy that many others do not, either within your immediate sphere or in the wider world. We all have much to be grateful for. Harness the power of that fact.

SECTION 3

The Big Ticket Items: Property, Motoring and Tax

1. Trading Places

When you decide to go out and buy your first home do all in your power to ensure you are also buying your last home. It used to be the case in the good old days when people had a bit of sense that when you bought a home it was for life. You stayed put and became part of the community. It was the exception rather than the rule to move. Then some clever dick, an auctioneer no doubt, coined that annoying phrase 'Trading up' and suddenly everyone had to start off with a shoebox, then five years later you 'upgrade' to a telephone kiosk and so on and so on, moving every five feckin' years with your ultimate aim being to end up in Malahide bloody castle to see out your dotage. The only net winners in this mindless race to the psychiatric ward are of course the parasites with respectable sounding titles like 'Solicitor' or 'Auctioneer' who are there to bamboozle you with endless reams of paperwork which they will so kindly be only to delighted to take care of for you – for the recommended fee of course. Oh, let's not forget the DIY and furniture chain stores whose goods are identical the world over; they'll be on hand to give helpful advice on how to decorate your new abode to your own unique, individual requirements. Time was when you got bored of your surroundings you went on your holliers for a wet week in Bundoran and that cured ye, you didn't go and sell the feckin' house from under yerself.

This is mass madness, you maniacs. Do you not realise

that moving house is the fourth most stressful life event it is ever likely to be your misfortune to experience, the other three being bereavement of a loved one, diagnosis of a life threatening condition and divorce. Meanwhile you're paying out thousands of euro for the privilege. By the way, with the new property tax now upon us you have another good reason to be modest in your housing requirements. Look, do a bit of 'forward planning' as the business editors like to call it, buy as much space as you're ever likely to use and make do with that. No family grows much bigger than 2.3 kids and half a Labrador these days so make sure you can accommodate this. Allow for the unlikely scenario of a lot of power cuts during your fertile years, so now you've ended up with 4.3 little brats, half a Labrador and a hamster. Fine. As long as you can convert the attic or stick up a bit of an extension without forfeiting the whole garden, you're sorted. But don't move. Dig in for the long haul and stay put. If by some chance you do land that dream job out in California by all means go, but don't sell. Hold what you have. Rent the house out. California's not all it's cracked up to be either; you'll get bored out there too and want to come home.

2. Flat Refusal

Do not under any circumstances buy yourself an apartment as your home. The management charges will be extortionate, certainly not less than €1,200 per annum and perhaps double this figure. This hefty, annual fee will be on-going for as long as you own the property. You will still be paying it in your dotage and the next generation will still be paying it in the unlikely event that you don't sell. You will also have multiple neighbours literally above, below and on all sides of you, increasing immensely your risk of sour relations with one or other of them due to noise or other disturbances. You will no doubt at some point in the not too distant future also need more room than any apartment – save perhaps a penthouse – can provide and when this time comes, because the option of extension or attic conversion is not open to you, there will be no alternative but to up sticks and sell with all the stress and expense that goes with it. On top of all this apartment living often rules out such simple things as a garden shed, dog ownership, a clothes line and so on which you may not feel the need for right now, but life changes and priorities shift. The simple solution therefore is to rule apartments out of the equation when considering your home purchase in the first place. If you are in this market bracket consider instead a semi-d or end of terrace house as an alternative. You will find there is no great price difference. Any extra you do pay will be more than worth it in the years that follow.

I am not by the way suggesting you rule out apartment buying as an investment. This is an entirely different proposition as you won't be living there yourself and your tenants by definition will only be relatively short-term residents. As an aside, I wonder when was it in our recent history that flats became apartments? No doubt some smart arse of an auctioneer started it around the same time the humble assistant behind the counter in your local café became a feckin' barista, thinking, quite accurately, that a simple change of name should add 20% at least to the asking price.

3. Protection Rackets

Many people, when taking out a mortgage take out mortgage protection insurance at the same time with the same provider and then just keep paying the premium along with the mortgage every month, never giving it another thought let alone shopping around for a cheaper alternative. This suits the banks nicely. It means there is little or no need to be competitive in pricing this product. Better still for them is the unethical fact that mortgage protection insurance is a legally binding requirement if you have a mortgage. So the first thing you should do if you are a victim of this cosy little arrangement between bank and state is to separate out your monthly mortgage payment from the insurance payment to see how much each is costing individually. Next, shop around to get the cheapest quote elsewhere for this product. I absolutely guarantee you the cheapest price for this insurance product will not be from your mortgage provider and not by some considerable margin at that. Another thing to bear in mind: most people take out the minimum legal protection here, which means they are only insured for the remaining balance on the mortgage in the event of death (this product is all about protecting the bank and very little to do with protecting the consumer). The remaining balance is of course constantly reducing each month, so why does the monthly insurance payment not reduce in tandem? Why indeed. My point here is that even if you shopped around several years ago and obtained the best available price at the time, it may well be worth your while revisiting this old chestnut as you would now be seeking to insure a lower sum and should therefore be able to extract a reduced premium.

Of course you might decide that you don't want any bloody mortgage insurance at all, perhaps you are a non-drinking, non-smoking twenty five year old fitness instructor with a twenty year mortgage whose grandparents are all still as fit as fiddles in their eighties. You know damn well you're not going to pop your clogs before the age of forty five, so for you this payment is a complete and utter waste of money. Or maybe you are single without any dependents and yes, you might die before your mortgage has been fully cleared but you couldn't care less! In that event your nephew or whoever you are leaving the house to can take on the debt with the asset and assuming the asset is greater he has little to complain about now, does he? It strikes me that this mortgage insurance is a bit insane. It's like trying to give yourself an incentive for reaching the dubious goal of an early grave. But what to do? We've already acknowledged it to be a legally binding requirement. Since this insurance payment is now going in a separate direction from your mortgage payment, is anybody checking to see if you are still paying it? What would happen if you simply cancelled it, nice and quietly? According to one bloke I know, absolutely nothing happened when he did exactly that – except of course he saved himself a few quid each month. But that would be illegal so you obviously shouldn't do it. Oh well, I can't think of any solution to the problem then. I guess you're stuck with it.

4. Sound the Silent Alarm

An alarm for your home is an expensive luxury at the best of times, but for the enthusiastic digester of this volume it is definitely surplus to requirements; after all you won't have a lot of valuables for the would be thief to steal now, will you? Still the local scum bag is not to know that before he breaks in and besides, being broken into is an expensive and traumatic experience even if very little is actually taken. So it is a good idea to take any cheap security measures which reduce our odds of attracting vermin. One simple idea is to put up a dummy alarm box on your house, the master criminal would see through this decoy but it should be enough to encourage the average druggy to look elsewhere for easier pickings. Another even simpler idea which amazingly also reduces your odds of incurring a break in is to stick up a 'Beware of the Dog' sign on your gate, regardless of whether or not you actually have a dog.

5. Blocking the Burglar In

We are told by the boys in blue that building high walls or growing tall trees or hedging around the perimeter of our property as a security measure is worse than a false economy; it actually encourages break-ins as it provides perfect cover from detection by neighbours for the publicity-shy thieves who can then do their job thoroughly and at their leisure. So save yourself the cost of building that wall and enjoy extra peace of mind on top. Keeping your house open to public view like this will also give you the added advantage of being able to spot the neighbourhood nosey, Nora, coming down the road for a 'friendly chat' in time to execute a well rehearsed escape drill. Of course you will be open to the odd embarrassing encounter as you walk buck naked out of the shower only to be confronted by your undrawn curtains and Mrs Murphy coming up the drive, readjusting her spectacles. Oh well, that'll give her something new to feel hard-done-by about!

6. Rent a Room

Everyone has heard the maxim: 'Time is money'. Well, 'Space is money' too. Have you got a spare bedroom in your home which you could rent out? If you have, after the quit smoking ultimatum, this is probably the most valuable suggestion in the book. Apart from the obvious rental income you will generate (renting a small double room in the Galway City suburbs can net you €240 monthly at the time of writing), there are other, added benefits. The most important of these is the fact that your new lodger will be splitting the utility bills with you. Granted there will be some increased usage with an extra person in the household but this should be negligible. Another advantage which is less tangible but often proves to be a Godsend is your new tenant's uniqueness. Everybody has their own particular abilities and talents so your family will benefit from whatever knowledge or strengths the newcomer provides in this regard. For example, I myself am a total technophobe so my tenants have in the past been invaluable to me when dealing with computer problems. Another tenant who was an electrician by trade fixed some faulty wiring for me. These benefits in kind are a two-way-street of course, ideally you become friendly with your new guests and you help one another out in the normal way. With an extra person in the house you will also have the added comfort of increased security from break-ins.

There can of course be problems associated with inviting a stranger into your home but these will be drastically reduced if you are very clear about the ground rules from the outset. Besides, it's your house so you're holding all the aces. There will be only one winner in any clash of personalities that occurs. I can honestly say I have had no major problems with any of my tenants over the years and there have been dozens of every gender, nationality and personality. The worst I had to deal with was when one fellow became a little shy about paying the rent. After a couple of warnings the situation hadn't improved so I asked him to leave, which he duly did. It was a tad awkward because he wasn't a bad lad but sure we have to handle slightly awkward situations like this all the time in life. On balance, with hand on heart I can honestly say this one is a no brainer, if you have the room to spare go for it and you won't look back. Oh, by the way did I mention this income is free from income tax? You can earn up to €10,000 tax free in rental income from your home. Sweet!

7. Variations on a (Rental) Theme

If you are a bit dubious about taking on a long term lodger you can always dip your toe in the water by making your spare rooms available as short-term accommodation for foreign students in the summer months. Equally you could let your rooms out for just a few nights or a week at a time to visitors. Are there particular times of the year when demand for accommodation exceeds supply in your locality due to sporting, cultural or other events taking place? If so you could command a premium price for providing desperate punters with room at the inn. You don't necessarily even have to own the gaff to do this. You just need a spare bed or possibly just a couch going a begging and a demand for your product. Best not to tell the landlord you are making money from your 'visitors' though, at best he'll want a cut of the action at worst he'll turf you out.

8. Sack the Management

If you are fortunate or unfortunate enough, as the case may be, to own a second or third property – perhaps like thousands of other poor schmucks you got caught up in the Celtic Tiger property bubble – you may have a management company in place to look after the day to day tenant issues such as the collecting of rent; repairs and maintenance; advertising the accommodation; signing of lease agreements and so on. This is especially likely to be the case if you live a good distance from your rental property. These management companies generally charge you 10% of the gross rental income in return for their services and many of them charge a set, separate and hefty fee for finding new tenants for you. My simple advice to you is sack the management company and depending on the rent you get for your property you could be quid's in to the tune of well over a grand a year. If you have never managed a property from a distance yourself before it will at first, like all new experiences to us adults, appear daunting, but I can assure you that after a little initial teething trouble there is nothing to it. First you advertise your property on Daft. This just involves a few minutes work and a fee of about

€35; you can stick a 'To Let' sign in the window and front garden of the property (for free) to help the process along. Next you have to show the property to prospective clients – this bit may be a pain in the ass if you live a long way off but you can minimize the work load by being organised and showing several people the house/apartment on each trip. It would also be extremely beneficial if you could befriend a neighbour of the property to help in this and other regards. At the very least you will probably want to develop a working relationship with a local handyman, (note: I said handyman not tradesman, they're cheaper) just in case you need to call someone to deal with an urgent issue.

The key to avoiding expense and difficulties with tenants is to be very clear from the outset that you are willing to be more than fair with them, after all a happy tenant is a long term tenant but they have to meet you half way. Make sure they understand that you live a long way away and you have an extremely busy life. It's no harm to exaggerate this point so they get the message that you don't want them phoning you up every other week about minor issues. Make it clear that as far as you are concerned minor breakages and wear and tear are their responsibility. Ideally the situation you want to encourage is, if the tenant requests some maintenance issue to be dealt with and let's say you agree to it – because if they are good guests that don't bother you too often you should humour their odd request even if you don't consider it strictly necessary or your responsibility (think carrot and stick). Then tell them you are far too busy to attend to the issue at that time but if they can wait a few weeks or so you will come down and sort out the painting or whatever. Alternatively, you offer them the option of shopping around, getting a few prices and going ahead with the work. Tell them they can then deduct the cost from the next rent. That way they do the legwork and you are not making unnecessary long and costly journeys back and forth to the property. In short, treat your tenants like responsible adults who are well capable of looking after the day to day running of their own home.

As for lease agreements, they can be downloaded from the internet and amended to suit you and your client. Obviously enough, in our situation of the absent landlord, you ideally want working tenants in full-time employment. Remember, start as you mean to go on; be fair but firm. It's like being a parent really; if you let them tenants will behave like demanding children, running rings around you – and why wouldn't they? I would too if I was in their shoes and thought I could get away with it. Another important advantage I have found since I sacked my management company is that I get a better quality tenant now. Why would this be? Surely management companies have the expertise to secure good quality tenants? Maybe, but we're forgetting, in today's world everyone is out for themselves and they don't give a hoot about the type of tenant they get. The only thing on their mind is the finder's fee and the 10% which they get regardless of what toe rag is ensconced in your house throwing cider parties.

If, for arguments sake, you have a modest three bed semi in Waterford to rent for €700 gross per month, by giving the management the boot you save €840 per annum straightaway on fees, another €200 on finder's fees when you find your own replacement tenants and I would estimate savings of about €300 per year in maintenance costs. On the flip side your work load in return for all these savings has increased, but only marginally. You will still travel to check on the property about twice a year which you always did anyway because you couldn't trust the shower employed to do it. When it comes to re-letting the property there are a few days extra work involved, travelling back and forth showing the property, but this only comes around every couple of years and is well worth the effort for the savings involved.

9. The Green, Green Grass of Home

If nobody in your family is an enthusiastic gardener a large garden is going to be a royal pain in the arse to maintain. The thing about plants you see is, the ones that you get for free, the weeds, never stop bloody growing and trying to take over the gaff and the ones you pay good money for wither and die before you can say 'my garden peaked last week, sorry you missed it'. It's a pointless bloody exercise designed to test your will to live. It's like Mayo playing in an All Ireland Final, poor buggers, there can be only one winner and it ain't gonna be you. And lawns, don't get me started about lawns! Particularly the large ones you see in the countryside. There should be an EU directive banning them. I mean to say what purpose do they serve? You cut the grass, you dump the grass, the grass grows and you cut the grass again. For what? Nobody actually enjoys these lawns!

If you don't believe me take a drive through the Irish countryside. You can drive past acres upon acres of perfectly manicured lawns. You'll even see plenty of poor sods out cutting and tending these barren green deserts, wasting that most precious and rare commodity, a fine Irish Sunday. But you'll see bugger all people out playing on, or otherwise enjoying, this pointless possession. They're not even attractive to look at for as soon as the first unfortunate daisy or dandelion pokes its head up to add a splash of colour, out comes the ride on. If I had my way I'd leave the sodden grass alone and let nature do as nature intended. Oh, but no! The Squinting Window Police would be after me then, when it would be more in their line to nominate me for a grant from the nature conservancy council. A meticulously manicured lawn is much like a perfect person: monotonous and impossible to maintain. What I can't understand for the life of me is how they ever became so feckin' popular? So buyer, beware the glossy brochure with the lovely house nestling on an acre of beautifully landscaped grounds. It looks like heaven but it may be about to become your living hell. Sometimes less is more.

10. Go Native

If you will insist on growing a few plants in your garden make sure you do your homework first. Find out what kind of soil you've got and so on and make sure your chosen specimens are hardy enough to survive the prevailing weather conditions; otherwise this plant husbandry lark will break both your purse strings and your spirit. The cheapest and most efficient thing to do is to have a look and see what grows naturally around you; take your cue from Mother Nature and go native. No point driving yourself to despair watching one harebrained exotic eyesore after another succumb to the rain soaked bog land that is your domain. Once you've planted it, your work should be done. If it can't look after itself it has no business in a tight git's garden.

11. Fruits of your Labour

Again, if for some inexplicable reason your idea of fun is crawling around the garden on all fours, getting muck stuck under your fingernails and in other orifices where the sun don't shine, then in the name of God will you at least please make sure you get a return for your efforts by planting a few fruit trees and shrubs such as apple, pear, raspberry or blackberry to name just a sample selection. The list of possibilities is long and varied. You might as well go the whole hog and grow the spuds and veg too while you're at it, especially if organic fare floats your boat. No point propagating Laurels and Rhododendrons, no feckin' atein' in those wastes of space. An added attraction of fruit trees is the aesthetic value of their colourful blooms in spring so you don't have to trade beauty for practicality. You can have your (fruit) cake and eat it too!

12. Compostable Cuts

If feasible, keep a compost heap in some out of the way corner of your garden. This doesn't have to involve any expense by way of fancy compost bins; they're all fine and dandy if you like that sort of thing but completely surplus to requirements. You can easily cobble together your own box for free or just leave it to ferment away to its heart's content in an open pile if it's hidden away. Composting waste in this way will often reduce your refuse charges and of course provides free fertiliser for your garden. Even if you're not particularly green fingered and a day spent gardening sounds like a worse fate than an afternoon in that other foul smelling environment, the Dáil bar, your compost is tradable currency and you should be able to curry favour with some local cauliflower curator in return for it – a free basket of organic veg, perhaps?

13. Do You Need a Car?

Between depreciation, maintenance, running costs, taxes and tolls your car is haemorrhaging money. In fact according to the AA's most recent annual motoring costs survey it now costs the average motorist €1,000 per month (and rising) to run their vehicle. So even though I admit that in this country with its pathetic public transportation infrastructure, it is a drastic suggestion, the question still has to be asked: do you need a car? If you are used to the convenience of having a car parked outside your door your instinctive immediate answer will almost certainly be yes. But to make sure this is an honest answer we need to ask a few more questions. Do you drive less than 10,000 miles per year? Do you live close to your workplace? Is it realistic to walk, cycle or bus it to work or other destinations? Do you live in a large urban environment with good infrastructure, close to most of your everyday amenities and with a half decent public transport operation? Are you a nervous driver? Do you dislike driving after dark? If you answered yes to most or even half of these questions you should probably sell your car because even though a car is a great comfort and convenience to have, it is also an extremely costly one and your money could most likely be better utilised in another area of your life. Perhaps you are retired with a free travel pass and rarely drive beyond a five mile radius of the house? Why do you have a car in this case? All I'm saying is think seriously about what it's costing you and what you actually get in return for that money.

14. Parking the Rent

Any city centre dwellers who have realised that their car was just an expensive fashion accessory which spent most of its time complimenting the flower bed in the front garden have now sold their vehicle. In so doing, apart from innumerable auto savings, they may have opened up another potential avenue of income. Do you have your own parking space in an urban centre which you are not utilising? If so, it is time you advertised this asset for rent. You have an in-demand asset going to waste; rent of a prime parking space could net you up to €1,000 per year. And what's more, this type of rental income is largely hassle free with no issues around repairs, maintenance, problematic tenants and so on which you usually associate with this stream of income. Park your reservations and rent that space pronto.

15. Buy a Banger

Unless you are in business and the vehicle you drive is likely to influence your customer's impressions one way or the other, there is only one reason for anyone to buy a new car and that is 'prestige'. This used to be called 'showing off' or 'keeping up with the Jones's'. A certain amount of one-up-manship always existed in every walk of life and no doubt always will but for new car sales in Ireland, this trend really took off with the new registration system that began in 1987. Now we could all see with a cursory glance at their reg how old our neighbour's car was. A brilliant little stroke between government and the motor industry! More power and good luck to them I say because this means a crazy number of people, in an endless, senseless cycle of trying to outdo or just keep up with their colleagues, are buying new cars every year (we've gone one step further now of course, from 2013 you'll have to change your motor every six months to keep ahead of the posse). Thankfully, this in turn results in a healthy supply of used cars, increasingly at better and better value, for the saner members of the motoring public. What people fail to realise is that the registration should not really affect the price of your car much at all. What's important is the mileage and condition of the vehicle. You can buy a three or four year old car with low mileage in near mint condition for half the price you'd have paid for it new. In other words it is almost the same vehicle in every respect bar one. It doesn't come with the perceived kudos of a new registration plate. What you have to ask yourself is this: is a newer registration plate worth €10,000 to €30,000 depending on the make and model in question? Of course we can continue this argument further and ask what is the advantage of buying a three year old car over say, a ten year old one? Now there are a few; you'll likely get a couple of extra years out of it and you won't have to pay the NCT tax as often and so on but these incentives are small potatoes indeed for shelling out an extra €10,000 or more.

Also, did you ever consider the other disadvantages of driving a newer vehicle over an older one? You will have increased insurance premiums for one thing. And just imagine the peace of mind that comes with driving a banger. Let me tell you a true story that happened to me just a couple of months ago. I was driving along a country bohreen (think grass in the middle) in my twelve year old battered but completely reliable Avensis when I came around a bend and ran into a young fella drivin' an eighteen year old Corolla. In truth we were both probably travelling a little harder than was optimal. We had both managed to brake and swerve in avoidance a little so the damage to each car was minor, just a little further denting along our respective wings. We got out of our vehicles, shook hands, surveyed the damage, agreed it was nothing to be wettin' our knickers about, bid one another good day and that was it. No need for guards being called (wasting taxpayers' money), insurance claims with increased premiums to follow, frustrating form filling or a week's depression as you kick yourself for your stupidity. Can you even begin to imagine how differently the scenario could have played out if we were both driving newer vehicles? It could've ended with a day in court, legal bills, sky high future insurance premiums and an intergenerational rift between previously friendly neighbours.

Another thing, as you smugly drive your new vehicle imagining all the positive impressions you are making on people: have you ever reflected upon the undesirable ideas your pride and joy puts in others heads? You will create envy in many shallow individual's minds for sure – and you may even consider this desirable – but envy will quickly turn into its uglier cousin, jealousy, in at least some of these vacuous minds. So now you have created ill will towards yourself in the minds of some people around you and you've paid through the nose for it too. This jealousy may manifest itself in a myriad of small ways such as bitchiness behind your back or minor vandalism to your vehicle. You probably won't even make the connection between these things and your car because the behaviour isn't logical or rational. If you have a very expensive motor parked outside your house it's certainly telling every reprobate in society that your house could be worth a visit after dark and the car itself would be a fun joyride for a few hours. Certainly if you drive a BMW or similar suitable 'getaway vehicle' don't leave it in any long-term car parks. Then there's the tradesmen and others that you get to call round to give you a quote for some job or other; we all know where they keep their code of ethics don't we – it's the reason why they're always hanging low. How do you think it'll affect their pricing policy when they pull up beside your new Jag in their battered transit? Whether they are tax compliant or not you can forget about getting the VAT knocked off. In conclusion then, whatever car you are driving don't change it 'til it calves, then buy yourself a low in mileage, high in years solid Japanese job.

16. Drive Diesel

Diesel cars just run and run forever. My auld rust bucket has notched up 330,000 careless miles and is still going strong. You'd be incredibly fortunate to get within sniffin' distance of 200,000 out of a petrol car. Plus it's a lot easier on the juice. Granted you'll pay a bit more for your diesel car in the first place but it's still no contest. In fairness people are copping on to this fact in large numbers in recent years but a sizeable minority still need to be converted. Some people will protest that they don't do enough mileage to justify a diesel; in that case I'd say you don't do enough miles to justify a car. Make your next car a diesel.

17. Top Dogs for Cars

You can't keep a good man down can you now? The cream always rises to the top no matter what you do! Take the Japs for instance; it's only 60 odd years since they were flattened at the end of the Second World War by not one but two atomic bombs. That's what it took to make these bucks realise the game was up; nobody could accuse them of being quitters anyway, they might be short little fellas but they have more backbone than a humpback whale and now look at them, they're back on top, taking over the gaff in a game of economic warfare and invading the world with their technological weaponry. Then there's the Germans; they've been crushed twice in the last century and here they are, back again, top dogs in Europe and dictating the rules to the rest of us as if it never happened – and why wouldn't they with their work ethic. They may not be much craic at a party but they know how to run things. Now it just so happens that these two nations make a few cars between them and as any farmer or taxi driver will tell you, (and who better to ask when buying a car) there's no need to look any further than the Jerry's or the Japs when deciding what make to go for. Reliability is their middle name. Whatever you do don't entertain the notion of buying a French car – even for five seconds! Sure you know what the frogs are like, all style but no substance and the worst of the lot is FIAT, you can guess, I'm sure, what those initials stand for? That's right: Fix It Again Tomorrow.

18. Last Chance Saloon

For those of you who've made it this far in my little utopian guide you're probably as well off to make that diesel car a saloon – especially if you have kids hogging the back seats – because by now you'll be developing a keen eye for a freebie and sometimes that freebie will be a mite bulky, so the bit of extra space will come in handy. I brought an intact wooden pallet home in the boot of my Avensis the other day after I spotted a notice in a shop window advertising them free to take away. While you're at it you should stick a hitch on the car too if it hasn't already got one; you never know when you'll need to haul some freebie home in a trailer.

19. Daylight Saving

Get into the habit of putting on your lights at all times while driving regardless of driving conditions, visibility or time of day. Even if it doesn't increase your visibility it will make you much more visible to others. Taking this simple measure has been shown to significantly reduce your chances of being involved in an accident. The cost of this measure is miniscule and therefore can be viewed as a sound investment as opposed to an added expense. I don't understand actually why our government doesn't make it compulsory for all new cars sold to carry this safety feature built in, so that as soon as you turn the ignition hey presto, your lights come on. They are supposed to be oh so concerned with our safety what with NCT's, penalty points and expensive road safety advertising campaigns. So why don't they bring in this simple measure which they are well aware would reduce accidents and which would be cost neutral to the long suffering taxpayer and virtually cost free to the individual motorist? I can think of no reason except the usual one for illogical government inaction: the motor industry mustn't want it and their powers of persuasion must be considerable. I take it the ubiquitous brown envelope wasn't buried with Charvet Charlie then.

20. Never Pay For Parking

A lot of people out there are under the misguided impression that parking fees are a necessary motoring expense. I assure you they are not. It is quite possible to park your car legally and for free in any town or city in Ireland. How do I know this? Because I do it regularly. Keep your eyes peeled, think laterally and you will be able to find free parking within a ten minute walk of almost any town or city centre in the country. In the event that you cannot do this, perhaps in Cork or Dublin, it is still a very good gamble to find a side street which is slightly off the beaten track and yet convenient to your destination and park there without displaying a ticket. You're chances of being ticketed are minimal and worth the risk. You need to become skilful at risk assessment to reduce the number of those €40 parking fines to a miniscule level. Think about your opponent, the much maligned traffic warden. Not the most motivated individual at the best of times, thank God, and so, if it's a wet day or if you park near the top of a steep hill your odds are improving. Equally if it's 4.30pm on a Friday afternoon this bored chap will be shuffling off home a little early on the QT. Conversely of course, if you leave your car double parked on the main street for four hours mid Monday you're gonna get – and richly deserve – a ticket. You get the picture?

There are many more ways to reduce or increase your chances of being ticketed, too numerous to mention here, but you'll get the hang of it. Remember the wardens primary concern is to make sure the traffic flows as freely as possible so almost all of his active work time will be taken up ticketing morons who're blocking traffic or making sure no few individuals are hogging the premium city centre parking bays all day. He's also a well known chap and generally quite sociable so a generous portion of his time will be given to meeting and greeting the public. The odds are in your favour; bet wisely.

21. Frugal Fuel Usage

There are numerous small ways to reduce your vehicle's fuel consumption. Having the air conditioning on or windows wound down increases fuel usage. Keeping the engine running when the car is idle creates more wastage, so if you expect to be stationary at a red light or road works for example for more than thirty seconds, turn your engine off. This point is ever more pertinent of course if your better half has 'just dashed into the shop for a second'. You know she's not gonna come outa there for a dog's age, so turn the engine off and relax. Also, excess weight in your car adds to your fuel consumption so shed those pounds, from the car I mean (although it wouldn't hurt to lose your own personal spare tyre while we're on the subject). Clear the clutter. If those golf clubs only see the light of day twice a year, take them out of the boot and store them in the shed. Better yet, sell the clubs altogether and take up something interesting (and cheaper) instead.

22. The Power to Perform

Of course the best way to burn money is to buy yourself a ridiculously high powered motor, let's say some three litre turbo yoke. Not alone will it eat the juice but your pocket will think your hand has gone mad as you fork out ridiculously excessive amounts for maintenance, insurance, tax, servicing and so on. What are you spending all this extra money for? Prestige, perhaps? We've already seen what that buys you in an earlier point. The power to get to your destination sooner, maybe? It's a nice idea in theory, but I don't think so – have you driven on Irish roads lately? You'll end up stuck behind the same slow coach as everyone else regardless of what you're driving. If you are fortunate enough to get onto a decent stretch and overtake, don't worry, we'll be right behind you a few miles up the motorway, ground to a halt at the same road works.

Then there's the 'Chelsea Tractors' – you know, those four wheel drive, ice cap melting monstrosities which were originally intended for rural donkey work, except these ones have never even seen a field let alone been in one. They tend to hang out in Marks n' Sparks car park and places like that. What kind of idiots drive these? Never mind the expense, just think of the hassle trying to manoeuvre a small tank around the city centre or worse, one of those underground shopping centre car parks. I drove a friend's Toyota Land Cruiser around Galway city one Sunday when my own car was out of action and let me tell you a more stressful day it'd be hard to have even if your wife went into premature labour. Here's my advice for what it's worth: get yourself a personality and some self-esteem so you don't have to over compensate for their lack with one of these gas guzzlers under your arse. Then sell the flippin' thing pronto while there are still a few fools rich enough left in the country to provide a market for your useless merchandise. Next get yourself a nice sensible Toyota Corolla and do your showing off through your talents and abilities instead.

23. The Fine Points of Motoring

There are a whole plethora of motoring fines you can pick up of course and in recent years, to exacerbate matters, we have seen the introduction and steady widening of the penalty point system. These points are an added headache as not alone will they negatively affect your next insurance premium but most likely your partner's as well (so Ally, for God's sake don't pick up any more of them, ok!). For the most part all these fines can be considered to be a voluntary tax which you have elected to pay as they are all behaviour related and therefore completely avoidable. I did say for the most part. We all know of some poor unfortunate who has picked up an €80 fine and three penalty points for doing fifty on a six lane motorway, just because some retard in the higher echelons of the civil service – who flies around the city in a taxi courtesy of the bus lanes and his taxpayers expense account – has decreed it to be a thirty mile zone. So avoid fines and perhaps even save your life by wearing your safety belt and keeping within the speed limits, at least when those limits are sane. Because the law is an ass you also have to exercise a bit of uncommon sense in relation to your speed. Again we can all cite examples of byroads with sixty mile limits that you'd want to be both suicidal and in a murderous rage to be travelling anything even remotely close to that figure on. I guess the government parties don't much like the nice folks living on these particular roads – they must be all shinners or worker's party voters. Remember there are bonus savings in keeping your speed in check because fifty to fifty five miles per hour is the optimal speed for fuel efficiency. So the law abiding motorist cuts his diesel bill, saves on repair and insurance costs from the otherwise inevitable crash he has avoided and, as if all that weren't incentive enough, he gets to keep all his limbs and internal organs as well.

24. Inflationary Pressure

Properly inflated tyres will not only reduce fuel consumption but will increase the lifespan of the tyres themselves. Find out the optimal tyre pressure for your vehicle and check your tyres occasionally to maintain them at that level. After all air is free, at least it is still free almost everywhere. One greedy git I came across who runs a service station in Roscommon town charges fifty cents to put air in your tyres (he must have migrated there from Cavan). Hard to believe, I know, but true. Who is responsible when we see outrageous developments like this in the market place? No, not the miserly bastard that introduced the charge, you! That's who! The customer who, despite fundamentally disagreeing with its practices, continues to support that business. This example is just the logical extension of 'The Fried Rice Syndrome' by that business. So please, where you come across business being done in a way you disagree with in principal, voice your discontent with a reasoned argument to the management. If the issue is not resolved to your satisfaction take your business elsewhere.

25. Used Buy

Many people never consider buying good quality used tyres when theirs need replacing. For some reason they automatically order new ones – some not even realising they have a cheaper option, I suspect. Good quality used tyres are widely available for less than half the price of new ones. They typically have perhaps 75% to 80% of their lifespan left in them. You don't have to be a mathematician to figure out that that is an improved return versus paying full price for a 100% tyre. As always if you shop around you can do even better than this. The cheapest new tyre for my car costs about €65 and I can usually get a decent used one for €20 to €30. Sometimes, as fate will have it, you inadvertently get the same usage from your used tyre as you would have from a new one. You may for instance get a rupture puncture which is too large to be repaired or you may have damaged the tyre beyond repair by driving on a flat for too long without realising. In these cases it won't matter whether you were driving on a €100 tyre or a €20 one, you're still going to have to shell out for a replacement. Use a coin to check the thread depth of a new tyre to compare with the used ones you're offered in order to gain the best value. The trick with this tip is to have your homework done before you find yourself driving on two bald back tyres with the spare punctured in the boot, so you know who to go to for a good deal.

26. Juicy Prices

I know I've already mentioned you should shop around regardless of what product or service you are after but the point deserves repeating in the context of fuelling your car. For some psychological reason even people who are quite savvy about bargain hunting in other contexts sometimes seem to be deserted by this ability when it comes to finding the cheapest juice in town to fill the car with (incidentally a similar phenomenon also commonly manifests itself in punters choosing which pub to socialise in). Maybe it's because we tend to put the same monetary amount into the tank when at the pumps? Allied to this, we can't physically see how much product we are getting so perhaps it feels like we are getting the same deal regardless of which forecourt we pull into. Alas we are not. If there is an eight cent per litre difference in price between one set of pumps and another and your fuel tank takes fifty litres or so then you are wasting €4 with every fill up. Sometimes the price difference in a small radius can be as much as ten cents or more.

By the way forget the advertising spiel from the various fuel companies; independent research suggests there is no appreciable difference in quality between one brand and another. This is a product whose purchase should be based solely on price. Buy from the cheapest supplier, period – unless of course you happen to know he has been convicted for fuel laundering. Actually shopping around for the cheapest fuel is a simple task and there is absolutely no excuse for not doing so because suppliers are now legally obliged to clearly display prices. So develop the habit of glancing at the prices as you drive about. Remember prices are constantly fluctuating. The guy who is cheapest today may not be tomorrow. If you cannot clearly see the price as you drive up to a garage then you can rest assured they are not competitive. The guy with the keenest prices will be shouting loudly about it.

27. Make Your Car Journeys Count

When going on a car journey for whatever reason try to kill two birds or more with the one stone, so to speak. In other words if you are going across town to meet a friend, pick up the groceries on your way back and time the trip to fit in with visiting time at the nearby hospital where your elderly aunt is a patient, that sort of thing. Never take the car out and come back having achieved only one task if at all possible. Plan ahead and get multiple jobs done with each journey.

28. How About a Good Servicing?

It is a false economy to keep putting off having your car serviced indefinitely. It will cost you more in the long run in repairs. That being said you should certainly not bring your old Jalopy within a headmaster's holler of a main dealer. Ask around among acquaintances and make enquiries with businesses themselves to find a good value, competent, back garden mechanic. The trick is to have this groundwork done before there's a problem, otherwise you risk being pressured into going to the first chancer you can find. Of course it could be a good idea to learn how to do a basic oil and filter change service on the car yourself. Even if like me, you've rarely poked your nose under the bonnet of a car and couldn't tell a carburettor from a clutch, a good instruction manual would go a long way in helping you and the initial cost of signing up for some evening classes on the subject would soon be recouped.

29. Annual Motor Tax

The clue to this tip is in the title. Tax your car annually, not half-yearly or quarterly. Why pay extra to go through this hassle four times a year instead of once? You know when the renewal is and you get an advance reminder notice in the post so be prepared when it falls due and take the pain in one go. Pay on time too, there's no benefit in putting this on the long finger. The establishment treat this one seriously so you're only risking a fine and penalty points on top of the tax if you delay. The obvious exception to this rule is of course if you believe there is a very strong likelihood that you'll be getting rid of your wheels in the next few months. The same principle applies to your insurance: be prepared, shop around for the best quote and pay the premium in one full whack. Do not even pause to consider those so called easy payment options involving monthly payments. As with the motor tax they will add between 10% and 20% to your annual bill. You may realise this point is another form of 'Buy in bulk' which was covered earlier but it's worth repeating here I think, because it's a very different context.

30. The National Car Tax

Simply put, the reasons given for bringing in that driver's migraine known as the NCT were – as is the case with most government explanations for anything – deliberately deceitful. Otherwise known as lies. The NCT is at best just another stealth tax and at worst a further cosy little arrangement between the motor industry and the Government to continue pushing and coercing the middle Ireland motorist into feeling he has no choice but to keep changing his car at ridiculously regular intervals. Imagine being legally obliged to test your car after four years – it's a sick joke! The car is still new; sure the plastic's hardly off the seats. In the case of some models the feckin' thing is still under the manufacturer's warranty for seven years. Jobs for the boys! That's the only useful purpose the National Car Tax serves. Anyway now that I've got that off my chest, I must begrudgingly accept that it is compulsory in this nanny state so we have to deal with it. Do not however, in the run up to your NCT date, fall into the trap of trying to second guess what faults might or might not need to be repaired. In other words don't bother your arse with those pre-NCT makeovers some car sharks try to sell you. Bring your car along to its appointed outpatient clinic as is. Let them tell you what, if anything, needs doing to it. You never know the car might even pass or it may only need to be brought back for a visual inspection after you change a bald tyre or something and there is no further charge or appointment needed for this. At worst you leave armed with a printout detailing precisely what work needs to be done to pass second time round. This is good ammunition for the mechanically challenged layman to have as he seeks out the keenest cost of getting the work done. Well worth the re-test fee of €28 as opposed to leaving yourself at the mercy of some imaginative or incompetent grease monkey in the first instance.

All this talk of repairing and replacing vehicles reminds me of a story which I think serves to highlight an alternative view of vehicle ownership that exists in the world. I was out in Kerala, India one time and I got to know this chap, Anil. Now Anil, being well off by local standards, drove a battered old four wheel drive (well you'd need one for the roads out there). One day in conversation I asked him in passing how old his vehicle was? He gave me a puzzled look and after scratching his head thoughtfully for a minute or two he said he didn't know how old it was. All he could tell me was that his father had bought this workhorse thirty five years earlier, second hand, from the American army (he didn't know how long the yanks had had it for) and had passed it on to him. In other words Anil was driving around in a family heirloom which he fully intended to pass down to his own son in time.

31. NCT Refund

Did you know that if you ring up to book your car in for its NCT and they cannot give you an appointment within four weeks, you are entitled to be provided with a test free of charge? Equally, if you bring your car along to be tested and you have to wait more than sixty minutes after the appointment time before the test begins then you are also entitled to a free test. Check out the NCT customer charter on their website for the exact wording regarding this entitlement. Of course you will have to ask for your refund as they are not likely to offer it to you otherwise. There are sixty two test centres around the country, so your challenge if you're up to it is to find the most inefficient shower near you and book your old jalopy in there for a free test. It's worth noting too that traditionally December and January are their busiest months.

32. Road Tax Rebate

So perhaps the cost of getting the auld jalopy past the NCT for another year is prohibitively expensive and you decide to send your faithful servant off to the big garage in the sky. If so, did you know that under certain circumstances you might be entitled to a road tax rebate? This is a well kept secret by the establishment. I was talking to a wily west of Ireland farmer from a place called Kiltivna in the county Galway recently; now you'd have to be up early in the morning to cod the fellas around there but even he didn't know about this possibility. Don't get too excited though, the conditions are numerous. First of all there must be a minimum of three full calendar months unexpired on your disc from the date your refund is calculated which, for reasons only known to the workaholics in the motor tax office, may not be until the first of the month following your application. But if you satisfy this criteria and your vehicle is going to be out of commission due to being scrapped, stolen, exported, an insurance write-off or it won't be driven due to your illness or absence from the state, then pick up a Form (RF120) from your local tax office (or email/phone to have one sent out) without delay to check if you are eligible – because it's not just about the money, is it? There's a special pleasure in prizing even a few measly euro from the vice like grip of a bureaucratic government department, even if it is your own money in the first place.

33. Getting Cleaned Out

Of course now that you are a jalopy driver and proud of it, you won't suffer from the same urgency to have the car valeted every other week as the Jones's do. This is a very positive thing too for it is impossible to figure out why exactly people are willing to pay such seismic sums to car valeting operators and I have pondered at length on this conundrum. Without a hint of irony they can often quote you €100 or so to clean out and hoover a space no more than a few feet square. That is what they are by the way; cleaners. Take away the posh sounding title and they are just cleaners, nothing more and nothing less. Now I can get a cleaner in to my four bedroom semi-d and she will clean it from top to bottom for about €50 at a rate of €10 an hour and if the auld banger does need a once over I can get her to do that too while she's at it for an extra €10 tops. Alternatively there must be some enterprising young fella living nearby that will be delighted to clean your car inside out for €5 to €10. Apart from the huge cost disparity the only differences to the service provided will be that he won't refer to himself as a 'valet engineer' when he calls round on his bicycle and secondly, he won't be including tax, VAT, insurance, advertising, rent costs and so on in his fee – not to mention paying the middle man or asking you to sign a disclaimer or other paperwork. Finally, he will call to your house to do the job with no expectation of a call out fee or overtime for working on a Sunday.

Taking yourself to the cleaners via the local car wash is another good way to separate yourself from your hard earned cash whilst getting little or nothing in return. You can't keep a car clean for any length here in muck splattered Ireland anyway and besides, now that we drive a battered auld rust bucket, the five minutes it remains clean in the wake of our visit to the forecourt car wash won't make much of a dent in people's impression of said vehicle. At some point, maybe on the eve of your NCT, you might want to give it a scrub and that's exactly what you should do. Give it a five minute going over with a mop or soft bristled brush and bucket of hot soapy water and Bob's your uncle, she'll be as clean as any was ever intended to be on an Irish road. You know, apart from anything else I rather fancy that the dirt on my car offers a very eco-friendly protective glaze from the harsh elements of loose chippings, hawthorn briars and the like.

34. Automatic Security

If you drive a vehicle closely fitting the profile of the one advised in the previous motoring related tips, you will gain the added bonus of never having to worry about alarming your car or messing about with steering locks or any other security measures for that matter because no self-respecting thief will give it a second glance. We aren't driving the typical getaway vehicle now are we? In fact it shouts loudly to anyone interested that you haven't two buttons to rub together. And this is precisely what you want to be saying to anyone interested in your finances because anybody dwelling on that subject is doing so for one reason and one reason only: to part you from as much of it as possible. So your vehicle is now adequately playing its part in protecting you not alone from ordinary decent criminals but also from their equally nasty counterparts such as bankers, various government departments and unscrupulous tradesmen to mention just a few.

35. Risky Insurance Manoeuvres

If for some reason you find you need to switch your car insurance cover to a different vehicle before your annual renewal date, don't make the mistake I did when changing my car. I just rang up the broker, gave them the details of my new car, cancelled the old policy and waited for the new contract to arrive in the post. This was an extremely efficient and hassle free process, unfortunately it was also prohibitively expensive. My original insurance had cost me €284 third party fire and theft for a year on a twelve year old 2ltr diesel Avensis. Five months into the policy I switched cover to a three year old motor; same make, model and horse power, but with comprehensive cover. I was charged a top up premium of €303 for the seven remaining months on the policy. I know I upgraded to a higher value car and extra cover with the comprehensive package but even so I got screwed. When I was on the phone changing the policy I was like a worm wriggling on a hook. I knew they were squeezing my balls but I felt I had little choice but to suck it up as I was collecting the new car that same morning. On mature reflection, when the pressure was off and I could think rationally once more, what I should have done was to shop around for a completely new full year insurance quote from all the usual suspects for the new car and opt for the best value on the open market, arranging for it to kick in from the time of my choosing. Then once I had the new car safely under my ass I should have cancelled the old insurance and waited for the rebate cheque. I'll never know exactly how much this would have saved me but I am confident I would have got the full years cover for no more than I paid for the 7 months. That wise old sage hindsight is a great man. I don't feel too bad about my folly though because a mistake which teaches you a valuable lesson isn't really a mistake at all now, is it?

36. On yer Bike

The humble High Nelly must be man's greatest invention since the wheel itself. Certainly as a mode of transport it has been popular for a very long time and seems, with good reason, to be holding its own – albeit with a few modern tweaks – in this technological age. The bicycle really is a cheap and versatile mode of transport. As with anything, it has its limitations which vary with each user but certainly any able-bodied person going on regular short journeys of four or five miles should own a bicycle. If you are not fit enough to cycle such distances you might want to consider the possibility that this is because you never move unless there's an engine firmly positioned under your fat posterior. In an urban environment this simple machine really comes into its own. No other form of transport can compete on so many fronts in the city. Switch to peddle power around town and:

(a) you will save money using this virtually free form of transport;

(b) you will become fitter and healthier as you incorporate this workout into your daily routine;

(c) you will get to your destination faster and feeling oh so superior as you whizz past the traffic and then chain the bike to its free parking space, the lamppost, right outside your place of work;

(d) now that you are keeping fit naturally you can cancel the gym membership. No more feeling like Mr Bean as you squirm with your head down, working out alongside the feckin' county hurlers.

I know that as you read this passage a dormant part of your brain is waking up and having a panic attack, doing overtime to raise conscientious objections to deter you from what it sees as a drastic medieval step backwards. It's saying things like, what about the fumes? Sorry to tell you but you're getting more of those cooped up in your metal box, sitting in endless tailbacks. It's too dangerous, it cries! No it's not, that's a myth propagated by fellows who can't fit onto a saddle anymore or by their lazy teenage children aghast at the thought of how, 'so, like ye know, uncool' they'll be in the eyes of their peers as they cycle in the school gates. Look, you're not going to be travelling around town at the speed of light, neither are the cars; plus you've got bus and cycle lanes as well as footpaths when necessary. Engage a little bit of caution and a modicum of common sense as you would in any other area of life and you'll be fine. You survived your own childhood didn't ya? And God help us all, you terrified half the neighbours as you tore around, airborne half the time, on your Raleigh Chopper back then. I'm not fit enough, I here you whine! Well how in blazes are you going to get fit? Here's the perfect opportunity and motivation for you. Fact: this tip is a genuine no brainer for most urban dwellers and plenty of rural ones too if you want to shave serious amounts of money off your annual transport costs as well as a few pounds off your backside. If not, sure the road into your dull job is paved with great excuses and tailbacks.

37. Tom Thumb

Whatever happened to thumbing a lift? Or hitch-hiking as the yanks have us calling it now. It used to be the most popular form of long distance travel within the state for youngsters with no car and little money. Kids these days are probably for the most part blissfully unaware that those two plump stumps known as thumbs are an extremely useful, versatile, readily available, lightweight, environmentally-friendly and all importantly free form of procuring transport. I know the objections but I'm not buying them. There's the 'it's too dangerous' argument which gets pulled out with a look of indignation every time some people fear they're being asked to inconvenience themselves, however slightly. Now I know there have been genuinely heart breaking stories of people, particularly young women, (why is it more tragic if some ill faith befalls an attractive young woman as opposed to say a balding slightly plump middle-aged man?) disappearing without trace and of course there are opportunistic predators out there such as paedophiles, rapists and muggers to name a few. The thing is these threats were always with us, even though in the old days we buried our heads in the sand and pretended they didn't exist – not a great defence mechanism I admit, but that's what we did.

The other point I would make about the risks involved is to ask, do you think hitch-hiking is a more dangerous activity overall than any number of other activities people spend their time engaged in? Is thumbing from Galway to Dublin a greater threat to the health and safety of your student daughter than say a typical student night out on the town? I don't know the answer to that question. I am just trying to emphasize the point that despite the very real dangers in society you cannot, with the best intentions in the world, wrap her in cotton wool, nor should you, and even if you could that would create greater dangers still. Quite simply, to live is to risk. What we can do however is reduce the risk by taking some simple precautionary measures like making sure your loved ones are aware of and alert to the dangers. Hitching with a friend should almost be considered compulsory by young girls; letting others know the expected route and timeframe involved; perhaps carrying a weapon of defence such as a pepper spray might be useful but I think having knowledge of some basic self-defence would be more helpful. Last but not least trust your instincts. This is a skill not utilised enough in the modern era but it's still there, perhaps dormant, but at your disposal. If you get a bad vibe or a negative feeling you don't need to understand or rationalise it, just trust it and don't get in that car. Then there's the whine 'nobody picks up hitch-hikers anymore'. That wasn't my experience. I recently had reason to thumb for the first time in years. I got a lift straight from Athlone to my destination, Grand Canal Dock in Dublin, within five minutes of sticking my thumb out. I probably beat taking public transport by an hour and saved about €15 into the bargain.

Like everything else in life there are ways to improve your odds. Put yourself inside the head of the drivers you are trying to reach. It's a simple sales technique. You are selling an idea to the motorist. Make it easy for him to pick you up. Encourage him to think it would be a pleasant experience if he stops for you and so on. In other words if you're a Dock Martin, leather jacket wearing male skinhead full of tattoos and piercings with a sour puss on you, I'm sure you're a lovely fellow but still and all you're probably as well off taking the bus.

38. Depreciating Assets

When considering whether or not to take out a loan one simple rule to live by which potentially, over a lifetime, will save you tens of thousands of euro is: never borrow for a depreciating asset. If you can reasonably expect the value of the asset you are acquiring to decrease in value over its lifetime – the classic example would be a car, apparently 80% of motorists borrow to finance a new vehicle – you should save for it rather than borrowing. Practising this form of delayed gratification not only saves you significant amounts in interest repayments but it also has the built in, added security of eliminating any risk of biting off more than you can chew or buying something when you can ill-afford to repay the debt. The exception to this rule might be if said asset was earning you an income over the course of its lifetime, for instance it could be reasonable for a taxi driver to borrow for a vehicle because the expense can be written off against tax, plus the product justifies itself by earning him an income.

So for the average Joe, as a rule of thumb I can only think of three scenarios where you might consider it reasonable to borrow: (a) To buy a house; (b) to pay for education expenses or (c) the setting up/expansion/improving of a business. Insofar as possible you should also plan ahead and save for these scenarios to avoid unnecessary expense and risk. Unless it is for business purposes, you should not under any circumstances borrow to buy a new motor vehicle. If you need a car urgently buy a cheap but reliable used model whilst saving, if you must, for a new one. Also, without exception – in case anybody is a little slow on the uptake – never, ever borrow to cover expenses such as a fitted kitchen, household furniture, Christmas, holidays, communions, confirmations or weddings (your own or anyone else's).

39. Freedom from Debt

The common man's goal should be to become and to remain debt free. To be indebted to is to be obliged. So if you are in debt you are in a compromised position. In other words you are no longer free. You have given up, at least partially, your freedom to the bank or whoever you have borrowed from in return for the money. Naturally the greater the level of debt the more enslaved you become. Now life is not always straightforward and sometimes to borrow may be the lesser of two evils. For example, you may decide to borrow for a mortgage because you have decided, after careful consideration, that it is better to be beholden to the bank than to another landlord. Fair enough but even in this case it should be a priority for you to repay this debt as quickly as humanly possible to buy yourself out of servitude and regain your freedom. In conclusion I would urge everyone reading this to prize that most precious gift, freedom. Please do not trade your freedom for a fitted kitchen.

40. The Lesser-Spotted Accountant

Sometimes if you need to engage the services of a professional you can use his somewhat lesser qualified equivalent to the same effect for a reduced fee. An example of this might be if you have some basic, not too complex, accounts to submit to revenue for tax purposes – an accountant's technician will probably suffice for your needs rather than the more qualified, more expensive but rather unnecessary accountant.

41. Thwart the Thieving Taxman

Some might say – and even revenue themselves claim – that it is a simple matter to conduct your own tax return without recourse to a professional at all, especially if you are a PAYE worker or your income is relatively straightforward to calculate. This regretfully is not true. The tax system is deliberately, dishonestly and unnecessarily complex for the benefit of the bureaucrats and their cronies at your expense. No ordinary punter could reasonably be expected to keep up to date with all the tax bands, breaks, exemptions, allowances and nobody knows what else – especially as the goalposts keep changing every year. So it is with reluctance that I would advise any taxpayer to engage the services of an accountant (or technician) at least once every few years to go through your family income and expenditure to try to identify where you are over-paying unnecessarily. Any accountant worth his salt will identify savings to justify his fee that you will have overlooked due to the complexity of the system. Even if you are the spawn of Einstein, I am convinced the once-off fee will prove to be a worthwhile investment. Of course the crime is in the fact that you are forced by the system to hire a professional simply to identify your entitlements. I think it would be safe to assume that if you investigated the matter you would find that a very high percentage of politicians and senior civil servants sons and daughters were accountants – how remarkably coincidental!

42. Mobile Property Savings

Filling out the hated property tax form, I noticed there are certain exemptions. The usual ones have been well publicised such as a property in certain specified ghost estates, properties bought by a first time buyer as their sole residence in 2013 and so on. All the exemptions – and you can rest assured exempt properties will be as rare as hen's teeth – are listed on the LPT (local property tax) website and in the guide which should have been posted out to you. Towards the end of the list one group of exempt properties caught my eye: mobile homes, vehicles or vessels. So it seems if you want to legally avoid the property tax you should consider living in a moveable home of some kind, such as a barge, camper van, caravan or indeed a mobile home. There would of course be many other associated savings with this lifestyle choice also. These home types are by definition small and generally without much if anything in the way of a garden so maintenance costs should be minimal, also of course if your home keeps moving it'll be hard for revenue or anybody else to pin you down to extract any other bills or taxes from you for which you may be liable. Levels of resentment towards this unfair arbitrarily applied tax are so high that far from the settled community being racist against travellers in the future, glares of disgust previously thrown in the direction of the local halting site may soon turn to looks of envy. Perhaps the government has unwittingly solved the age old divide between these two communities. Could it be that we will all soon be in the market for our own wanderly wagon, re-joining our estranged countrymen and toasting marshmallows by the roadside campfire? I admit it's an extreme solution but the austere demands being piled upon the shoulders of your average working man are also extreme and only going to get worse.

43. Don't Defer

A certain few individuals will be entitled to a full or partial deferral of their property tax liability. If you are one of these it is easy to see how you would be tempted to avail of the option. But don't. The deferral comes at a price. Interest will be charged on the due amount at a rate of 4% per annum and of course the fee itself will rollover and snowball year on year. Before long the amount owing will become insurmountable and yet it has to be paid at some point. The house cannot be sold for example, without clearing the outstanding debt. The debt remains even after death. This is a deferral, not a waiver. A waiver means the charge has been cancelled; a deferral unfortunately only means you have kicked the offending ball down the road and to continue that analogy, this ball will soon turn into a ball of lead to which you will be shackled by the ankle via a very heavy chain. This is an unfair, unethical tax for a number of reasons, one of which is it seems to take no account whatsoever of your income or ability to pay (except for the deferral non-option) and you should register your disgust with your political representatives both now and at election and referendum time.

I would further advise, albeit reluctantly, that regardless of how limited your means are cut costs elsewhere if you must but pay this extortion charge to Nero. Do not let it build up to the point where the family home is at risk. There are, as usual, exceptions to this advice. If, for example, you are quite satisfied that you won't want to sell the property in your lifetime and you know who you are leaving the property to in your will, then it would not be unreasonable to inform this person or persons of your decision not to pay the tax, offering them the option of paying it for you rather than facing a lump sum liability at the time of inheritance.

44. Review Revenues Arithmetic

Now that you have reluctantly agreed to pay the blasted property tax do not simply accept revenue's valuation. I conducted a little amateur research amongst a few dozen friends and acquaintances to see if revenue's guesstimate of property values were accurate. What I discovered was that they got the valuation, and therefore the liability, correct about 50% of the time and the other 50% of the time they had valued the property one band too highly. There were no examples of revenue underestimating the value of a property in my little investigation. Funny that, isn't it? What this means is that revenue's method of calculation errs in their own favour when in doubt or when the value is borderline. So check out Daft and other websites, have a chat with the neighbours and bend the ear of a local estate agent (but don't pay for an official valuation, that's totally unnecessary) to determine the correct value of your house. If you find the value is borderline follow revenue's example and err on the side of caution in your own favour. It is a self-assessment tax after all so unless you're completely taking the mickey they'll accept your valuation. They've said as much.

45. Merchants of Misery

Now we all know bankers are wankers, I think it's in their

DNA. Anyway, it's an accepted fact recorded throughout history since time immemorial. However, when compared to moneylenders, they are saints in shoe leather. These parasitic bloodsuckers prey on the soft targets of society by lending to poor schmucks with poor credit ratings who simply cannot afford to borrow at any interest rate let alone the insurmountable loadings these guys apply. But I'm not going to dwell here on the nasty reprehensible nature of moneylenders – I think the world and her mother are in unanimous agreement on that score. There are more than forty legal money lenders licensed by the central bank along with countless illegal operators. The biggest of these companies has more than 100,000 customers on its books. This company typically gives loans of up to €500, charging €56 interest per €100 borrowed over a year. The interest rate rises to over 187% on shorter six month terms meaning the punter will pay €30 interest on a €100 loan. This company seems to be thriving in the recession as it has grown its customer base year on year from 75,000 in 2009.

It is estimated that there are more than 200,000 people in Ireland using moneylenders and this is likely to be a conservative estimate. To put that in context there are only just over 1.6 million households in the state. So according to these figures one in eight households could be in debt to loan sharks charging interest rates of up to 200% or more. I was dumbstruck by these figures when I first saw them. It's all very well vilifying the nasty moneylenders (and while conducting my research I found plenty of commentators who were willing to do just that), but there was a marked silence about the behaviour of the customers of these operators. This I find strange; after all it takes two to tango.

It has to be asked what kind of idiotic imbecile borrows these miniscule amounts at such outlandish interest rates. There is nothing you could want on this earth which justifies borrowing from a moneylender. Every citizen in the state receives enough money for basic essentials either through wages or social welfare. The amounts in question (rarely more than €1,000) can be saved relatively easily in advance compared to the effort required to repay the loan after the event.

So what is the money being borrowed for in the first place? For occasions such as Christmas, communions, christenings, weddings and worse. These annual life events do not need to cost much in the first place. If you cannot afford to save for these parties you should simply keep them low key and inexpensive. I will repeat for the slow learners reading this: under no circumstances whatsoever should you ever borrow from a moneylender. The mentality of someone contemplating borrowing from one of these leeches is similar to a person who cuts off his own hand so that he can claim disability benefit. If you choose – and remember it is exactly that, an act of free choice made by you, and you alone – to borrow from these doorstep lenders you are stating that it is your fervent wish to spend your life broke and in fear of the doorbell ringing. Even though it is politically correct to sympathise with the plight of people caught up in this vicious cycle of debt, if you discard your own peace of mind so willingly how can anybody help you? It isn't possible to legislate for stupidity, so you're on your own. You have to break this cycle yourself. Good luck.

46. One-off Windfalls

Current expenditure should always be covered by current income. I would include in this expenditure anything which needs to be repaired, improved or replaced at regular or even vaguely quantifiable intervals. And also not just weekly, monthly or annual bills such as food, mortgage payments, utilities, insurance and holidays but also things like home improvements, car replacement, kids college years or household technological gadgetry. All these things should be planned and saved for out of your families regular income sources. As mentioned previously, they should not be borrowed for as this only serves to make such purchases an even greater financial burden with interest being added to the pain. If you are the fortunate recipient of an unexpected financial windfall – as many people can expect to be at some point in their lives due to redundancy, inheritance, insurance payment, a win in the 3.30 at Chepstow or some other source – please resist the temptation to blow it on a round the world cruise, a new motor, fitted kitchen or a shopping trip to New York with the girls. Remember this is, as the name implies, a once-in-a-lifetime lucky financial break. Lightening rarely strikes twice so it won't be coming round again. With this in mind what you want to do is invest your money in a way that will allow you to continue feeling the warm, beneficial trickle of it for the rest of your natural in the form of a regular return on your investment to supplement your income. Alternatively you may decide to clear your mortgage or a portion of it to reduce your outgoings. What you decide to do will of course depend on the sum involved and your own personal circumstances. Get some solid independent financial advice, look at all your options and remember: invest don't spend.

47. Cracker Trackers

If you are one of those mortgage holders fortunate enough to have a tracker mortgage do not give it up under any circumstances. The banks are losing money hand over fist on these loans and so are constantly scheming and trying to come up with devious ploys to hoodwink unwary customers into changing their current tracker mortgage to a different arrangement. The very fact that they are doing this tells you that the tracker is a great deal for you. You can take it as a rule that anything which the bank perceives as a negative is extremely positive for you, the customer. The poor old bankers you see can't increase the interest rate on your tracker willy nilly whenever they feel they need more money, as they can and are doing with other mortgage types. Your tracker is protected because it is linked to the ECB (European Central Bank) rate. So let's reiterate the point to make sure you are crystal clear about this. If you are discussing any aspect of your finances with your bank make sure the first question on your lips is: how will this affect my tracker mortgage? Without exception, walk away from anything which separates you from your beloved tracker. You and tracker are wedded for life. There is no divorce for this union. Tracker mortgages are so valuable that even if you were to come into a lump sum financial windfall which enabled you to clear your mortgage it would most likely not be advisable to do so. You can probably earn more investing the money elsewhere than you would save in mortgage repayments.

48. Money Talks

If you are about to embark on a major financial commitment such as taking out a mortgage, pension plan or share buying it would be foolhardy not to seek independent financial advice before doing so. The key word here is 'independent'. There is plenty of 'free' advice to be had from banks and others in this field but sadly the truth in this case is if it comes for free, at best it has no value and at worst it could cost you dearly. You see these 'free' advisors obviously have to be paid by somebody so if you're not paying them who is? I'll bet you a pound to a penny their paymaster is the same bank that they just advised you to take out your mortgage with. The simple truth here is money buys loyalty so sadly, even though these guy's fees could sometimes bring tears to a wooden Buddha, if you want impartial professional financial advice from someone who only has your monetary health in mind resist the temptation to opt for the freebie. Bite the bullet, pay for an hour or two's consultation for a once-off fee or you could be paying handsomely every month for the next thirty years.

49. Debit beats Credit

To be certain that you never incur the penal interest rate charges which apply to credit card debt I suggest it is simpler and safer to simply switch or stick to using a debit card instead. Even if you are more organised than an Ikea manager of German extraction who always clears the balance on his credit card without incurring any interest, there are still extra bank and government charges incurred on credit cards. At one time there were arguments in favour of credit -v- debit but these have essentially all been eliminated with the new generation visa debit cards. I suppose I should admit to not being an authority on credit cards as at the tender age of forty three I have never had one. But neither in all my years have I ever felt in any way inconvenienced by its absence. That probably says it all really. There is one exception to the advice just offered. If you are for any reason worried about the security of a card transaction you may want to use a credit card for the peace of mind that comes with it. Alternatively you may want to question why you are risking a doubtful financial transaction with any type of card.

50. Intermittent Financial Review

You should review all your financial commitments at least annually in an attempt to spot potential savings or stop financial leakages via unnecessary charges. For instance, you may have set up a regular savings account last year paying 4% interest but when you review it you might discover it now only pays 2.5%. You think this is odd because you are sure you received no notification from the bank informing you of the rate change, not even a simple email. Don't worry, you are not going senile. The reason you have no memory of correspondence from the bank is because there was none. Incredibly, despite what we've seen as the end result of lax financial regulation in this country, the bank is under no legal obligation to inform you when it changes the details of your financial arrangement with them. Of course they won't inform you out of common decency and respect either because they don't possess either quality.

Banks sometimes advertise or phone you offering an appointment to conduct such a financial review but this will be of extremely limited value as they are unlikely, in all fairness, to point out any good offers their competitors have. In other words their advice will be the very definition of the word biased. So once again you are on your own and must conduct your own independent annual financial review. I would be very surprised if after thorough investigation you don't discover savings enough to make the effort worthwhile.

51. Your Word is your Bond

If you are fortunate enough to be able to borrow money interest-free from a family member or any other party for that matter whilst simultaneously unfortunate enough to need to, it will in all likelihood be a casual arrangement agreed with a handshake as opposed to a formal legally binding loan. This being the case, there is a very serious risk of the agreed repayment timeframe not being adhered to by you as it is so easy to illicit sympathy from friends and colleagues with one plausible excuse or another, and to keep kicking the repayment date down the infernal road to perdition. In the name of all that's sacred do not under any circumstances let that happen. You will be cutting off your nose to spite your face by blacklisting yourself from the perfect credit source (not to mention discarding a genuine friendship). So, to make sure we are crystal clear: any such loans you are privy to are as hard to come by as Viagra in the Vatican so treat them as your utmost financial priority to be repaid before all and any other commitments.

52. Don't Lose all your Marbles

When I was a nipper and no more than knee high to a grasshopper I learned a valuable financial lesson in the school yard from Mitch Mulhall, during a marble season. Mitch you see was a very good marble player and winning almost every game he played he went home from school most afternoons with two bulging pockets full of his spoils. The unusual thing about Mitch though, was that he would always arrive back into school the next morning with only one marble whereas everyone else, including yours truly, would be carrying all in their possession. If he lost his first game (an extreme rarity) Mitch was done for the day. If he won he now had two marbles to play with and so on. In other words, this cute farmer's son – who dropped out of school after his inter cert – was demonstrating to the rest of us an early example of risk assessment and damage limitation. Mitch was putting a strict limit on his potential daily losses, yet at the same time his potential gain was unlimited. I don't know whatever became of Mitch's vast marble collection but I can tell you the crafty fox went on to become a multi-millionaire when he rezoned a few acres of farmland as residential during the insanity of the boom. There's no fleas on that fella and if there are, they're all paying rent!

53. Look your Goliath in the Eye

I've never had the pleasure of witnessing an ostrich sticking his head in the sand but that is what they are reputed to do when danger is imminent, the theory being that the poor misguided creature believes if he doesn't see the danger then it doesn't exist. Such behaviour would make a bird look dumb, even next to his cousins in the animal kingdom who are themselves considered to be of only limited intelligence. What then would we think of a human being behaving in this manner? As I say, I've never caught an ostrich in the act but I have come across a few Homo sapiens who have thwarted evolution to such a degree as to consider this an intelligent survival strategy. In fairness, it's not their fault. This is the end result when you think yourself smarter than Mother Nature and so you turn her flawless 'survival of the fittest' design on its head by introducing a new strategy for living called 'survival of the grossly unfit'. You do this through our new age sponsorship of breeding wasters via the social welfare system. You see this system is the precise opposite of everything Darwin's theory of evolution taught us. With this new approach the strongest, most intelligent able-bodied members of the pack are penalised to the point where they cannot afford to reproduce many more of their own kind, with their spoils being handed out to welfare lifers to enable them to produce half a dozen feral youths apiece with the IQ of a partridge between them. This lot have evolved a highly sophisticated and complex reasoning, which was ably demonstrated in a recent survey of the demographic. The first question in the study asked the participant to scratch his arse, to which 86% of respondents refused, citing fear of having their dole cut for working. The second challenge put to the group was to pick their nose, again a majority, 92%, refused as they believed this could be considered a 'benefit in kind' and therefore could impact on their medical card eligibility.

Anyway, that was just a little background history to

explain how the human ostrich evolved. But what is the human ostrich? Well, this is the guy who, when faced with a difficult situation in life, ignores it in what he considers to be the not unreasonable assumption that it will just go away. If his problem was marital, he ends up divorced. If it was financial he ends up bankrupt or even homeless. He carefully considers his options, he correctly predicts that any action he takes carries an element of risk, so 'logically' he concludes he should do nothing at all, thereby taking no risk. I know; it's enough to make you fear for the human race but sadly there are a lot of these ostriches about – after all they have state-sponsored, incentivised breeding programmes. I'm sure you've come across one or two of this breed yourself?

So, let's cut to the chase. Are you an ostrich? Are you avoiding creditors? Ignoring bills? Paying penal credit card interest? If so you are heading for financial oblivion. Look, no matter how much of a financial hole you've dug for yourself, there is a way out. But first you have to stop digging. You are David. You're creditors are Goliath. You have to stand and face them fearlessly. If you confront any problem – financial or otherwise – with honesty, it loses most of its power. Anything which is brought out into the open in this way becomes manageable. Please note, I didn't say it would make it easy, but manageable. You may still have a difficult challenge but take it step by step; deals can be done. When you face your Goliath the playing field is levelled somewhat. A portion of debts can be written off, timeframes extended, everything is up for negotiation because whether your opponent likes it or not, he knows only too well that he can't get blood from a turnip (and a turnip's is precisely the intelligence level you were operating at to have gotten yourself into this mess in the first place). Most importantly, as you work through your woes, learn the important lessons contained in the process and you will never have financial difficulties in your life again. Isn't that a prize worth winning for the short-term pain and inconvenience? Oh and don't be as hard on yourself as I have been; if you have been bankrupt, wear it as a badge of honour, after all you've joined the ranks of an elite society. It's a bit like being a member of Mensa when you think about it like that. And besides, the man (or woman) who never made a mistake never made feck all.

54. Cashing out of Cheques

If you are a member of that dying breed who still write cheques in payment for goods and services it is time to cease this senseless habit. It is an expensive pastime these days with government stamp duty of fifty cents on each one you write plus bank charges of up to twenty eight cents on top of that. Use your debit card instead if you must but better still, go back to using the auld reliable: cash. Cash payments incur no charges of any kind and increase your bargaining power in many instances.

55. Daily Mail

The postal service in Ireland, I am happy to report, is very punctual and reliable. Almost all items of mail you post will in my considerable experience arrive the next day and therefore there is little or no point in paying a surcharge for the service of guaranteeing a next day delivery. In fact I once received a letter which was addressed simply to PJ More, The Burren, on the day following postage. There was no delay despite the fact that, as most of you know from your primary school geography, the Burren is an area of about 250km sq. The sender even misspelt my surname and I for my part hadn't even got a letter box at my address. None of this deterred my wily west of Ireland post mistress in her determination to execute her duties. So a regular stamp will suffice for your postal requirements; spending more just guarantees you that which you would have received regardless.

Also as mail almost never goes missing in transit, the only good reason for paying a premium to register a letter or package is if the sender or the recipient has some doubt about the other's trustworthiness. In fact registered mail is extra hassle as it has to be signed for at the time of delivery or alternatively collected at the local mail sorting office within three working days. The same package sent by regular mail costing €4 will cost €10 sent registered and let's say the contents are valued at €100. What this means is you are paying 150% extra to guarantee the safe delivery of goods which were at least 99% safe in the first place. So on the law of averages and using these rough figures, for every 100 packages you send you will pay an extra €600 to guarantee their safe delivery but if you had not bothered with this expensive form of insurance you would only have lost one package costing you just €100.

56. Allowance for Saving

Save the children's allowance from day dot. You'll never miss what you never had and little Einstein's third level education is going to have to be paid for somehow. No point putting off the inevitable and causing yourself extra pain and sleepless nights in the future. Trust me this is the easiest most stress free way of doing it. The money goes directly into your current account and you have a regular savings account set up, paying a half decent rate of interest, which it is automatically transferred to. The money accumulates away painlessly, although you do have to keep an odd eye on it to make sure the bank is not screwing you on the interest rate. At today's rates if you save little Johnny's monthly money, which currently stands at €140 each for the first and second children even with recent cuts, in eighteen year's time you'll have amassed a nice little nest egg of over €30,000. This is a simplistic example of course, leaving aside the interest and inflationary factors but it amply demonstrates the benefits of this policy. With this amount you'll even be able to keep the little limpet out from under your feet after his graduation with a deposit for his own gaff, if you so choose. I must reiterate the key to this plan is to put it into action the day the little monster enters the world. Starting this plan some years later is akin to the difference between the guy who never smoked and the fella who quits in his thirties: they both end up as non-smokers but the smarter chap did it the painless way. Mind you if we continue this analogy both these guys are much better off than the one who never quit until the eleventh hour when the Doctor told him he had cancer.

57. An Unexpected Certainty

In life we are told there are no certainties except for death and taxes. This is not entirely true, there is another certainty:

you will have unexpected expenses and they will occur at fairly regular intervals. You might say that this is a contradiction in terms but what I mean by this statement is that even with the best planning, budgeting and future forecasting in the world there will be expenses which you overlooked or which you could not possibly have known about in advance. However it doesn't matter so much that you don't know what the mystery bills will be so long as you acknowledge they will come and allow a reasonable contingency figure for them in your budgeting. Now that you know this, it isn't an acceptable excuse to moan that you had to max out your credit card at ridiculous interest rates north of 20% to attend the funeral of your great uncle Cecil in Birmingham after his sudden and unexpected demise at the early age of ninety two. Seriously, forewarned is forearmed; expect the unexpected. It will erase sleepless nights and ease the balancing of your finances.

58. Gambling Excess

The first and most important rule when investing a sum of money – and remember investing is another word for gambling as we are all very painfully aware here in Ireland – is only risk that which you can afford to lose. So regardless of whether you are putting your money on a horse running in the 2.45 at Punchestown, investing in some er, blue chip 'can't lose' bank shares or putting your hard earned cash into bricks and mortar, before you do the deal ask yourself what will be the effect on you and your family if you lose all of this money? Can you take it on the chin? In other words, imagine the worst case scenario happening to your investment and even though this eventuality would be a serious pain in the posterior, if it would not negatively affect your day to day standard of living then at least you can probably afford to take your gamble. This does not necessarily mean it is a good idea, only that you can afford it. The opposite is naturally also true; if losing your entire investment would result in serious financial difficulties then the only sane course of action is to walk away no matter how good the 'opportunity' seems.

59. Know When to Walk Away

If a particular deal – be it an investment offer or product for sale – appears far too good to be true then you need give it no further thought; it is safe to assume that it is too good to be true. It is a 99.9% certainty that there are hidden catches which will cost you dearly. So walk away without so much as a backward glance. We all have a strong self-preservation instinct which, put another way, means we are self-centred. Whilst being natural and normal this trait can sometimes become overly dominant, to the point where we are blinded by greed almost to the exclusion of other, counter-balancing instincts. Greed may dominate to the exclusion of our other attributes such as logical reasoning and treading warily with a degree of healthy scepticism. This is what happens when people invest in pyramid schemes or get rich quick scams of all kinds. Ireland's recent property bubble experience was a prime example of this albeit on a larger and more widespread scale. So remember: fools rush in where angels fear to tread.

60. A Pound in the Hand is worth Two on the Payslip

It has often been remarked by a tight, bright B Level student that a euro saved is equivalent to a euro earned. An interesting observation, but only true in the black market economy. His A Level peer would have further elaborated that a euro saved was, in mainstream economic life, actually worth up to two euro earned. By the time you deduct regular income tax, the other income tax known as USC (universal social charge), PRSI, other work related costs such as travel and the divil knows what else, you may well have to earn more than two euro for every one that eventually reaches your overworked paw. Before hastily parting with your hard earned cash on some impulsive purchase it is worthwhile pondering this nugget of wisdom and doing a quick mental calculation to convert the cost of your impending purchase from Euro to hours worked for your Faganesque employer. No doubt, in some cases this will lead to a swift revision of your decision.

61. Doing Your Homework

Have you ever considered working from home? Would it be possible in your profession? This is becoming an ever more popular option for many people and it is not difficult to see why. There are many attractions such as cost and time savings on the commute, further savings on lunch, snacks, take away coffees and the like. If you can work from home you are also to a large extent protected from the temptations of the relentless retail onslaught of the modern day urban environment. If you are self-employed and renting office or other work space such as is the case with many advisory jobs, consulting professions, alternative practitioners of various kinds and so on, there are substantial potential savings in rent to be had by relocating your business to home. Allied to all this there is the prospect of clothing and dry cleaning cost cuttings to be had if you are not going to be entertaining clients or customers in your new home/work space. Of course there are pitfalls to be wary of when mixing business and leisure space like this. It goes without saying that whatever part of your home is given over for work must be used solely for that express purpose. Ideally, if space permitted, your 'office' would be a separate building entirely from your living quarters. Regardless, it is imperative that a distinct separation be maintained between your home and work life. There is also the very real risk of going stir crazy if working reclusively in isolation for weeks on end without physical interaction with professional colleagues, especially if you are now operating from a rural retreat so make sure to break out occasionally from your new monastic work day setting to make a beeline for the concrete jungle to hook up with your fellow carnivorous business predators. If this option is at all possible for you, even for a portion of your working week, do give it your most serious consideration as the potential savings can sometimes run to in excess of €10,000 per annum. One acquaintance of mine who made the transition initially invested in a wooden home office costing in the region of €20,000. A lot of money says you and you're not wrong, but with the savings he's making it will have paid for itself in a couple of years. He calculates his annual savings to be €3,960 rent, €4,250 commuting and a €2,000 saving on lunches and coffees along with numerous other smaller savings. Even though this crafty fellow is saving a small fortune from his ingenuity and initiative, he tells me the real payoff is the improvement in his quality of life. He has clawed back two hours a day in commuting time to spend with his family and his stress levels have reduced to a rate comparable to a Buddha's.

SECTION 4

Out & About on a Shoestring

1. Get Flirty

The art of flirting is as old as time itself – I'm sure that's how Eve got poor old Adam to pick the feckin' apple that caused all the trouble. Still, don't let one little mishap put you off; flirting is a powerful persuasion tool which everyone has at their disposal (obviously to greater or lesser degrees). Women of course – and attractive young women particularly – have a greater potential in putting this ancient art into action and who are we men to begrudge them seeing as how the fairer sex are disadvantaged in so many other walks of life. This is not to say flirting is the sole preserve of the mini skirt and fluttering eyelash brigade, it is not; anyone can flirt with flirting. Most women probably employ this technique from time to time maybe even without realising they're doing it. I would urge you all to harness this latent talent and use it to maximum effect to obtain everything from job promotions to discounts and even freebies. It's also a lot of fun and wouldn't the world be a nicer place if everyone dumped the solemn look for a cheeky grin and a glint in their eye.

2. Cash in on your Smile

Nowadays you are probably on camera all the time; sitting on the jacks just isn't the same peaceful, private alone time it once was. Anyway, not much we can do about it – except milk it. Big brother is most definitely watching you 24/7 so you may as well put on your best smile for the lens and watch in delighted amazement at how the simple act of smiling impacts positively on your financial dealings and every other aspect of your life for that matter. A study was conducted in America some years ago involving the waiting staff in a restaurant. On one predetermined day of the week, the staff were asked to carry out their work as usual, efficiently, courteously and pleasantly, but they were not to smile. The following week on the same day, with the same staff and all other things being equal in so far as is possible, the same request was made of the staff, except this time they were encouraged to make every effort to smile as much as possible. What was the result? On the evening the staff were smiling their tips were more than double that of the previous week. The moral of the story is straightforward. It pays to smile. It also actually makes you feel better and amazingly this is true even if it's a false smile so, even if you don't feel like smiling, fake it 'til you make it!

3. Random Acts of Kindness

Commit random acts of kindness every day, not just because it's nice to be nice or even to put a smile on yours and the recipient's faces – although these are excellent reasons in and of themselves to follow this advice – but also because you will be repaid many times over in unexpected ways for your generosity of spirit by the universal flow. These acts do not of course necessarily have to cost you anything in the monetary sense. They might simply involve a kind word of praise, encouragement or advice; letting someone go ahead of you in a queue; picking an item of litter off the street to put in the bin. The list of possibilities is endless. Go on, put it into practice. Only good can come of it.

4. Doggy Bags

Ok, so you've been off the fags for six months and you've saved €2,000. You decide to celebrate your success by bringing herself out to a restaurant for a slap-up meal. Fair enough, we all have to let our hair down now and again and admittedly you couldn't have a better reason, but don't lose the run of yourself altogether. Make sure that when you've stuffed yourself and can't eat another morsel, if there's food still left then ask for a 'doggy bag' to bring home the leftovers. Some people cringe with embarrassment at this thought but believe me there is no need. This is quite a common practice and the staff won't bat an eyelid at the request.

5. Early Birds

Your mother always told you it wasn't good for your digestion to eat late at night – that's true, she knew what she was talking about – but when it comes to eating out, late dining is also harder on your pocket. Did you ever notice how the same meal in the same restaurant cooked by the same chef can cost almost twice the price depending on what time of day you eat it. Defies logic I know, but compare lunchtime prices with evening menus in a few culinary establishments and you'll see what I mean. I guess the reasoning is just supply and demand; it's probably easier to get bums on seats in the evening so a premium can be charged. What all this means for you, my penny pinching friend, is if you have cause for a celebration and you want to mark it with a nice meal out, consider organising your gastronomic get-together at lunchtime to save a few bob – particularly if you are the one picking up the tab for all the snouts at the trough. Your esteemed guests will also be more likely to go easy on the vino at an earlier hour which should save you and them both from your respective hangovers.

6. Skip the Tip

Tipping as a phenomenon is one which is growing more commonplace in western society, indeed it is the norm now and expected behaviour in certain service industries. As a widespread practice I am opposed to it and not just for the obvious reason of saving money. I think the original premise was fair enough; one where you gave a voluntary unexpected extra bonus payment to someone for a job exceptionally well done or where somebody went beyond their job description to facilitate you, the customer, in some way. If that happens by all means a little expression of gratitude is appropriate and what better way to express your appreciation than by putting your money where your mouth is with a little financial thanksgiving, especially where a low wage service worker is involved. Indeed, in such instances, it's a win-win situation as the person whom you've tipped will likely remember you favourably and be encouraged to bend over backwards to be helpful when next your paths happen to cross. But as with many a good and noble practice the art of tipping has been corrupted beyond recognition. We are now expected, for example, to tip every waitress and hotel porter regardless of what kind of shoddy service they dish up to us. Far from being a 'discretionary gratuity' it has become simply a stealth hike in the price of your dinner. Now that would be bad enough if the pimply student waiter was the beneficiary – you could console yourself with the thought that the money was helping him to achieve his degree so that one day he would be able to get a job which he actually had a smidgeon of interest in and which furthermore didn't require the compulsory giving of tips to supplement his wages. Alas, the only beneficiary of the 'compulsory tip' phenomenon is the fat cat employer as it enables him to squeeze further the already paltry wages he pays to his staff. Some employers actually brazenly confiscate the contents of the tip jar for themselves. I was told this was common practice in a Chinese restaurant where an acquaintance of mine worked. In this particular case the employer then added insult to injury by returning half of the December tips to the staff and calling it their Christmas bonus!

Another common practice is for tips to be shared equally between all staff members regardless of who receives them. I understand the intention here is probably honourable as some staff such as chefs are not on the frontline and therefore won't receive tips very often, regardless of service, but this practice is flawed as the layabout and the diligent are rewarded equally. Under this system regular tipping is exposed for what it is: a percentage of the staffs basic wage but paid by the customer rather than the employer. So I have two tips on tipping here, if you'll pardon the pun. Firstly, only tip an individual for exceptional service which you deem to be above and beyond the call of duty otherwise their wages should suffice for services rendered. Secondly, if you do still wish to tip make sure your hard earned money is actually going to the intended recipient and not being diverted to the greasy glove box of their employer's Merc.

7. Don't Play the Lottery

Speaking of voluntary taxes, here's another one. Someone once provocatively described the national lottery as 'a tax for stupid people'. The most committed subscribers to this tax ironically tend to come from the lower socio-economic groupings in society. Is this a coincidence? Or could it be that far from making you rich beyond your wildest dreams it is far more likely to contribute to keeping you broke all the time. Look, despite the above quote you aren't that thick. You know you haven't a rat's chance in a barrel of terriers of hitting the jackpot but you're buying a dream, a few quid for a little escapist fantasy. Fair enough, we can all use a bit of that, right?

All I'm saying is that dreams and fantasies don't have to cost money – you can have them for free. You can even make them come true sometimes. Every one of us has a secret wish or dream which we've been putting off doing anything about. I've been blathering on about running the New York City marathon for years, sure I'm exhausted just thinking about it, but I've also had dreams on my 'bucket list' which I have ticked off. Instead of putting your time, energy and money into the pipe dream of winning euro millions, which let's face it if it came true would, in reality, cause a lot more problems than it would solve for the ordinary Joe Soap, why not divert those same resources into taking a first baby step towards your most desirable, real, achievable and worthwhile fantasy. Of course it will be daunting and difficult; the risk of failure will be ever present. That's as it should be, sure if it was easy everyone'd be doing it and it wouldn't be much kop as a dream then. Maybe the national lottery shouldn't have been described as a tax for stupid people after all. Perhaps it should be considered a tax for the unimaginative.

8. Free to Enter

Enter free competitions if you wish. Do not however pay for a ticket to enter any draw, raffle or lottery; by definition they never represent value for money. Even if by some miracle you were to win, the prize quite often is something which is of no benefit to you, such as the teetotaller winning a bottle of twenty-five year old scotch or the rotund lady whose feet reside permanently in the shade securing second prize, a box of chocolates, at the village fete. I once knew a bloke living in a terraced city council house who was thrown into a quandary as to what to do with his lucky win of a bouncing baby calf. But what if it's for a good cause, I hear you cry! See my next point for a solution to that conundrum.

9. Charitable Souls

Now you might think that being of a charitable disposition and being a tight bastard were mutually exclusive. This, I am glad to say, is not the case. There is a limited and lazy definition of charity which sees it as giving a financial contribution to some perceived good cause, either real or imaginary. This is all very well, but if you don't want to or haven't got the cash to part with there are a myriad other ways of being charitable, usually involving the giving of your time or talents. If you don't have a pet cause already just type volunteer into your search engine and you'll soon find plenty of worthy requests. This is a very good idea if you have the time for it, not alone for the obvious reasons but even though it is not your intended goal you will be rewarded with feelings of satisfaction and achievement, which are not to be sniffed at; these are health giving properties. You will also most likely learn new skills and make new friends. In short your life will become richer and your pocket no poorer. I love a win-win situation, don't you? Just a note of caution: if you give to charity and then publicise the fact, it is not charity. It is advertising. I'm not saying there's anything wrong in doing this. I just wouldn't want you to confuse charity with self-promotion.

10. Third World without End

With great regret, I have concluded, for the ordinary man on the street, donating money to third world charities is akin to throwing it into a bottomless pit. There appears to be much the same benefit. How long has this problem been with us? Longer than my forty three year history anyway. Are we any closer to a solution? Are world hunger levels reducing? The answer to both these questions is an emphatic no. So if giving your €50 to Concern is not doing any good your reluctant response should be to stop wasting your money. Please don't mistake me for a heartless bastard here, believe me I was that soldier, giving my tuppence worth to every emergency relief operation, call me slow on the uptake, but forty years later I've twigged, nothing has changed, the developing nation's (as the PR people now like to call them) bowels are still rumbling with hunger, louder than ever. I'm not saying world hunger can't be eradicated, it can and quite quickly too. Human beings are incredibly resourceful and inventive. If the political will was there, particularly from Europe and America, the issues causing the hunger (which is not the illness, but only the symptom) could be tackled in a meaningful and productive way.

Alas the political will is non-existent. There can of course be only one reason world poverty is not on the political agenda and that is because there are no votes in it. When was the last time you noticed that starving Africans was an election issue? Never! Why ever could that be? Again there can be only one answer, because Joe Public doesn't give a tuppenny toss what happens in Africa or anywhere else for that matter as long as his own nest is feathered, that's why. But that doesn't make sense, sure isn't Johnny Average the very decent fellow, the same man who's throwing money into a collection for Trocaire every other week? Aren't the Irish renowned the world over for being the most generous donators to catastrophe relief efforts, time and time again? How do we square these conflicting evidences?

I respectfully suggest that our generous 'charitable' donations are designed to assuage our guilty consciences for, at some level – perhaps even sub-consciously – we all know we are the beneficiaries of the world political systems which are in place at the expense of many other nations. Every action has cause and effect built in. If we live disproportionate and unsustainable lives (and we do) then something has to give elsewhere. Someone else has to do without. We are not in fact a million miles removed from the much reviled colonial landlords of our recent history. We throw a few token scraps from our banquet table to the diseased creatures cowering underneath, and then clap ourselves on the back for it, before continuing to gorge upon our obesity. So if you genuinely want to do your bit to fight world poverty, the good news is you can keep your money in your pocket, begin instead to lobby your local, national and european representatives on the issues. Educate yourself on the subject wherever possible so that your actions are not contributing to, rather than alleviating, the issues.

11. Charity Shops

Following on from the earlier charity point and for some of the same reasons, you should become a customer and supplier of charity shops. Hell why not become a staff member to boot while you're at it? You can get great bargains in some of these shops and the pain of parting with your cash here is eased by the knowledge that it is being directed away from 'The Machine' and towards someone worthy of it. All that being said, charity shops should not enjoy any amnesty from the haggler in you. Their overheads are small compared to other businesses since they get their stock free and many of the staff are volunteers so they should be fertile ground for a bit of friendly bargaining.

12. Give Blood

Giving blood is a great way of giving something invaluable to others; in fact you are giving the gift of life itself. What greater gift is there? Yet it isn't costing you a penny. Brilliant in its simplicity! And that's not all; after you donate your pint of blood (actually it's only three quarters of a pint they take, I believe) you get to hang about, just as a precautionary measure, swilling free Guinness and munching all the crisps and biscuits you can handle, all the while in the seductive presence of friendly young nurses in uniform. Oh and they'll probably give you a few pencils and maybe an auld ruler for the young fella on the way out. 'How bad, butty' as they say down in Waterford!

13. Milking the Oldies

A great 'charitable' habit for the apprentice 'Tight Bastard' to cultivate is that of making time to visit elderly neighbours or relatives. I am of course being disingenuous when I call this a charitable act because you will be getting a return for your time investment here. Firstly, it can be a perfectly pleasant cost-free way to spend an evening, with lashings of complimentary tea and buns or maybe a little something stronger if you time it right. But that's not the real object of this exercise, no Sirree Bob. What we are really about here is trying to tap into that grey bottomless ocean of thriftiness that is the Irish pensioner. Think about the years in which the average seventy year old grew up. If you are seventy today you were born in 1943, right in the middle of World War Two, and so you grew up in the 40's and 50's. You were a young adult in the 60's. Apart from having some great stories from an era so alien to today's world, these people grew up in a time when nobody had a pot to piss in (quite literally in some cases), and therefore almost every elderly Irish person is thriftiness through and through. Even if life has been good to them and they have become wealthy, it's in their bones, in their very DNA. Necessity is the mother of invention and when these people were young it was necessary for their very survival to be careful with every penny, so they became extremely inventive in relation to getting the most out of everything. This knowledge is largely untapped; for the most part it is not even considered as having a value in today's disposable and throwaway society. Hmm! I wonder now who it suits to let all that invaluable knowledge go to the grave with the emergency generation?

So don't delay, visit the old timers today; no need either to limit your visits to neighbours, get yourself down to the nearest old folks home. They will be delighted with the company and pleasantly surprised that someone is interested in their lives, not to mention amazed that the younger generation has woken up to realise they have something valuable to contribute. Besides being wonderfully entertained, get them onto the subject of making ends meet in their youth and you will be richly rewarded with nuggets of penny pinching wisdom. After all who doesn't like talking about themselves – particularly when it's an Irish person being afforded the opportunity to have a good moan about life's difficulties?

14. Support for the Arts

Keep an eye out in the local press and notice boards for listings of official openings of art exhibitions, book launches and so on. Go along, look with thoughtful expression at the paintings or whatever it is they are plugging, throw in the odd knowing nod, all the while downing the free wine and nibbles with enthusiastic and appreciative relish. What more pleasant way to spend an hour or two in the company of good art, conversation and wine and all on the house. Even if the wine is sure to be cheap plonk – so what! Beggars can't be choosers and anyway, it'll taste great, because to be free is divine.

15. Go Back To College

No, I'm not suggesting you enrol in a third level course here, although now that I mention it, that mightn't be a bad place to hide out to see off the recession over the next few years. No, what I'm suggesting is just dropping in and swaggering around with a backpack and a folder under your arm just to see what free or subsidised stuff might be on offer. It is a particularly good idea to drop in on their open days for freebies. You'll probably get a discounted copy of the Irish Times or a subsidised meal in the cafeteria if nothing else (of course as with all purchases, these are only savings if you were planning to buy them at full price in the first instance).

16. Mature Students

If you do decide to return to education to get a belated degree make sure you are seen to be unemployed for some time before your course starts. It's probably best if you are classed as long term unemployed, which is to say you haven't worked for fifteen months or more, as this grouping are entitled to every grant and benefit under the sun – and then some. Whatever you do, don't make the mistake of working part-time while attending college with the idea that your earnings will help with the expense. You'll just be shooting yourself in the foot and will be penalised by the grants system for having a bit of get up and go about you. A friend of mine recently returned to college to do a masters, money was tight and a masters isn't cheap, especially with monthly trips up and down to Dublin from the west necessitating numerous overnights on top of the course fee of €6,170, not to mention expensive text books and so on. She was unemployed for all intents and purposes, but was getting some casual employment which amounted to, on average, three hours per week. She took it as a given that she would receive the full grant of €6,170 which would just cover the fees, all other associated expenses she was prepared to beg and borrow to cover privately. Anyway, to cut a long story short she was in for a shock. SUZI, the grants body, awarded her only €2,000 because they classed her as employed due to the paltry three hours work she had. She appealed but was again refused. Also, the course was two thirds complete before the miserly two grand was sent out. I think the moral of the story is clear: honesty and effort in this instance don't pay. There's an old saying which came to mind when I heard this story: 'Never let the right hand know what the left is doing'.

17. Join the Local Library

This really is a must for any self-respecting penny pincher. It's practically free. Membership costs €5 for a year or €2 at the subsidised rate and pensioners and children are free – so tell them you are unemployed whether you are or not when joining to avail of the cheaper fee, they won't look for proof. Regardless of what membership rate you decide to pay it is incredible value indeed. Obviously you can now read free books for the rest of your natural but more than that, the library also stocks DVDs, audio tapes, computers for use by members and you can go in there and relax with a free read of the daily paper or certain weekly/monthly magazines. Sometimes there are poetry or other reading events held in your public library which are almost always free to attend. Before leaving this den of FREEdom check out the notice board, a great source of information concerning inexpensive or free upcoming events. Finally, if looking for a particular book title that's not in stock ask the staff if it can be ordered for you, this is often possible or it could just be that the book you require is out on loan in which case the staff will hold it for you upon its return.

18. Beat the Bookie

Don't worry, I'm not suddenly suggesting you take up gambling and blow all our hard saved money on the nags. Coming out of a bookies better off than when you entered is almost as difficult as getting a politician to say 'I'm sorry you asked me that'. Difficult, but not impossible. The first rule for the mere mortal who suffers normal temptations of the flesh is to enter this den of iniquity with no money, cards or other means of spending on your person. Look around and avail of only what is going for free, before thanking the kind staff and leaving. You should be able to enjoy a free read of the paper and a cup of tea, maybe even with a chocolate biscuit thrown in while sheltering from a shower, at the very least. I must warn you, to my taste buds, Paddy Powers' coffee is putrid, although his mocha is almost palatable. Still you can't complain, it is free after all. There are free biros to be had as well. Sometimes on a busy bookie day like on Grand National day or during the Cheltenham festival some bookies will offer free sandwiches or other snacks to keep their victims captive. Also bookies often offer free bets to punters in much the same way a pusher offers you free drugs to get you hooked. Take the freebies but under no circumstances part with any cash, that way you can't lose. One trick you can try is to open an account with all the various high street bookies, lodging the minimum required amount. Very soon after you withdraw all you have lodged, so that you have no money in the account but you are still on their system as an account holding customer. As a result you will occasionally receive texts from some of these outlets offering you a free bet which, of course, you gratefully accept. Be warned however that you are playing with fire and need to be on your guard against this devious opponent. I'll repeat this again for anyone who didn't understand its importance: never, ever spend money with the bookie thinking you are smarter. You are not JP McManus; you will lose.

Okay, so there's a big match on and yourself and your pals would like to have a flutter but you want to stick to the advice given previously. Just bet among yourselves! Check out the odds the bookies are giving via your cashless account and offer the same odds among yourselves, thereby cutting out the middleman. On the law of averages, since there is now no profit maker in the equation you should, over a period of time, break even in your gambles whilst still enjoying the added excitement of putting a few quid on that neutral match. If after an extended period of time you notice you seem to have an abnormally poor return rate compared to your colleagues it will be safe to assume that gambling is not your forte and you should quit.

19. In for the Long Haul

Alright so you've decided to ignore my earlier advice; you reckon a little flutter in the bookies once in a blue moon won't lead to personal insolvency. Besides, a bird just shit on your best suit and when you looked up the culprit was none other than one of a pair of magpies flying overhead, two simultaneous sure-fire signs of good fortune to follow. Fair enough, we all have to live by some belief system I suppose. Still, you should as always seek value for money so if you must have a punt why put your cash on a horse race which will be over in less than five minutes? Why not back a soccer match which will net you ninety minutes of tense drama? That's eighteen times more excitement for the same money. Maybe more if it goes to extra time. Of course the logical extension of this policy would be to back the overall tournament outcome (such as the premier or champion's leagues). This way you get months of interest in multiple match outcomes for your single initial stake. Mighty; just throw your tenner on Man United or whoever in August before the start of the league and the same note will, with a little luck, be keeping you on the edge of your seat 'til May. Win or lose, you will have got your money's worth several times over.

20. Delayed Gratification

It appears to me that our out of control consumer society is fuelled by a sense of entitlement and an absolute belief that our every whim should be instantaneously gratified. These feelings have of course been carefully planted in us by the modern brainwashing techniques of our manipulative rulers. But regardless of why we have these feelings it's no use passing the buck. That's too easy. Instead, each individual must take control of and ultimate responsibility for his or her own thoughts and feelings. In fact despite the huge efforts that the multinationals expend to try to control your mind (with quite a lot of success it has to be said), it is the one thing they cannot control without your permission. Numerous survivors of the holocaust have attested to this fact; despite everything the Nazis took from them, in many cases they retained independence of mind and thought. If they succeeded against such odds surely you and I can do likewise in the face of our would-be masters. So please spend time each day in critical and reflective thinking – not about others, God knows we do too much of that – but about ourselves. Ask why do I feel I am entitled to this or that? Why must I have it immediately? If I spend my money on X instead of Y what are the consequences, intended or otherwise, likely to be? In other words practice delayed gratification. Look (and think) before you leap. Trust me the pleasure will be all the more intense for the waiting. Of course it would be wise to take this advice beyond financial parameters and into all other areas affecting your life. Remember, anything worth having is worth waiting for. If it is not worth waiting for you never wanted it in the first place – it was just a thoughtless whim.

Besides, instant gratification of your desires denies you the wonderful pleasure of anticipation.

21. Pricey Popcorn

Okay, I know that technically, going to the cinema with your partner at the princely sum of €25 for the pair of you is a waste of money since you'll be able to watch that same film for free at home on the goggle box before you know it and anyway, you know it'll never live up to the hype. If it came out of Hollywood and has an A list star in it then by definition, it has to be a load of tosh for the brainless teenage market as that's the only way the studio will recoup its investment and make a profit. All the same, sometimes that's just what you need: a night out at the flicks where you can leave your brain at home and just chill like a zombie in front of the big screen. Fair enough, but please don't extend the night's financial promiscuity to the exorbitant price of the popcorn at your local picture palace. If you really can't exercise a little delayed gratification by getting your sugar fix afterwards then please smuggle those noisy munchies in with you to annoy the bejaysus out of all your fellow cinema goers within earshot. Seriously, the simple act of bringing your own coke and popcorn will save you a tenner or more. You will also get the pick of the best seats in the auditorium as you walk with a superior air past the captive queue at the sugar trough.

If you are on a first date and therefore out to impress (with an impossible to live up to false impression of yourself) then the situation is a little trickier but by no means impossible to negotiate. You could turn up with your own home made popcorn and drink, garnering the sympathy vote with a sad tale of how you stoically suffer some malady or other like eczema and have to be extremely careful about the ingredients you ingest into your poor body. That should have her eating (the homemade popcorn) out of your exploring hand in the back seats.

22. Grace of the Concessional

When buying tickets for anything be it cinema, theatre, concert or whatever, look for the concession price if there is one regardless of whether you are, strictly speaking, entitled to it or not. Tell them you are a mature student but you don't have your student card to hand. In my experience you will be given the discounted price without any hassle or checks more often than not. Particularly in a situation where the vendor is keenly aware that he is not going to have a full house for an event; he is unlikely to risk the loss of precious bums on seats by arguing the toss with you over a couple of euro. Go on, give it a go, sure you have nothing to lose. Don't worry if you do get a refusal, it's nothing personal, just business; have another go next time.

23. Road Clothes

When you are out and about on the highways, byways, parks and beaches of the land taking your daily constitutional, keep your eyes peeled and a bag handy for free clobber. It appears to me we are a fairly absent-minded, careless lot judging by the amount of abandoned hats, scarves and other attire you come across on the roadside or at popular picnic spots. If the cap fits as they say, wear it. If you're worried about dirt or germs just bung any finds in a ninety degree wash when you get home and they'll be good as new.

24. Tents R Us

If you need a few tents for the upcoming welly wedding or any other outdoor pursuits, get yourself off down to the grounds of the latest weekend music festival such as oxygen or the electric picnic early on the morning after it finishes. You'll get all the free tents you want in there. Half the lazy teenage tykes are too spoiled to bother packing theirs up and bringing it home with them. You never know what other useful items you'll be able to scavenge while you're there as well. You might even pick up the wellies. God bless the disposable age I say.

25. Early Birds

As for a supply of drinks glasses for whatever happy occasion you have coming up or if you just want to replace the ones the ankle biters keep breaking, just take an early Sunday morning stroll around any urban centre making sure to pass the now closed doors of the most popular watering holes in town. You'll pick up any number left behind by last night's revellers. You'll be providing a free community service into the bargain, saving the council in overtime clean-up bills. You might even find a few quid scattered on the pavements, left behind by yesterday's careless yobs.

26. Take a Break from Holidays

Before booking yet another two weeks in Gran Canaria again this year ask yourself why you are going? Why would you want to spend a fortnight impersonating a beached whale whilst reminding the locals of a pot of par boiled lobsters as they pass along the beach? Think back, what did you actually get from last year's holiday? Okay, so you read Cecilia Ahern's annual offering. You could have done that with your feet up on the couch at home. You got a 'good colour' – otherwise called being burnt to a crisp and increasing your odds of a stint in St Luke's cancer hospital. All I'm saying is stop and think. Has your annual 'Flight of the Earls' become just a weary habit? Something you do because well, you can't remember when you didn't do it or what it would be like not to go on holiday. Worse still, do you take off every year just so that you can name drop to the neighbours on your return? 'Oh we took the kids to Barbados this year, it was absolutely fabulous!' Was it indeed? Ask them what they know about Barbados after spending fourteen days and nights there and all they can come up with is the name of the local beer and a description of the quaint little restaurant they found on the first evening and ate in every night. They feel blessed to have secured this at the last minute bargain basement price of €1,500 a head (excluding taxes and charges, excess luggage fines, €50 Dublin airport parking fee and spending money of course). Some wise fellow whose name escapes me once said: 'The unexamined life is not worth living'. Whoever he was that fellow was no daw. Heed his advice; examine the motivation for your actions and what better place to start than the annual family pilgrimage.

27. Tantrum Travellers

If you are the proud parents of infants that's wonderful, congratulations, but as you know having kids is largely about sacrifice. One of the first things to go out the window when the newborn comes in the door is the notion of an enjoyable family holiday. Many apprentice parents are in denial about this at first and they stubbornly try to insist they can still carry on as before. Well maybe you can – if you can afford to have a live in nanny in tow. Otherwise save yourself the heartache and long drawn out suffering of trying to attain the impossible. Plenty before you have tried and failed. Tiny tots simply do not like travelling. What they want and need to feel secure is consistency and familiarity. Family holidays provide the precise opposite of this and so if you take them out of their comfort zone by jaysus are they going to make you pay for it. They may not yet have the power of speech but rest assured they will communicate their distress and teach you the error of your actions so effectively that all but the true sadists among you will never entertain the idea of a family vacation for years to come. Don't take my word for it, after all I've never had the dubious pleasure of the nappy years but just ask any parent recently returned from a trip, especially abroad, with infants in tow and the best slant the most optimistic of them will put on it is that it was 'challenging' or they'd 'do it differently next time'. You know yourself these are just euphemisms for what they really feel but cannot express about the apple of their eye. What they are really thinking is how does the adoption process work? So to recap, if you have nappy-wearing ankle biters forget family holidays, full stop. The two just do not mix. You'll just be paying through the nose to torture yourself.

28. Be at Home with Yourself

Whatever you do, don't go travelling to try to find yourself because you are not *there*. Believe me I looked. I went to Thailand, India, Iceland, South Africa, you name it, lookin' for meself and there wasn't a sign of me anywhere. I even went on an expedition to the feckin' Antarctic to see was I down there, but no, plenty of icebergs and Penguins, alas no sign of P.J. When I got home and plonked down on the couch exhausted, too tired to think, stillness entered and… Well blow me down with a (Penguin) feather but there I was all the time!

29. Christmas Holidays

Well alright then, if you will insist on having your holiday why not consider jetting off over the Christmas and new year period as that way, the cost of the holiday will be offset by the savings you make by disappearing for Christmas. Brilliant, eh? You can be the real life scrooge who cancelled Christmas but nobody will be any the wiser as you'll have the perfect cover story.

30. Bucking Credit

At the time of writing, if you book a flight with that well known, considerate airline, Ryanair by credit card you will be charged a 2% surcharge. If you book with a debit card there is no added fee. No doubt you will find a similar story regarding other airlines and indeed businesses of all kinds. Nobody however is quite as enthusiastic as Leary-air for added extras and it was of course a recent court ruling which forced this policy on the airline and not some strange benevolent feeling towards those like myself who are allergic to credit cards.

31. Go To Roam

If you must have a holiday – and remember holidays are a luxury not a necessity; after all you won't find your annual trip to the Canaries enshrined in the Declaration of Human Rights – consider going to Roam – roam around the back garden that is. By this I am suggesting your metaphoric back yard. It is amazing the number of people who have been to every continent in the world on numerous occasions but have not considered exploring Connaught at all. We are all guilty at times of taking for granted that which is readily available. Every country is fascinating in its own right and that includes your own. If you have never done so, give the idea careful consideration as there are after all, some very obvious benefits.

Number one amongst these is avoiding airports. The most annoying (and expensive) feature of foreign travel in recent years has to be the necessity of dealing with that most disingenuous, devious and dishonest shower of companies known as 'the airlines' and king of the pricks among these in my estimation is of course, Ryanair. Oh I know they have brought down the cost of air travel hugely and we are supposed to consider ourselves forever in their debt. But what bloody good is that if the experience always puts us in a foul mood, leaving us bickering with the missus before the feckin' holiday has even begun with our difficulties then replicated on the return journey, meaning our holiday begins and ends with domestic strife and somehow we have been conned into thinking it's a privilege to part with our hard earned cash for this experience! Other fringe benefits can include not being ripped off by the banks on currency exchange transactions or by foreign locals who would have you believe their grasp of English is very poor despite dealing with 3,000 English speakers every week. Car hire will naturally be rendered unnecessary also. The list of potential savings is long. Now I know Ireland is an expensive little corruption but nonetheless the financial benefits of holidaying at home rather than away should generally be significant. Also there is no need to feel you are missing out on the benefits of being exposed to foreign cultures while exploring Erin's Isle. After all if you are from the heart of Dublin for example, and you take the trouble and strife off to the back arse of Leitrim let's say, you couldn't have found yourself in a more foreign, dare I say alien landscape of locals if you'd gone round the world with Jules Verne that time. If it's foreign languages you're after take yourself off to the wilds of Connemara and mix it up with a few untamed local fishermen. You'll get on only mighty, on account of, in order to fall out with someone you have to be able to translate their insults.

32. Camp Ideas

A major expense to be budgeted for when travelling is accommodation. There are of course ways to minimise or eliminate this burden. The simplest and most basic of these is to go on a camping holiday. If you have never tried it, this suggestion is likely to be dismissed as a fate worse than spending the fortnight with your divorced sister-in-law and her terrible twins. But hold on a minute, it could be just the ticket with a little planning. For some reason it is only the possible downside that immediately springs to mind such as possible adverse weather or the potential for an uncomfortable night's sleep. Stop though and keep an open mind. What about the advantages? If you have kids and particularly boys of a certain age, say between about seven and thirteen, they will love the sense of adventure that comes with camping. Why do you think the scouts (and girl guides) have enjoyed such enduring popularity? This accommodation is of course free and there is no need to book your trip in advance meaning you can't lose any hefty deposit for unavoidable short notice cancellations. Neither are there any penal surcharges for camping in peak season and you can time your trip to take maximum advantage of any favourable weather forecast. Part of the fun of course is cooking your food on an open fire so you will have eliminated costly restaurant trips for the family as well. Needless to say your suite arrangement is completely flexible and you can upgrade to a better view at a moment's notice free of charge.

33. Check Out the Couch

Anyone interested in free travel accommodation might want to check out the online community that is couchsurfing.com to see if it is for them. This is a worldwide community of people – the majority of whom would appear to be twentysomethings it has to be noted – who open their doors (and hearts, apparently) to fellow travellers for free. You will also have the added invaluable advantage of being able to avail of your hosts local knowledge and tips. I can only imagine this resource would be priceless when travelling in unfamiliar territory. The idea being, in order for it to work you would also host other travellers in your home in return. It sounds like a great idea although I must confess I haven't put it to the test myself as yet. I'm sure it won't be everybody's cup of tea but hey, it costs nought to check it out. If this is a novel idea to you remember as with anything new, you are bound to have reservations about it. We are naturally conservative creatures but please do not dismiss the notion purely out of instinct. Go to the website, inform yourself of the facts, give it all time to sink in and make an informed decision. Happy surfing, dude!

34. Do the Daft Thing

If you are looking for a nice holiday cottage or apartment for your family vacation this year instead of going through the usual accommodation brochures and websites, think outside the box. Where could you find cheaper, alternative accommodation which provides you with your requirements? Ask yourself, how is it at a time when the country is awash with vacant property that people can charge sums of €600 or more for a week's stay in a remote bungalow while others are struggling to get that per month for a city pad? The answer is simple: it's just a question of labelling and marketing. Present your property as an idyllic rural romantic holiday retreat and advertise it in that niche and you charge a premium for your trouble. But you don't need to pay that premium when there are plenty of desperate landlords all over the country with vacant property of every hue advertised on Daft.ie and elsewhere. True, these landlords are ideally looking for long-term tenants while you are merely looking to rent for a week or two. That is just a minor detail; plenty of these properties will have been vacant for extended periods in the current economic climate, especially the remote variety which are in such demand by holidaymakers. The owners in some cases will be desperate enough to listen to your proposal if you call them up and make a cash offer to rent their pad for a short family break. You can be perfectly honest in your introduction, acknowledging and apologising for the unorthodox approach, admitting that you are unwilling or unable to pay the market rate for your annual sabbatical. Then offer them a quarter of what they were asking per month to let you have the place for a week plus a few euro added on to make it an attractive offer for them. Not everyone you approach will be open to your proposal of course but if you are a little flexible about the precise location and type of place you require you will, after a number of calls, get a taker. You may have to bring your own bed clothes and so on but that's a small inconvenience I think for a reduction of a few hundred euro in your holiday budget.

35. Sponsored Sightseeing

One way to see exotic locations around the world and have the whole itinerary, flights, accommodation, sightseeing, meals, entertainment, the lot organised for you is to sign up for one of the many charity walks which have become increasingly popular in recent years. The basic deal is simple enough: you the punter agree to raise a minimum specified sum, often around €5,000, through various fundraising initiatives (for this pretty much anything goes as long as you're making money at it). The charity for its part will cover the cost of your fare, accommodation and possibly some meals and excursions out of this. They will also organise the whole itinerary. You will be required to complete some sort of challenge as part of the trip, usually this involves walking a number of miles each day (there are of course cycling, running and other types of sponsored trips available also). If you feel you wouldn't be fit enough or are too old for this type of trip, think again. There are many charities operating these fundraising initiatives annually so there are trips available to cater for every age and fitness level you could think of. You have everything from the endurance tests designed for serious athletes to the walk in the park type doddle which is dressed up to sound like a challenge worth sponsoring for the benefit of the paying public and there is every in-between level of endurance trip. Truly if you are in the least bit mobile at all there is one to suit you. If you are still not convinced please be further reassured that there are always medically qualified personnel and support vehicles travelling in situ on these jaunts. Charities after all are just as terrified of litigation as everyone else these days and they need the bad publicity of one of their walkers arriving back at Dublin airport in a wheelchair or worse, in a box, like they need a hole in the head so believe me, you will be very well minded.

As for the fundraising side of it, this can admittedly seem like a daunting challenge but like all seemingly insurmountable challenges the trick is to break it down into bite sized pieces. Allow yourself plenty of time with a realistic, achievable but not too easy monthly fundraising goal. Again be reassured that the organisers will give you every possible assistance with this and remember this is what they do for a living so you will have the full support of experienced professionals behind you to tap into. Don't forget, they want you to reach your target possibly even more than you do yourself. A personal failure on your part amounts to (a degree of) professional failure on theirs. Admittedly this form of travel isn't for everyone but if you enjoy new challenges, meeting new and interesting people and seeing new parts of the world in intimate detail on foot then this could be for you. You will feel like a new person yourself at the end of it all. Of course you will have figured out by now that this is not a free holiday at all but instead of paying with your money you pay with your time and therefore it may suit those of you who are time rich but cash poor. This kind of travel may also appeal to adventurous souls who don't want to travel alone but know nobody willing or able to go with them on such exotic treks as the Inca trail in Peru or the Camino De Santiago in Spain.

36. Limit Your Losses

Is there anyone among you who, hand on heart, can say you've never accidentally left any belongings behind you in a hotel room or other temporary accommodation? Well if there are, I'm impressed. I've left dozens of items behind over the years, anything from the obvious toothbrush and towels to books and jewellery – the list is embarrassingly long. So what's my point? How do we stop these losses? The truth is I don't know. I still sometimes forget stuff but I will say in my defence that

I have improved greatly. The key to this is to be aware of and accept your shortcomings or weaknesses, as I now do in this regard, so I will check and recheck my accommodation for personal belongings before checking out, even searching drawers which I 'know for a fact' I haven't used during my stay (often eerily finding belongings here). I leave no stone unturned and nothing to chance. In fact I only just stop short of bringing in a team of forensics with metal detectors.

So how in the name of Jerusalem can it be that I still have the occasional ability to arrive home only to discover some item of apparel has been accidentally abandoned? I don't think I will ever know the answer to that conundrum. My personal belief is that some sinister paranormal force is present in hotel rooms around the world whose idea of fun it is to fuck with our stuff. This being the case I can only advise that – in the interest of damage limitation – when you are away on short trips do not bring expensive paraphernalia with you insofar as possible. Leave the Gillette razor at home and pack a pound shop disposable or two instead, bring cheap and dispensable bedside reading material as opposed to expensive lovingly thumbed texts, that kind of thing. Another tip is when you are nearing the end of a bottle of aftershave or perfume at home, do not empty it completely; leave it aside to use on holiday so that in the unfortunate event of you mislaying or losing it on your travels the financial fallout is miniscule.

37. Forget the Travel Insurance

If you are going traipsing around India alone for two months or if you are planning on a fortnight's white water rafting in the Canadian Rockies then fair enough, you might want to consider taking out some kind of insurance cover before you leave. But if like many people your idea of an annual vacation is to lie by the pool and then the beach on alternate days on some sun kissed Island resort for two weeks then you really don't need travel insurance. Use the bit of grey matter God gave you; take all reasonable precautions to keep yourself safe, just as you would at home, then relax and enjoy yourself. The likelihood of any catastrophe befalling you is negligible and certainly does not warrant the ridiculous insurance premium. Minor claims would be more hassle than they were worth anyway and would most likely lead to a deterioration of your health as a result of the stress of processing your claim. Besides if you are holidaying in the EU you'll be looked after as one of their own seeing as how we are all happy little Europeans together nowadays. Come to think of it, given the state of our own health service, you are probably as well off to get your stroke out of the way while on your annual sabbatical rather than waiting until you return to the chaos that is the HSE. Sales of travel insurance policies like many other goods and services are mainly secured on fear and an illogical fear of something that is less likely to happen than a blue moon on a warm Wednesday in February at that.

38. Obnoxious Ornaments

When you're on your holidays in the Lake District why on earth would you want to buy a mass produced 'made in Taiwan' plastic souvenir as a reminder of your romantic break to take pride of place on your mantelpiece when you get back home? Come on, we can do better (and cheaper) than that. You can't cross the same river twice – or so said some famous philosopher whose name I've forgotten – and neither can two people have the same holiday experience. Therefore they shouldn't have the same bloody Russian dolls in the living room cabinet. You can find any amount of attractive and unique ornaments on your travels in the form of unusual shells, attractive stones or pine cones. Your own photographs are of course unique mementos in themselves. If you keep a weather eye to the ground while out walking in the wilds (or just the city park) you may come across gems such as deer antlers or a well preserved piece of bog wood. If visiting the zoo or an estate house with ornamental birds be alert for swan, pheasant and peacock feathers, they could come in handy for one of those collages we were talking about earlier.

If you still feel obliged to buy something from that malnourished-looking souvenir stallholder in Malaga, I recommend a fridge magnet; they're cheerfully cheap, won't clutter the place up too much and can double as a hold it for shopping lists or utility bills. By the way, that guy you felt so sorry for wasn't under fed at all – he was a perfectly healthy weight for his five foot eight frame. He just appeared to be a stick insect compared to all the fat frumps you're used to looking at back home so there was no need for the sympathy purchase at all at all.

39. Park the Charges

Do not drive to the airport in your own car. Take the bus or get a friend to drop you off to avoid the extortionate parking charges. I know I've already mentioned earlier that paying for parking is unnecessary at any time but I think it justifies repeated special mention in this context as the cost really mounts up when you leave your old banger at the airport for a fortnight. You could arrive back to a €100 fee on your return. That's all you need to cheer you up at the end of your holiday with Monday morning looming and four months of monotony facing you before your next break at Christmas.

40. A Sterling Idea

If you travel to Britain or Northern Ireland occasionally, as a lot of us do, you probably often arrive home with Sterling left over from your trip. You would be well advised to hold on to this money until your next hop across the pond rather than converting it back into Euro, thereby saving yourself bank currency exchange charges twice on the sum in question. If you are a regular visitor to your anglicised relations it would also be prudent to keep an eye on the exchange rates in order to 'bulk buy' your sterling when the market is favourable to you. These suggestions may also be applicable in the case of other currencies, such as the US Dollar, depending on your own particular travelling habits.

41. Sing For Your Supper

Music is truly our global language; it transcends all borders, cultures and races. To have some musical ability has always been a wonderful talent to possess and is even more so now in this modern age of international globetrotting. If you have a good voice it's a bonus but if, like me, your singing would put the crows out of business don't despair, you can still be musical. It is within everyone's ability to learn to play a musical instrument and what's more it is a very smart move to do so. Apart at all from the sheer enjoyment it can bring and the fact that it will increase your confidence and your attractiveness to the opposite sex when you perform your party piece, this is a talent which can be utilised in the form of busking all over the world to earn a few quid. Mighty handy if you are stuck for the price of a hostel or a bit of dinner on your wanderings. Who knows where it'll take you – many's the famous band whose earliest performances were on a street corner for the princely price of a few pints that night.

42. It's only my Opinion

One way to make a bit of extra cash that I was told about was by filling out online surveys. Sounds good. Get paid for your opinion! Everyone's got one of those, right? Certainly you can make a few shillings at this malarkey but you definitely won't get rich. I signed up with irishopinions.ie as an experiment to see if I could get rich on the bosses time. Well it's easy enough to sign up and everyone is welcome. You spend quite a few minutes giving them some personal information and then sit back and wait for the surveys/money to roll in. They sent me plenty of surveys but the pay was paltry, anything from fifty cents to €3.50, depending on how long they estimate it should take you. One example of a survey sent paid €1 at an estimated time of 15 minutes, that's €4 an hour or about half the minimum wage. Pretty miserable, but it gets worse; that survey actually took me 33 minutes – that's less than €2 per hour for those of you that aren't the brightest bulbs in the pack. Oftentimes you spend several minutes answering questions only to be told you are not suitable for that particular poll, no explanation is given and you receive nada for your time in these instances. Your money is not earned in cash either but rather in vouchers for the likes of Tesco and other big retailers. You have to earn €10 before you can claim your first voucher to that value. So if you decide you actually have something more worthwhile to be doing than filling out ridiculous, mind-numbingly boring questionnaires for a pittance before you reach this princely sum, you will presumably receive diddly squat for your efforts.

In fairness, I have been told there are better paying survey companies out there; the number of companies to choose from is certainly numerous and there is nothing to stop the insanely idle signing up to them all but I have not been able to put myself through the mental torture of joining their ranks, even in the noble pursuit of saving a few other poor paupers the trouble by reporting back. At the time of writing I have just completed over €10 worth of surveys with irishopinions.ie, having spent six weeks as a member, some of my earnings have not been cleared yet so I'm still awaiting my first big 'paycheque'. This will, without doubt, have been the hardest earned tenner of my life.

Having got all that negativity off my chest, to look on the bright side I suppose there are worse things you could do with your time, almost all the crap on TV is for example an even bigger waste of time and you get nothing at all in return for that; or perhaps you find yourself stuck on a long bus journey alone except for your smartarse phone so completing one or two of these surveys could be the thing to while away an hour or so. Besides, I'm assured some people enjoy filling them in and even get a sense of wellbeing by contributing to the improvement of products and services as a result of the information they provide – God help us all, there's now't so queer as folk. Anyway, I guess you've nothing to lose but a little time if you want to give this idea a bash. If it keeps you out of the pub of an evening or from going shopping it'll be the best little earner ever, despite all I've said.

43. Glorified Wallpaper

Here's a job anyone can do and you don't need any training or experience. It's open to any age, gender or creed from eight to eighty and you might even get to rub shoulders with a few famous actors in the course of your work. What is this job? Working as an extra in the film industry. If you keep an eye out in the papers, particularly the arts and entertainment sections, you will occasionally see notices advertising open casting days for extras to which anybody can go along to have their picture taken and fill out a single sheet form with some details, mostly measurement and physical size details pertaining to costume. A short time later, perhaps a week or two, you may receive a call from the extras' co-ordinator to see if you are available on a certain date or dates for shooting. These calls will usually come at very short notice so if you generally need a lot of advance warning to reorganise your schedule, this work won't be for you. You may also like to check out www.moviextras.ie who are the leading suppliers of extras to the film industry in Ireland. Be warned though, it costs €99 to join (very often reduced to €89 on offer) and have your profile added to their database. Pay rates for extras aren't glamorous and can vary greatly, usually anything from about €70 to €85 gross for a day. If you're working day runs over 10 hours you may be into overtime at a rate of perhaps €14 per hour. The work is also quite intermittent so won't provide a regular, reliable income. On the plus side though you will get fed and watered on set, it's an opportunity to get a glimpse behind the lens of the film industry and it's not as if you have to over-exert yourself for the wages. You will generally be used as glorified wallpaper, filling in the background of a scene. It is not uncommon to be on set all day without being used at all, you'll still be paid in this case but it can be rather boring. It can happen, rarely, that you will be called as a special extra, this means you will have a line or two of dialogue to deliver. This of course makes for a more interesting days work and also for an increased pay rate. From personal experience I can tell you the two most important tools of this trade are a good book and a deck of cards. You could perhaps earn on the double, filling out some of those online surveys while hanging about on set.

Do not make the mistake of thinking this is glamorous work, it's anything but. You are likely only to spend a tiny fraction of your day in front of camera. Occasionally however you might get lucky and find yourself getting paid, as I did, for touching up a sexy Irish actress (who shall remain nameless) in a brothel scene. If nothing else you can use your experiences as conversation pieces, saying you worked on such and such a movie. Who knows maybe you're the next great undiscovered star in waiting! After all, many famous faces started out as extras. Don't quit the day job though, just in case.

44. Tap into your Inner Entrepreneur

If you are unemployed and genuinely cannot find employment but would like to do so then become your own employer. There is absolutely no acceptable reason for anyone to be continuously unemployed all day, every day. There are literally hundreds of small enterprises you could start up regardless of your formal qualifications or personal circumstances, even your below average IQ level, God between us and all harm, is no impediment to running a profitable enterprise. I'm sure we can all think of a few examples as testament to that truth. Have you got a saleable skill which you could advertise? Are you good with computers for instance? Because if that is the case there are plenty of prehistoric schmucks like me out there who need your help. Can you play a musical instrument? Are you qualified to give grinds in any subject? If you do a reasonable paint or DIY job at home you can do it for the neighbours for a small fee. Cash in hand to begin with like, just 'til you get on your feet, of course. Do you like animals? Perhaps you could walk dogs for a living. Believe it or not there are a lot of people out there who are either too busy or lazy to exercise their own pooch. Why they got one in the first place is anybody's guess, who cares, the point is you can turn it to your advantage by offering your professional dog walking services for a modest fee. Alternatively you could advertise your services as a babysitter. Apart from the fact that you can earn up to €50 for a few hours of hogging your hosts sofa, watching their movie channels whilst simultaneously stuffing your face with the contents of their fridge, this idea could prove to bring about a windfall the equivalent of winning the lotto. If babysitting a set of twins suffering from the terrible two's syndrome has the unintended consequence of putting you off children for life, you can consider it the most financially rewarding job it is ever likely to be your good fortune to land. The savings accruing to you from this early enlightenment will run to hundreds of thousands of euro in the ensuing decades.

Turn the car into cash. No I'm not suggesting you sell your auld jalopy. We've already discussed that possibility earlier but since you decided to hang onto it perhaps it could earn its keep. Could you run a few errands in it for elderly neighbours for example? Stick a hitch and trailer on the back and hey presto you're a removal man or a courier. Now I know there are rules and regulations around these things, sure you can't take a leak these days without needing fifteen different feckin' kinds of permit for it (they wonder then why the economy is about as active as a stagnant pond in mid-Winter) but still, you can always put it under the heading of 'doing a turn for a friend' until you've tested the viability of the enterprise. Besides if you're a man of straw what are they going to do, sue ya? Trust me the powers that be have bigger fish to fry.

Picture this, can you take a half decent photograph? If the answer is yes then congratulations, you're a photographer. Off you go and make a few quid doing something you like. Remember the wise maxim; 'Find a job you enjoy and you'll never have to do a day's work in your life'. I know I'm being overly simplistic here but hopefully you get the point. This is not about photography per se but rather about thinking outside the box. Look around, what assets or resources have you got which can be harnessed and with a little effort converted into cash? Don't forget 'life helps those who help themselves'.

45. Stop Spending In Protest

Pretty much every Tom, Dick and Harry (not to mention Mary and Jane) in the country is pissed off with our Government right now and rightly so. If you are not incensed about paying billions to the faceless bondholders whose names we are not allowed even to enquire about then you are surely getting your knickers in a twist over the various new inventive and seemingly never ending taxes this shower of wasters keep raining down upon us. The 'universal social charge' is a great long winded name for what amounts to extra income tax. Of course the really controversial beauty is the new property tax which is an attack on the very roofs over our heads. All the while the gravy train keeps rolling in the form of fat wages, expense accounts, brown envelopes and astronomical pension packages for our parasitic representatives. How in God's name do our elected puppet parties or their masters think that taxing the bejaysus out of us is going to help the economy? I mean you don't have to be Eddie Hobbs to know that won't work. It was already tried and failed a couple of short decades ago back in the 80's; some of these Muppets were in the Dáil back then, including our man Enda. Do they have sieves for memories or what the feck is wrong with them? I won't even get into the scandal of Apple and the other multi nationals moving billions of euro in profits through Ireland without paying diddly squat in tax either to us or anyone else – now will you believe me about who calls the shots in our brave new world?

Anyway enough with the rant, all I want to say here is that if that's the game they want to play then you can go along with it. You can make a few 'cuts' of your own in protest at Government policy. Why not go to your local elected representative and inform him or her that you are going to desist from all optional spending until such time as for example, the property tax at the very least is reversed. If people did this en mass I guarantee you the government would soon sit up and take notice because this simple action would have the potential to totally banjax the country. But don't worry, that is not my aim and anyway, our spineless officials would cave in long before any major damage was done. It would be a lot more effective than blocking up Dublin city centre for a few hours with all the trucks and tractors from counties Cavan and Leitrim combined at any rate. Even if my suggestion doesn't take off and you find yourself a lone voice in the wilderness pissing against the wind at least you will be able to defend yourself against comparisons with scrooge. If anybody accuses you of being too tight to spend Christmas you can reply in a superior tone that you are a conscientious objector and far from accusing you of being tighter than a nun's knickers they should instead be applauding the patriotism of your self-sacrifice for your country. At the very least, if you don't save the country you'll certainly save yourself a small fortune in unnecessary spending. You will also quickly realise you don't even miss a lot of the rubbish you used to fritter your money away on.

46. Taxing Times

The long suffering, average worker is under ever increasing pressure these recessionary days being squeezed relentlessly on all sides by, on the one hand the out of control all-consuming monster which is our social welfare system and on the other by the ugly, over inflated egos which power the public service gravy train. The earner stuck in the middle isle of Erin is the most financially abused and taken for granted character in the EU. A single person in this economy for example, enters the top tier of PAYE (Pay All You Earn) income tax at 41% on any income above a measly €32,800. That's only €2,733 per month. He will also pay the USC charge of anything between 2% and 10% on top of this, after which he must deduct genuine work related expenses some of which are not tax deductible. This of course excludes the dizzying array of stealth taxes, both new and old, which our lawmakers are increasingly pummelling Joe Public with. This poor victim of a grand state-sponsored protection racket will not make it home with even 50% of his hard earned money intact. It all looks rather bleak from the point of view of the habitually abused of middle earth. Some would say it looks rather like a black economy for them.

47. Just the Job for Joe Public

If you are not a highly motivated workaholic and therefore disinclined towards self-employment the best place for you to while away your working life is in the public sector. According to figures just released from the CSO (Central

Statistics Office) average weekly earnings in the private sector in the first three months of this year (2013) were €628.26 as against a whopping €913.25 in the public sector. I should mention both figures are gross amounts before tax and other deductions have pillaged their respective pay packets. That's a hell of a premium the public boys are on, not far off 50% over and above poor paddy private's paltry sum. We haven't even tried of course to calculate what the almost cast iron job security of a cushy government number might be valued at. Unless you are an alcoholic paedophile you're unlikely to get the boot and even then it'll take years of bureaucratic adherence to 'correct procedure' to evict your limpet ass from its post. Then there are of course a mind boggling myriad of extra privileges, perks and expense claims to which you are 'entitled' and are not included in your official wage figure. I knew a fella in Dublin who, just a couple of years ago took a three year paid sabbatical from his public job. No, that wasn't a misprint. I did say <u>three full years paid career break.</u> Apparently though, these are all fair reward as the public working week is just shy of a full half hour extra toil more than the private recruit. Of course it's not that simple to board the public gravy train as it's overflowing to capacity – in fact it's like one of those overcrowded buses you'd see out in India or the like with passengers sitting on the roof and hanging out the windows holding on for dear life – so it ain't gonna be stopping at a station near you any time soon (unless of course you happen to share the drivers DNA).

Still, booms and busts are like time and tide; they're cyclical things. History always repeats itself (especially as our electoral system doesn't allow for learning of hard lessons) so as soon as they've pensioned off all the old guard and money once more allows, our esteemed politicians will be back, like Páidín's party, buying elections once more with promises of jobs galore. When they do you should be ready to pounce. You might even want to start applying now so that in a few years time when you finally get that coveted interview there will be a record of your longstanding enthusiasm for the position. A word to the wise though, if you are indeed savvy enough to wrangle your way into a permanent, pensionable, public job remember, everything has a price. You will be detained there in your five star open prison for the rest of your natural. With the rare exception of the occasional crazy not possessed of normal materialistic instincts, nobody leaves. Regardless of how unfulfilled you feel you will stay put. No more than Rex the pet pooch you're not gonna budge from your pampered door step zoo cage to compete with the wild wolves of the privately owned open prairie.

48. Find It For Free

Another website which is always worth checking out before parting with hard earned cash for goods is www.freecycle.org. Members join their local group and post notices either to say they have an unwanted item to give away or to ask for some product which they require in the hope some other member will have one they are not using. I have used this site recently to both receive and gift goods and my experience was positive and hassle free.

Naturally enough you have to be realistic in your expectations with a site like this, there is a limit to the value and quality of goods you can reasonably expect people to part with for free. None the less the site is free to join so you have absolutely nothing to lose. I've picked up a fridge in working order, coffee machine, cooking pots, box containing 75 books and a budgie cage no less over the past few months. Just last night a bloke had advertised a two-man boat in sound working order with oars and the works. Naturally enough I politely applied for this generous freebie but alas no joy, I guess some fortunate fella got in before me. Oh well, you win some ye lose some but it costs nothing to try. Interestingly enough my experience of freecycle strongly suggests it is a facility used mainly by middle and higher income individuals. I have yet to come across much evidence of people of a lower socio-economic background availing of the free gifts offered here. You can draw your own conclusions about what that tells us.

49. Cut out the Middle Man

Everybody involved in the process of ensuring goods reach the consumer has to get a slice of the pie, naturally enough. What you as the consumer should be trying to do where possible is to cut as many unnecessary links as possible from this chain of distribution with a view to reducing the price you pay. What do you care if two or ten people were employed in the process so long as you get the cheapest price possible after all, you're not a bloody one man local employment agency, or are you? With this in mind you should check out whether the goods you require can be purchased more cheaply direct from the manufacturer or wholesaler, particularly with expensive items, but it may also be possible to do this with cheaper products, especially if you are prepared to buy in bulk.

50. Keep Boredom at Bay

Being bored is a dangerous condition, financially, to find yourself in any more than very occasionally. When you are bored your desperation to alleviate the situation will drive the temptation to spend money to a critically high level, even if, or perhaps especially if, you can ill afford it. This desperation can manifest itself in a multitude of ways; for one person it might be 'retail therapy' while for another it might mean going to the pub in the middle of the day only to stagger home, broke, at closing time. For yet another it might just mean they don't feel they could live without that Sky TV package which comes with a hefty monthly subscription and renders it's victim comatose on the couch five evenings a week. These solutions and others of their ilk are not acceptable financially to us tight bastards and furthermore should not be acceptable to anyone who wishes to live as opposed to merely existing. The solution then, as with most problems, is firstly one of recognition. Ask yourself, do I have long standing habits laid down which involve spending money for little reason other than the ritual killing of time? Do I go to the cinema every Friday night to see the latest release regardless of its content? Am I constantly redecorating and changing the furniture 'to freshen the place up'? Do I automatically light up a cigarette after my dinner without even asking myself whether I want it or not? These are just a few examples to get you thinking The list of possible questions is almost endless and will vary with each individual but you should have the gist of the idea and so be able to critically reflect, with honesty, on whether this is a trap you fall into often or not. I'm sure we all do from time to time. It will be for you to decide how often is too often. There are so many pointless pursuits which people can and do engage in that you might as well at the very least take up the free ones instead of the expensive variety.

Anyway, having identified a pattern, we now need a plan to rectify it. First off write down where and when in the week you are leaking time and money to little or no useful effect. Next you need to come up with a long list of cheap or free, useful, alternative practises as replacements for those patterns you hope to phase out. On this list could be included things like going for walks, reading, visiting family or friends, playing with the kids, watching (intelligent, non-subscription) TV, meditating, making love or whatever you're having yourself. You get the idea. Remember Rome wasn't built in a day so depending upon how much of your routine you hope to alter you may need to phase in the changes gradually; too severe and sudden a change to your addictive habits will result in withdrawal symptoms which will prove too difficult to surmount and ultimately failure in your objective, therefore gently does it. As a word of caution before you rush in optimistically with all guns blazing, remember the old adage: 'Time wasted isn't necessarily a waste of time'. Occasionally doing absolutely nothing is just what the doctor ordered; a little meaningless trivial pursuit can be a wonderful thing.

51. Caged Consumers

The poor unsuspecting public are under constant bombardment from corporations plying their wares; it is unrelenting and no space goes untargeted, no trick left untried to part you from your hard earned cash. But at least if you are aware of this fact (information is power) you can defend yourself from the onslaught to a reasonable degree. There are however some instances when, even armed with this invaluable awareness, you are still extremely vulnerable to being preyed and feasted upon by the insatiable conglomerates. These are occasions when you are held captive for a period of time and rather like a caged animal you may engage in atypical behaviour out of sheer frustration or boredom. This explains why in these situations you are willing to pay perhaps a 50% premium over and above the normal price for certain products. You may even purchase goods which, as soon as you are released, you realise you don't want at all.

The classic example of such a situation is at airports. You are required by the airline to check in up to two hours before the flight, on top of which you leave for your destination deliberately early in case of delays – which of course there won't be now because you've allowed for them. So there you are in the airport twiddling your thumbs three hours before your flight departs. What are you going to do? Start spending money, that's what! And haven't they lined up a fine array of ways for you to do just that. First there's the duty free and other shops where you find yourself buying 200 fags and a litre bottle of vodka when you don't even drink or smoke (it's for aunty Theresa whose minding your twin terriers back home), isn't it dirt cheap sure? Then there's the café where you'll fork out €6.50 for a plain ham sandwich, which was only buttered on one side and after all that you'll need a €3 cup of black coffee (milk and sugar are extra) to calm the nerves. You get the picture. We've all been that soldier. You'd think we'd cop on to the con eventually but no, very few ever do. Look, it's not that difficult to protect yourself from this torture. Arrive prepared with a good book or two and your own generous, homemade sambos. Once you've checked in and found your departure gate, settle in to a comfortable seat and do not take your nose out of that book for love nor money 'til they announce it's time for boarding. There are other situations where the same rules apply such as on trains, at the zoo, in the cinema and basically any place where the powers that be believe they have a captive audience and can try it on. In all these situations initiate the scout's motto – 'Be Prepared'.

52. Ying and Yang of Spending

It is worth remembering that every time you choose to spend money on a certain product or service, assuming you are like most mere mortals and have a somewhat limited income, you are simultaneously choosing to deny yourself some other item which you would no doubt like to acquire. So be careful before you buy. If you spend money on the lotto, Chinese takeaways, twenty fags and a bottle of wine on pay day and then find your electricity being cut off before the end of the month, you have chosen this. You have stated clearly by your actions that those things were of a higher value to you than anything which electricity provides you with. You may not be in the habit of thinking about it in those terms but you should. It's called cause and effect and is otherwise known as bad budgeting. Thankfully everyone in Ireland receives enough money to cover at least the bare essentials (food, shelter, clothing, heat and light).

If for some reason you find you cannot afford to make ends meet, somebody somewhere is guilty of bad budgeting. You will most likely discover who the guilty party is by looking in the mirror. I don't mention this in such a cold hearted fashion to make you feel bad but rather to arrest your denial. Budgeting is a skill and like any other skill it requires a certain amount of tuition and practice. If this skill is one which has thus far evaded you not to worry, help is at hand. Make an appointment today with MABS (Money Advice and Budgeting Service). This is a free service which is available to all. In fact even if you are not in financial difficulties it is no harm for anyone to check out their website www.mabs.ie as they provide a wide range of useful advisory services. The helpline number is 0761072000.

53. Buying and Selling Votes

Please always remain conscious of the fact that when you purchase any product or service or indeed part with cash for any reason you are exercising your democratic right to vote. Purchasing any item is to vote in favour of that product and anyone or any company involved in any way in the production or supply of it. Equally to decline a purchase is to vote against. Every spending opportunity then is a mini referendum for you to record your opinion and make your minor impact on how society should or should not operate. Therefore when you buy twenty fags you are saying clearly and unequivocally that you are in favour of and support the tobacco industry and all it stands for; when you throw a few quid into the church plate collection or pay a priest to conduct your wedding you are saying you are happy with the Catholic church and its current policies at present. I could continue with more examples in that vein but there should be no need, I hope you get the point. Capitalism is the ultimate democratic system. You literally get what you pay for. Just a little something for you to ponder while waiting in the queue to make your next purchase.

54. A Right Turn Off

Lads, do your self-esteem a big favour and do not engage with the world's oldest profession, prostitution – well not as a paying customer anyway (if you want to try your hand at selling your wares I've no comment to make about that here). Seriously though, why would you pay large sums of money to somebody who clearly does not want to be there and is most likely repulsed by you, to hop into bed for twenty minutes? That by the way is giving your staying power the benefit of some considerable doubt. To pay for sex is to miss the point and all the fun of the whole exercise. It's a bit like paying to go in to see a movie with only ten minutes remaining; you get to witness the climax but your pleasure is seriously curtailed because you missed the two hours of drama which preceded it. You're left feeling short changed and perplexed, wondering how come everyone else enjoyed the experience so much more than you.

You see by paying for sex you've missed out on all the fun and heart pounding excitement of the chase. The will she or won't she? The unexpected twists and turns, the hopes dashed and the expectations raised as the drama unfolds. No amount of money can buy you those thrills 'n spills. So come on lads (and ladies too, if you're tempted to buy such services), there are many ways to skin a cat and it seems clear to me that paying a 'working girl' is the most expensive and least enjoyable option. You might as well just buy a skin mag and pull your plonker, you get just about the same level of intimacy and engagement and with a similar end result, namely staring at yourself in the bathroom mirror a little deflated but hey, it'll have cost a lot less, you'll have satiated Johnson temporarily and there's no risk of you having to explain away an STD to the missus. Plus you can call on your magazine girls again, night or day, for no extra charge.

55. Tie a Knot in It

Of course the single most expensive decision you are ever likely to make is to have a child or worse, children. I read one article which estimated the cost of rearing a child from cradle to graduation at €250,000. I'd say that's a gross underestimation myself especially as nowadays the little feckin' financial black holes seem to go to college forever. An honest to goodness degree is of no use anymore, you have to go on to get a masters, a PHD, a doctorate and the divil knows what else before you're considered fit and ready to do a day's work. That's not to say anything of the piano lessons and the karate classes which are compulsory purchases for all would-be 'parent of the year' contenders. God be with the days when extracurricular activity meant running around the fields or a spot of fishing in the local pond. I could go on endlessly on this topic but you know yourself they're bloody expensive little tykes and you don't know the half of it if you haven't had 'em yet.

If you are going to persist with this parenthood plan at least make sure it is just that: a plan and not an accident. There's really no excuse for an unplanned pregnancy these days, is there? Not now that we've all figured out we won't actually burn in hell for eternity for putting a bit of rubber over Johnson. The other thing about kids is that the world is overrun with them. The world population is exploding at an alarming rate. We just topped the 7 billion mark a short while back (2011). There were only 2 billion of us in 1927 when my father was 4; by 1974 when I was a 4 year old the number had doubled to 4 billion and it's predicted to double again to 8,000,000,000 by the year 2025. Lads, I'm no mathematician or world expert on food productivity but I can categorically tell you this has to stop. We can't keep multiplying our numbers indefinitely without catastrophic consequences. It's time to tie a knot in it. At the very most nobody should have more than three kids by the normal biological means. One to replace each of the parents and a spare one so to speak to allow for those that for one reason or another never procreate. Producing any more little ankle biters than this is, apart from being quite sadistic, downright selfish. If you really are a glutton for punishment and wanting more than three offspring you should adopt one or two of those poor little buggers from a Russian orphanage or one of those unfortunate urchins from a famine ravaged African country who can't reasonably expect to live to see their fifth birthday. Of course if you are a fulltime, long-term recipient of social welfare or if you are otherwise incapable of financing yourself let alone the rearing of children then you have absolutely no business having any. Why should I have to pay to rear your sprogs especially when the world needs more mouths to feed like it needs another hole in the bleedin' ozone?

56. Employ a Granny

The cost of availing of crèche facilities for the little apples of your eye while yourself and herself head off to wear yourselves out on your respective career treadmills must seem extortionate and completely out of proportion relative to other essential expenses for anyone earning anything approximating an average wage. Yet what can you do? You can't bring the little trolls to work with you, and love them as you may you are certainly not sacrificing your career for them; they have already taken over every other aspect of your now unrecognisable life. I suggest what you should do is, ask yourself what people did for childminding services before the term 'crèche' was invented. That's right, they got the granny or other elderly neighbour to mind the kids and what's more she did it efficiently, happily and for free. Unfortunately for many of you those days are gone and granny is no longer with us or she lives in Poland or on the far side of our little island. At any rate she is not available to do the school run five mornings a week. That is a pity because there goes your free minder. Still though, there must be plenty of other people's grannies you could utilise who would be only too delighted to supplement their pension for a token gesture of say €100 per week doing the one thing they know how to do better than anything else: minding little sprogs. After all the average Irish gran has been minding generations of children for over fifty years starting with her own siblings when she was little more than a nipper herself. I'll bet you a pound to a penny there's a woman (or even a man, let's not be sexist, eh!) living near you who is probably missing the excitement of kids about the place and who would give her false teeth for the chance to supplement her widow's pension doing the one thing she loves best in the world.

Your mission then, should you choose to accept it, is to find this woman. Put up a few wanted ads on local shop notice boards. Try to think of other places where oldies hang out. That's right, put up notices in the local GP's waiting room, bingo hall and anywhere else you think they might be seen by your target audience. Get the word out among friends and colleagues, advertise in the local press and distribute flyers in yours and nearby estates. Do whatever it takes; she's out there and you just have to find her. Naturally enough it goes without saying that when you have narrowed the field of candidates you should take every prudent precaution, have them Garda vetted, check their references and be very clear about the rules of engagement and terms of business from the outset to avoid problems later on. You could also do a few unannounced spot checks early on, arriving home sooner than expected to make sure she hasn't got them locked in the attic and after that, as long as she is sound of mind and limb, you have yourself the finest of childminders for a song.

57. Running to Stand Still

Many of us grew up with the mantra 'work hard and live frugally' which is pretty solid advice for remaining financially solvent – foolproof in fact, you would think, for improving one's wealth index. Alas there are exceptions to every rule and if you are someone who works in the official economy for €10 euro per hour or less, apart from the fact that you are being undervalued and unappreciated by your employer, you may actually be worse off financially than if you were sitting on your arse at home. Or perhaps you do earn a half decent wage but you have a large family or other dependents. It is time to get out the calculator, put on the thinking cap and tot up what your real net income is after all taxes and job related costs such as travel, work clothes, lunches and so on. What do you have left for yourself after your forty hour (or perhaps fifty hours including commuting to and fro) working week? Next compare and deduct from this what you would receive in handouts if you were to cease your employment. As a single person for example, you would currently receive €188 dole which may be over half the amount you currently work for. You are also entitled to €20 for fuel during the winter months, then there is the rent allowance of course and don't forget the health board are always on hand to help you out with utility bills or unexpected lump sum payments if you are persistent and persuasive enough. There are back to education allowances, carer's allowances and bereavement

310

payments and the divil knows what else going a-begging. On top of all this being labelled a social welfare recipient protects you from most of the stealth taxes the government have or are about to bring in such as the USC (universal social charge) and water charges to name just a couple. There's a lot to be said for being a man of straw in today's Ireland.

Look, I'm no expert on the inner workings of the social welfare system; in fact the people working for this bureaucratic, dysfunctional and many-tentacled monster only seem to have the vaguest idea of how it operates. What you want to do is befriend an experienced social welfare lifer to teach you how to extract the maximum juice from this ripe-for-the-plucking, low hanging succulent fruit. Once you have compared and contrasted the figures for work versus early retirement you may still be better off by tuppence ha'penny keeping your nose to the grind but what value should you place on those fifty hours of freedom unemployment offers?

In fairness though, before you throw in the employment towel there are all kinds of perks to having a job that are difficult to quantify such as the social interaction, skills development, promotion prospects, self-esteem building and just preserving your sanity by having a goal in life. In short there is no dole for the soul but it is possible to develop all of these positives through other avenues besides the traditional employment route. Another consideration in favour of keeping the job is the fact that there are sometimes income supplement payments available as a top-up for those who are gainfully employed but on a low income. If you are walking this tricky little borderline tightrope and unsure how to proceed I cannot tell you which the best way to jump is, nobody can, but do not act in haste. Think through all the implications carefully; research ways in which you might utilise your time more rewardingly if your job pays peanuts and leaves you unfulfilled. Check out education, self-employment and volunteering opportunities. I know that some poor, much crucified taxpayers reading this will be incensed and quick to point out to me that the dole is not a lifestyle choice. While I have every sympathy for your position you are only right in theory. Regretfully for a whole host of reasons, in practice it is a very valid lifestyle choice for many.

58. Falling into False Economies

Are you engaging in any false economies? Perhaps you have become blinded to your own financial detriment by your over eager pursuit of frugality. For example if it takes you an eight hour day to clean your house from top to bottom and you are far from fond of domestic chores then it would be prudent indeed to engage the services of a professional cleaner who will relieve you of your monotonous task for about €50. At a rate of €10 per hour she will complete the job to a higher standard in less than half the time it would have taken you, she being an efficient, experienced professional. You will also have cut out all the procrastination and ingenious avoidance techniques we all employ when an unavoidable but mind-numbingly boring task is looming. So you have now bought back more than a day of your life for the princely sum of €50. Bearing in mind, if like me you are a forty something Irish male, you only have about 10,000 to

12,000 such days left to you on the law of averages, what value will you put on one of them? How much, for instance, do you get paid for a day's work? Certainly if it is more than fifty quid you have just bought yourself a bargain and that's without even attempting to put a value on the successful evasion of a much maligned chore. Can you think of other examples where you are currently operating a false economy?

What is and is not a false economy will of course vary from individual to individual. Some of you lunatics out there probably consider shining the bathroom floor 'til you can see your face glowing in it the very definition of domestic bliss and would therefore be better off flushing your fifty down the toilet than plucking a domestic hygienist from the classifieds. Re-evaluate the things you spend your time and energy on to make sure you are not falling into the self-defeating trap of false economics.

59. Expensive Convenience

It occurs to me that much of the money we spend is not really buying us a product or service as such. We may be purchasing physical goods but when we ask ourselves what is it we expect to get from these goods in return for parting with our cash, the answer is often convenience. We are simply buying back time or sub-contracting effort, or both. A classic and perfect example of this would be the humble washing machine, so much a part of everyday life now that it is totally taken for granted. While we are blissfully oblivious to its wonder the elderly women of this country in particular can tell you, in descriptive detail, what this modest machine has meant for the domestic labourer. The mountains of work time and knuckle-skinning graft this unassuming invention has erased in a single generation would be nigh on impossible to exaggerate. Only a sadist would think this inspired creation was not a household essential. That is an example at one extreme end of buying convenience, there are however endless ways and means in which we are sold this invisible commodity.

When you park your car in a city centre car park for instance you are not paying €2.50 an hour for a parking space, you are paying it to absolve yourself from parking a little further out along the road and therefore you are buying the doubtful convenience of avoiding a little free healthy light exercise by walking ten minutes each way to and from your vehicle. You won't even have saved any time avoiding the stroll due to urban traffic congestion. Depending on the width of your girth you may well then have absent-mindedly dealt yourself a double whammy disservice by paying for the dubious privilege of depriving your poor body of some much needed exercise. I'm sure if you put your thinking cap on you will be able to identify other examples where we unthinkingly shell out good money to our own detriment by buying a false illusion of convenience. Of course there are times when you willingly pay a premium to genuinely buy back time, such as any occasion when you frequent your local corner shop rather than going to the nearest supermarket; when you microwave ready meals (at what long term cost to your health?) rather than cooking from scratch or when you take the car instead of the bus. Anyway the list of such occasions is long and having reviewed your own regular patterns of behaviour you may well conclude that the scarce and precious time returned to you in some of these instances is well worth the financial cost.

That's all well and good but before we leave this subject with you reclining smugly on your self-satisfied laurels it would be prudent to take a look at how you then utilise this hard bought, recaptured resource. Supposing you have paid out €20, either directly or indirectly, to claw back an hour of your invaluable time on a given day, what then are you going to 'purchase' with that hour? After all you cannot salt it away in some bank of time deposit account. You must spend it on something. Since you have paid a not insignificant sum for this time it would be wise I suggest to consciously question what then becomes of it. If for example, later that evening you spend an hour watching back to back soaps on the goggle box, you have decreed two episodes of fairly shitty or Corrie or whatever is worth the handsome fee of €20. Ask yourself would you rent a DVD containing 60 minutes of your favourite soap for €20? If you are of anything remotely resembling average means and possess a modicum of sanity I respectfully suggest you would not. Pause for thought, is it not? So by all means where you deem it prudent pay for convenience, but thoughtfully, whilst simultaneously remembering how you spend your time is worthy of just as much attention as how you part with your shillings.

60. Degrees of Success

If there is one piece of irrefutably sound financial advice which is universally accepted by everyone with even half a brain, it is that investing in your education is a sound investment. It pays handsome dividends indeed. For the discomfort of going to college and having to endure a few years of wild parties, developing lifelong friendships and opening your mind to a whole world of previously unimagined possibilities, the average successful graduate will not alone be much more likely to find gainful employment when compared to his classmate who went straight into the workforce after the leaving cert, but can also expect to earn twice as much as his less well-educated friend. To put this in context the non-graduate might earn €25,000 a year if he's lucky while his friend who is the same age, not dissimilar intellectually but slightly better educated can expect to earn €50,000. Not alone this but our college guy will also most likely enjoy a more intellectually stimulating career with all kinds of perks and privileges our other poor schmuck can only look on in envy at. The flip side of this is that our sad degreeless sap's work will also likely be more physically demanding and dangerous in nature, quite possibly with no protections or pensions of any kind in place. Our college friend, on the other hand, is already cruising along nicely on the gravy train of life, economy class, and can upgrade to first class by going further and completing a master's degree or even PhD.

We all know of high profile exceptions to this rule; Bill Gates is the prime example of one who dropped out of college to go on to become the world's richest man. There is an exception to every rule but citing Bill Gates as a reason not to go to college is rather like pointing to the one eighty five year old smoker still standing in defence of that habit and ignoring the thousands in the graveyard. You are not Bill Gates! Go to college, if you are too short sighted to go for the money then go for the girls but for God's sake go and get that cash cow degree. If you missed the first college cruise liner a few years back there's another one available for boarding every September. Better late than never! And yes, you will be sickeningly nervous and anxious initially at taking that bold step off reassuringly familiar terra firma, particularly if you have been out of education for a long time. But we are not living at all only merely existing if we don't take occasional terrifying leaps into the unknown. Besides it will soon become easier, enjoyable even. The first step is always the hardest. Of course right now the timing for such a jump couldn't be better with the whole country up shit creek without a paddle, while Eamonn and Enda are busy boring holes in the canoe. What better time to hide out in a centrally heated, modern university availing of grants and subsidised grub and maybe even learning something useful along with your degree.

61. Well Read Street Cred

Formal academic qualifications are all good and to be encouraged but it represents only one side of a well-rounded education for life. On its own it is a very rigid suffocating type of knowledge and it needs to be blended with the other, more important side of this coin which is the continuous assessment, self-taught skill set of negotiating everyday life. There is no graduating from this particular course, this is lifelong learning and to become accomplished the first attribute you will need is to have an open mind. You must also learn to question everything. Remember there are no facts, only opinion. You must expose yourself to as rich and as wide a variety of information as possible. Doing this you will quickly learn that most of what you are told is untrue or only partly true or true but not applicable to you. Your challenge is to separate out these truths, half-truths and outright lies. Remember everyone has an agenda; everybody is trying to sell you something. This is not a criticism but simply human nature. Nobody can see the world precisely from your perspective so at best two people endeavouring to be honest with each other will say 'this is my truth, tell me yours'. In an argument it is possible for both parties to be right and even more likely for both sides to be wrong, if only everyone realised this how many wars could have been averted, not to mention family feuds? The world is constantly in a state of flux, always changing and therefore even that which you accept to be true today may not be so tomorrow.

What has all this got to do with savvy financial management you may be wondering? Everything! The world is full of people on the make from politicians, bankers, businesses and chancers of every hue. A fool and his money are easily parted, which is exactly what you will be if you do not keep yourself well informed and up to date with what is going on in the wider world around you, beyond your own little cocoon. When you, the broken, swindled fool come whinging, looking for sympathy and demanding compensation you should receive neither. It is your own fault; learn the hard lesson and move on. So to avoid that last harsh scenario, you cannot afford to waste your evenings watching Egofactor, I'm a Has-been, get me on the Telly, Stars in me Arse or any other moronic rubbish which is passed off as entertainment these days. Equally don't throw away your valuable time reading tabloid tat, you can ill afford it. Instead you should spend these hours reading quality books and newspapers with intelligent, well-articulated, useful opinions. The television is still a great resource but only when used in a thoughtful manner. Watch informative documentaries, news and current affairs programmes. Never forget, information equals power and power equals money. If this advice strikes a chord, two good places to begin your new daily diet curriculum are I suggest RTE radio one and the Irish Times newspaper.

62. Taking it on the Chin

If you are sacked or simply let go from your job it would be wise to bear in mind that a shut mouth catches no flies and keep your counsel on the subject. Even if you feel you have a legitimate gripe, Facebook and twitter are not the places for airing it; neither is texting your now former colleagues to piss and moan in an attempt to elicit sympathy. Tempting as it probably is, putting a brick through your former boss's window is of course even worse. Bad mouthing your former boss is not going to endear you to prospective future employers, particularly if you are hoping to find work within the same industry from whence you've just been unceremoniously ejected, or you are trying to find employment in the same small town. Remember, Ireland is an incestuous little country with everyone seemingly related or connected to everyone else. If you feel you were unfairly dismissed, your only sensible recourse to justice is through official channels and even then it would be advisable to think long and hard before embarking on the modern day equivalent of the Christian crusades. It is sure to be a lonely, frustrating, stressful and dissatisfying journey – and that's if you win. By all means seek legal advice if your level of anguish truly is at an octave which warrants it but be sure to realise your solicitor will only be concerned with how likely you are to win an unfair dismissal case, how much it's likely to cost and so on. But what about the emotional, social and domestic costs and not least the cost to your future employment prospects having gone to war in public with a past employer? Would you take on someone you knew to have hauled their last boss through the courts? Would you care about the merits or outcome of their case? In a recession, when you have 500 other applicants to choose from, I for one certainly wouldn't. So think before you leap, and then don't. Chalk it up to experience and move on.

63. Petty Trifles

If you find yourself in dispute with another party, be it a business or an individual, over a relatively minor sum, and having repeatedly tried in vain to resolve the matter to your satisfaction via the usual initial personal approaches one makes in these situations, you find you are stuck in a classic stalemate of 'irresistible force meets immovable object', then assuming you honestly believe you have a half decent case to put forward, you might want to consider taking your gripe to the small claims court.

Now don't break out in a cold sweat at the mention of the word 'court'. This is nothing like the nightmare scenario of a normal law suit with all the attendant vultures, stress and expense. According to the website www.courts.ie 'the small claims court is designed to handle consumer and business claims cheaply without involving a solicitor' and 'the procedure is there to help you make your small claim with a minimum of procedural red tape and at little cost'. Fortunately I have never personally had the dubious pleasure of using this service myself but when I checked out the process online it did indeed seem to be a relatively painless, possible way forward for anyone stuck in the aforementioned bind. Claims must not exceed €2,000 and the fee is a very reasonable €25. Having paid your fee you fill out a simple claim form and forward this to the district court clerk (aka the small claims court Registrar). He/she will, where possible, negotiate a settlement between the warring factions without the need for a court hearing. If the matter cannot be resolved the Registrar will bring your case before the district court to be adjudicated upon. Personally I reckon if you really feel you've been screwed over by someone to the tune of €500 or worse €2,000 it'd be worth gambling another petty €25 to get it back and even if you lost the satisfaction of knowing you hadn't quit without a fight would buy you a heck of a lot more than €25 worth of self-esteem. Win or lose you can then put it behind you and walk away with your pride intact.

64. Don't go in There

If you are strapped for cash and you find yourself walking into a newsagents or corner shop, don't. Stop and think. They have nothing for sale which you need or want. Think about it, what do people buy in a newsagents? Cigarettes, soft drinks, newspapers and magazines, lottery tickets, greeting cards, crisps and confectionary – these products would cover the vast bulk of their sales. Some of these items are downright damaging to your health, others serve no useful purpose and *none* are essentials. On the rare occasion that you do find yourself buying a useful product from a corner shop, such as a box of teabags, remember you could almost certainly have bought a similar product for half the price elsewhere.

Again the same rule applies to fast food outlets of all kinds; these establishments have absolutely no value to the consumer at all. At least the corner shop might occasionally sell you something useful like a banana or an apple. What does the greasy chipper sell? Burgers and other reconstituted crap which have roughly the same nutritional content and are about as tasty as a salted soggy cardboard egg carton. The only reason you think this barely edible fare is tasty is because either you are inebriated or there is so much salt and MSG added that you can't actually taste the burger itself. So if you find yourself walking towards a chipper with a view to entering it to make a purchase, don't. You'd be better off to simply throw your money down the nearest drain, that way you save yourself from having to queue and whilst you are still putting your money into shit at least you are not putting the shit into you.

65. TD or not TD?

You might want to consider running for election next time round as your ordinary, average muck savage T.D gets a salary of about €90,000. That'd be fair enough if it was the end of the matter as the poor craters have a thankless job listening to an endless stream of punters pissing and moaning about their woes – and that's on the weekend when they're back down in their constituencies from the pale after a week in the Dáil, listening to endless auld balderdash from the likes of Healy Rae rabbiting on about eating his dinner in the middle of the day. No, in all fairity now I for one wouldn't begrudge them their near two grand a week wages, salubrious a sum an' all as it may be. The twist in the tail that really encourages the opportunist with an eye to the main chance into this profession though is the average €50,000 or so claimed in expenses by 165 of our 166 sitting TD's. So the average TD is spending a thousand euro a week in the carrying out of his day to day duties and presumably we're expected to believe he can't get by without it? The only thing is one labour TD, namely Eamonn Maloney, quietly gives the lie to this assertion. He has not claimed a single red cent in expenses since entering the Dáil at the last election in early 2011. What's more any time I've seen his mug turn up in the media he seems impeccably well turned out and adequately versed on the topic under discussion. How does he do it on a meagre €245 a day or so? What other profession gets paid half their salary again just for turning up to work? In a recession your perk for arriving into work with some consistency is normally that you get to keep your job. So start your campaign now in time for the next general election, you could be quid's in, €140,000 annually for cracking jokes down the back of the class with Ming, Pinkie and all the other independent messers. Seriously there's never been a better time to run as an independent, sure the whole country is disillusioned with the party political system and in their desperation are turning to pot head boggers and flamboyant tax evaders for deliverance. Meanwhile, if by chance you fail in your bid to serve your nation patriotically perhaps you should look closely, as a private citizen, at where your hard earned tax dollars are being collected and spent. Then ask yourself, is the government spending my money wisely and justly? If the answer is yes then great, no problem. If the answer is no, what then? What can you do about it? I'm afraid I must leave that to each individuals ingenuity and conscience.

66. Money on the Line

Book your train or bus fares online in advance as you will get a cheaper deal than if you just turn up and pay at the station. You won't save as much as their adverts suggest because there will likely be transaction charges involved when booking online which the company just neglected to mention but nonetheless you should still save a few euro off your ticket price. This tip can equally apply at times for other purchases too such as tickets to a show or air fares but double check all other options in these cases as it is not an absolute given that online is cheapest here.

67. Start a Swop Shop

Do you have a saleable skill or service which you could trade with others in return for their time or expertise in an area which you require? You could try swopping a dog minding service for someone else's gardening skills or whatever. The possibilities are endless. The tricky part is making initial contact with likeminded individuals living close enough for you to trade with. The more densely populated an area you live in the greater the possibilities with this idea of course but it can still work in more rural communities. Decide what talents, abilities or products you have to offer and then go about publicising yourself anywhere you can think of. Utilise Facebook and other social media sites to get the word out, advertise on local notice boards or free ad newspapers. This of course is not a new idea and there are already a number of websites set up to encourage this activity, some that may be worth checking out to help get you started are u-exchange.com, Adverts.ie (buy and sell website) www.clonfavour.com (This is a Clonakilty, Co Cork based group, but they are supportive of others wishing to replicate their model) and www.swaportrade.ie (this last one seems to be mostly Cork based also but not exclusively so). There are also ad hoc local groups popping up on Facebook which are worth seeking out, two that I've come across are 'The Malahide things for sale, swap or free group' and 'The Greystones area buy sell or swap group'. I'm sure there are lots more out there so try to find a group local to you and if you can't why not consider starting one of your own? Some of the groups already mentioned say they are very happy to offer support and advice to other communities trying to follow suit. Apart from saving you money, getting involved in this form of trade which is as old as humanity itself helps forge strong friendships and a sense of community spirit which are of course priceless.

68. Death without Debt, Amen to That

In the event of your death or that of a loved one there are a number of bereavement grants available depending on individual circumstances. You should check out The Citizens Information website for details of these. They are not all dependent on your ability to pay. There is something there for almost everyone ranging from once off payments of €850 to €6,000. If it is your own death which is in question it would of course be advisable to have done this in advance.

Another avenue to explore in an attempt to avoid funeral expenses is to consider donating your body to medical science. If your body is accepted (there are numerous reasons why it may not be) by one of the five medical research colleges in Ireland, they'll look after your disposal when they're done with you, saving your estate the expense. The college may hold a memorial service for donor family members at some point and it may also be possible to have your loved ones ashes returned to you in the event they are cremated, should you so wish. Each school has its own procedures for entering into an agreement with you. The five colleges in question are University Colleges Dublin, Cork and Galway as well as Trinity College Dublin and The Royal College of Surgeons, Dublin. What better legacy to leave behind than making a contribution to our understanding of the human body. It could be the perfect solution for the agnostic or atheist looking to avoid a religious ceremony whilst not wanting to upset his devout spouse with a humanist service. You can contact the colleges directly for more detailed information and of course you can also tap into that fountain of knowledge that is The Citizens Information website once more.

69. Avoiding a Grave Expense

There are various pros and cons to weigh up when deciding what should become of your remains once you exhale your last, expire upon this mortal stage and the curtain closes on your great performance, a masterpiece of that favoured genre, the black comedy. If I had my way I'd continue as I had lived and make sure someone or something gets use of my spare parts when I no longer need them. Once the medical profession had taken anything of use to them I'd like, as was a tradition in Tibet I believe, to be placed upon a sturdy funeral pyre (of biodegradable natural materials of course) and left there for the birds and beasts to feast upon, carrying my spirit far and wide on wing and hide. Well, can't be any worse than letting the worms have ye. It's a perfect environmentally green solution to my disposal too, in keeping with this century's buzzwords. Alas no, there are laws against that kind of thing, supposedly for that catch all reason 'health and safety' but in reality, as always, those three little words are just code for 'there's no money in that class of thing for any powerful vested interests'. A pity though; it'd be brilliant just have the missus stick you up there, out the back, the family could bid farewell slowly, a little at a time. No need for six grand to get rid of ya either. Maybe some cute whore of a minister will see the logic of legalising my pragmatic wish – they could save a packet on those funeral grants!

In the meantime, if you are lying there on your deathbed reading this you might want to consider cremation instead of a traditional burial. Admittedly, both are expensive solutions to your upcoming dilemma, although cremation is generally less expensive, particularly if you simplify the process by opting out of the palaver of a religious service. Also, with cremation there are no on-going grave maintenance costs or issues to trouble your descendants for generations to come, which is as it should be, I mean to say it's bad enough to be a financial burden on those you love (or are just quite fond of) when you are living, but really once you pop your clogs nobody should feel obliged to fork out in your memory. Let death be the end of you, as was originally intended. Of course if you are willing to be so magnanimous towards your kinfolk it would seem reasonable to suggest that it should be a two way street. Why not spark a money-saving family tradition?

70. Don't Box me In

Well praise be to Mohamed! There is a new law, just come into force which allows you to be buried without a coffin. This is thanks to the Muslim community who traditionally prefer to be buried without one if local laws allow but is open to people of all religions and none to avail of. It is up to individual cemeteries and local health authorities to decide if they will facilitate this change in the law. Still, it's worth checking out this possible option of cutting one expensive part of the funeral procedure, after all the coffin is not serving any useful purpose once it is buried six feet under. Alas, for so-called, catch all 'health and safety' reasons a coffin will still be required during the funeral service so savings may be limited. Presumably though, from now on if you still want the traditional graveyard burial you can hire your final wooden suit rather than having to pay full whack for the purchase price.

71. Thy Will be Done

The vast majority of adults, unbelievably, have not made a will. There are a number of reasons for this such as people believing they don't have any assets to leave or just foolishly assuming that their estate will be divided in the manner they would wish, regardless. The main reason, I suspect, for the low propensity for will making is apathy and our intriguing, modern day denial of the only certainty in life. So pull your ostrich head out of the sand and listen to me. You are going to die whether you acknowledge the fact or not. Also you have assets to distribute in the event of your death even if these only amount to your collection of DVD's, a wardrobe of flares from the seventies and your ten year old corolla. So we have established two things 1. You will die. 2. You have assets to bequeath. The only question left to answer then is whether you think you or some stranger with a funny wig in a court are best placed to decide what should become of your worldly possessions (not to mention dependent children) in the event of your untimely demise? I think you know the answer.

Go on, make that will. You know it makes sense even if it does feel a little morbid. While you are at it, making your own will and discussing its contents with those affected (this is also very important to avoid your loved ones spending half their inheritance arguing the toss in front of the guy in the funny wig and paying for his kids to smoke pot in law school), it is a good time to make sure your nearest and dearest, whose passing will have a bearing on you financially and otherwise, grasp this thorny issue as well, leaving you all well protected and in the loop regardless of who takes the great leap into the unknown first.

72. Let them Rest in Peace

Have you ever taken a glance at all those pages of anniversary notices of deceased loved ones in the back pages of newspapers? Sometimes the person has been dead for thirty years or more. It's sad isn't it? You find yourself wondering when are the living going to let them go. By all means spend a few quiet moments thinking of your deceased relatives or friends on their anniversary; light a candle or perform some other symbolic gesture for them if you must. But if you ask me, putting expensive adverts with photos and the whole works in the national paper every year for several decades after their departure from this world (to say nothing of paying to have masses said for them) is several steps too far and smacks of behaviour which suggests that somebody has become unhappily stuck at some point in the grieving process. I don't mean to sound harsh, I know we hate the thought of our loved ones being forgotten but I'm afraid it is inevitable that, sooner or later, everyone is forgotten. At the very latest once everyone who ever knew you has passed away then it is safe to say all conscious memory of you has been erased. It is counterproductive, painful and emotionally draining to cling on desperately and indefinitely to that which has already slipped from our grasp. Gently, let the dead go and if they still exist in any realm you will be reunited soon enough. For now, put your energies into life and the living.

73. Thrifty Text Alerts

They say birds of a feather flock together. This being the case, now that you are a fully-fledged tight bastard you will probably notice that you have made the acquaintance of, even become friendly with, a few like-minded individuals. If not you should try harder as they can be a useful resource. One simple idea a gang of thrifty individuals can put into practice is for each member to agree to send around a group text alert to all the others whenever they come across a genuine too good to miss offer while out and about. If you are looking for a particular item but are holding out for a bargain price you can use the other members of the group as extra sets of perceptive eyes in your search. Needless to say this idea will only work if all the members engage with it in the right spirit which is one of camaraderie and helpfulness. You could have as your motivational theme a variation of the old Smiths' song called 'Tight Bastards of the World Unite and Take Over'.

74. Don't Get Burnt

The summer is on the way! How can I tell? Not because of the bleedin' sun anyway, that's a certainty. The reason I know summer's on the way is because the shelves are filling up fast with a dazzling array of those brightly coloured tubes, bottles and sprays collectively known as 'sunscreen'. We are assured that summer this year will arrive on the Tuesday following the whit bank holiday weekend and last right through until Thursday. It's not even Paddy's day yet and already the shops are full of blasted sunscreen. We will be warned repeatedly between now and then through every media and marketing outlet imaginable that we face a lingering and excruciatingly painful death before the church bell strikes midnight on mid-summers eve should we be foolhardy enough to dare stick even our big toe out, unprotected, into the deadly glare of the noonday sun.

Seriously it's a bit over the top all this doom and gloom about the killer cancer rays of the sun. How the hell did our poor forefathers ever see a day past thirty? Remember, no air conditioned handy nine to five office job for them, no way, they were out sweatin' in the fields from dawn 'til dusk. Do you think they were covered from head to foot in factor sixty sun (and air) block? Not on your Nellie, you can bet your last horse drawn plough the only protection they had was the honest sweat of their brow. And what about the Aussies? How come they haven't all been fried to a cinder? Someone told me they get 300 days of serious sunshine a year in Melbourne. Gets up to 50 degrees Celsius down there I believe. Come on, when you are in Boots sheltering from a torrential downpour and you see a tube of this stuff costing up to €20 do you not smell a corporate rat infesting our minds, twisting the facts to put the fear of God into us? After sex the next best way to shift product is after all through that other old reliable, fear! I know the Health Police will give me chapter and verse about it all being to do with the hole in the ozone; how our natural protection mechanisms are defenceless against it etc., etc. Call me a sceptic if you like but I'm a bit suspect about how this hole in the ozone appeared at round about the same time sun block landed. Was it up there in outer space all the time just waiting for an opening to make its grand entrance? Listen, just in case I'm wrong, I don't want to be the cause of half the country getting cancer, so to be on the safe side wear a nice wide brimmed hat and long sleeved t-shirt (I know that's a contradiction in terms but that's what the smiling shop assistant called them, without any hint of irony) this summer. I know, I know, it's not going to help your cool factor but it's only for a couple of days and it'll save ye twenty quid or more, not to mention the money you'll save on shirts – it's a real bugger trying to get the stains from that sun lotion out of your clothes. By the way, a final word of warning: dispel any thoughts of a harmless bit of 'how's your father' in the dunes with herself while wearing sun cream. The sand will stick to everything and I mean everything. If this happens, then you will truly understand the meaning of the words excruciating, lingering and painful. Don't ask how I know this, I just do.

75. Country Cousins beat City Slickers

Pretty much every professional (or even unprofessional) service you could care to mention will cost you a lot more inside the Pale than outside it. Dublin city prices for everything from hairdos to having your corns removed cost more than the same service down the country. The reason of course is that all the associated costs of doing business such as rent, insurance and labour are greater in an urban setting and have to be passed on to the consumer. In theory at least the cheapest professional services you can find should generally be those provided from the practitioners own home in a remote rural setting, because this person has almost no associated costs and her local customer base has a much lower disposable income than her city counterparts.

I had reason recently to avail of the professional services of a rural Co Galway Chiropodist and she charged me all of €20 for a very satisfactory service. How much would I have paid in Dublin? I'll never know for sure but according to a quick search online it would be somewhere in the region of €60. That's all good and well if you live half way between Ballydehob and Ballyfeckoff I hear you complain but if you live and work in the city aren't you stuck with city prices? Not necessarily. What's to stop a city dweller incorporating a visit to the dentist or acupuncture clinic into their next trip to visit granny down in the sticks? Just do a bit of online research and/or put the word out with rural relations or friends regarding the service you require to see what kind of quotes come back. Make sure to compare and contrast with the city offers because there's an exception to every rule; the townies may have a cut price deal which beats the culchie competition on occasion.

76. Bending Genders

It's becoming increasingly difficult out there on the high street and shopping mall jungles to separate the rose from the briar. Often, as a gang of youths pass by, you have to do a double take to tell if they are guys or girls. My eyesight is perfect in case you're wondering; no, the confusion arises as the marketing moguls are finally seeing dividends for their long running campaign to double the prospective customer base for products traditionally only sold to the fairer sex. So now we don't bat a false eyelash when a young fella passes wearing anything from earrings to hair extensions. They've got handbags (manbags) which contain their perfume (cologne), scented deodorant sprays and breath fresheners. I'm quite sure some of these guys are wearing foundation, eyeliner and lipstick. They can be seen hanging out in trendy art nouveau coffee emporiums (whatever they are?) and if you do a little eaves dropping (well I had to, strictly for research purposes, you understand) you'll hear the conversation turn to the pain of full body waxing or the price of a decent fake tan. Older members of this strange new breed, you know the twenty eight or twenty nine year olds fearing they're past it are booking appointments for nips, tucks and hair transplants with the relaxed manner of a bloke going down to the barber for a short back and sides.

And I'm not talking about the ones kicking with the left boot either; these are otherwise average, reasonably balanced young men without any major, known psychological issues. I reckon that guy – the lead singer with The Cure back in the 80's, Robert Smith, has a lot to answer for. It's him I blame for planting the seed in the corporate heads. Of course the likes of David Beckham didn't help, prancing around in a skirt (a sarong the media called it but it looked like a feckin' skirt from where I was sittin'). Does he not realise that he is a role model for millions of football-mad cavemen who are only paid from the shoulders down and don't actually entertain independent thought? But of course he does, hasn't he got Beckham perfume out now and he finished out his playing career in the fashion capitals of the world. No wonder he did so well on the pitch – how would you keep a straight face, never mind engaging with his tackle as you see him and his hairdo dribbling his balls in only one direction? Seriously lads, please step back from this lunacy. I'm all for equality of the sexes but equal to doesn't mean the same as. You wouldn't date a six pack-laden, broad shouldered, hairy Helena now would you? No feckin way! So don't expect the more discerning gender to fancy a deep-voiced, overgrown version of themselves. Women generally like their men a little rough around the edges, so give yourself a break, save a mint of money and quit this pulling and preening at yourself. You're not some kind of prize peacock. Have a shower every day, with a bar of coconut oil body shop soap if you must, shave every other day, shampoo once a week and you're ready to knock 'em dead. If you really want to impress the ladies do a bit of reading to develop an intellect as everyone with half a brain knows women are more turned on by your personality, wit and intelligence than by your appearance. You see I told you they were different, they don't keep their brains down their pants like we do.

77. Don't Spend a Penny

It is true that the best things in life are free and there are few better feelings in the world than the relief of relieving oneself having been burstin' for some considerable time beforehand. It's a sweet and blessed outpouring indeed! Still if you get caught short while out and about there's no reason to pay for your pleasure in some public jacks when there are pubs, bookies and coffee shops with free facilities at every turn. If, upon venturing in to use the convenience of one of these establishments you are confronted with that ubiquitous grumpy proprietors sign 'Toilets for customers use only' take no notice, sure you're bound to be a customer sometime either directly or indirectly so you're covered and besides, if you get pulled up on your way out they can hardly ask you to take it back, can they?

78. A Wealth of Ugliness

Should you be one of the fortunate few well-to-do readers of this pedantic script, congratulations, more power to your elbow! A word to the wise though, please avoid like the plague engaging in ostentatious displays of wealth – otherwise known as rubbing your neighbours noses in it. This behaviour will not do you any favours here. That kind of carry on might be alright for the Yanks but in Ireland it is considered by any right thinking individual to be an ugly and vulgar display of bad taste, especially in the current climate when so many of the coping class are struggling to pay the mortgage. Half the population will resent you for wearing your wealth on your sleeve and the other half will be kept awake nights, scheming ways to topple you from your ivory perch while pocketing a share of your spoils in the process. You will have enemies you've never even met waiting in the long grass to trip you up at every turn. Don't forget at the back of all our smiling Irish eyes is a begrudging little so and so with a boulder sized chip on his shoulder. Who needs that kind of attention? Understated elegance is a far more attractive attribute, don't you think?

Do you know what is even more annoying – not to mention perplexing – than people wearing their wealth on their sleeves? It is idiots trying to display wealth they don't have on their sleeves. You know the imbeciles I'm talking about, the ones who hire a limousine for little Brittany's communion bash at a cost of €500 euro when they only live 5 minutes from the church. That's €100 a minute folks. Are you impressed yet? What about those gargantuan monuments to their departed ancestors which a certain, nameless section of society erect, blighting graveyards around the country? The same people who splash the cash on these ridiculous displays of 'ooh look at me, I'm a tasteless tart, who would be thick if only I were a little more intelligent' will be down with the poor, long suffering community welfare guy the following week frantically waving their electricity bill final demand and inconsolable in their grief at the prospect of not being able to afford the basic essentials which no humane society would deny them. It's enough to make you throw up in despair for our once proud nation. If it's humanity they want, I'm tempted to think they should be dispatched humanely by lethal injection to put them out of their misery or at least to put the poor broken hod carrying humpback taxpayer out of his.

79. Home Fires Burning from Britain

Many people who have worked in Britain but have now retired to Ireland are eligible for the British winter fuel allowance. The payment varies between £100 and £300 depending on individual circumstances. Lots of people have been receiving this payment for years but only if they first claimed it while living in Britain and then transferred it to Ireland when they moved back. Now, following a ruling of the European Court of Justice in early 2013, it is possible to claim this payment from Ireland for the first time. The main criteria for a claimant are that they were born before July 6th 1951 and that you can demonstrate a genuine and sufficient connection to the UK. I reckon Ireland and particularly the West of Ireland must be full of auld geezers who fit that description. If you think there is even a chance of eligibility you should check it out on https://www.gov.uk/winter-fuel-payment/how-to-claim or alternatively make an appointment with your local public representative for help with the application process. Go on, you've feck all to lose and there's nothing like a little unexpected windfall to warm the cockles of your heart.

80. Good Sports

Okay, so getting involved in sports activity is supposed to be a good thing, especially with today's obesity epidemic widening at the girth in an ever-expanding, endless spiral. However I would just like to point out that any physical exertion which works up a sweat will deliver the desired effect upon the bathroom scales plus other, associated health benefits. It doesn't have to be one which involves the acquisition of broken noses, cauliflower ears, brain damage, replacement hips and the early onset of excruciating arthritic pain brought about by repeated breakages and fractures.

According to one article I read on the subject, the average Irish sports person suffers from two significant injuries annually. Another study involving seventy four hurling players over an eight month period recorded 135 injuries in total, 41% of which were attributed to foul play. The GAA alone pays out about 6,000 claims per year under its player injury scheme. From these random statistics, which I had to search hard to find, we can conclude that the risk of acute (sudden onset) injury is a very real and present danger in many sporting disciplines. Furthermore, we haven't even mentioned overuse injuries, wear and tear problems which may only reveal themselves when the participant has hung up his boots for the last time and is no longer in the limelight or the psychological pressures on youngsters to perform at ever higher levels of competency. Almost all the focus of sporting competition is on winning and yet by definition there can only be one winning team or participant in any tournament. That leaves you with a hell of a lot of losers. Anecdotally, at least it seems to me, when I hear the reported death of a once famous sports star, more often than not it appears to be an untimely, early demise.

This is the dark side of sport which is rarely discussed in the media or public sphere because it doesn't do anything for the image of sport as a sexy, wholesome, healthy and life-affirming area of modern living. But what can you do? According to this you're damned if you do and damned if you don't as we've already agreed that mimicking a sloth is not the answer. At the very least you should obviously inform yourself about best practice around injury prevention measures in your chosen sport whether this be the wearing of appropriate protective gear or following advised training and warm-up guidelines, because, as I keep repeating, prevention is cheaper and in this case a hell of a lot less painful than cure. You should also keep a healthy perspective; moderation is a good motto in all things. Personally, I'm taking no chances; I'm going to stick to letting the dog bring me for a few brisk walks every week – off road of course for fear of being run over by a bus – in my on-going battle with the bulge.

81. Dream Purchases

The idea of buying exercise sounds a bit ridiculous, doesn't it? I mean how can you buy something intangible like that? It's a bit like buying air isn't it – marketing bottled fresh air has been done, believe it or not. It's a doddle though to the corporations; they have moved on you see from selling products to selling ideas, dreams, images and illusions, so for example when you pay €2 for a bottle of water which you could have had for free from your own tap with added time and environmental savings included for good measure, you haven't actually paid €2 for the product, you've paid it for an image of purity, fitness and healthy living which was sold to you long before you walked into the shop for your purchase. The same is true of almost anything you purchase. Think about some of the things you shell out for. Gym membership and Nike trainers, what are you buying? Health and fitness, brilliant! Sure, being fit and healthy is wonderful except you didn't need to pay for it. Hop on your bike or go for a few more walks and eat a bit more fruit and veg instead of sausages and chips and hey presto, you'll have your heart's desire and not alone did you not have to pay for it you actually saved money by buying the healthy foods.

Why do you pay a hefty monthly fee for 100 TV channels from Sky which, if you are animal rather than vegetable you simply haven't got time to watch. Again you've been sold a pup, an illusion. One good book from the library would be more entertaining and educational than the top twenty most popular programmes on telly combined. Why does someone pay €40,000 for a car, spending money (in most cases borrowed) they don't have – the kind of money which would have paid for a house in some parts of the country – when they only drive 10,000 miles a year and the car they traded in was perfectly adequate for their transport requirements. Again, they bought an image, not a car; a novelty which wears off after a couple of months. Unfortunately the financial burden takes quite a lot longer to offload. What image is perpetrated by the purveyors of alcoholic products? Have you found that reality concurs with the myth on the morning after the night before? No way! You find yourself reaching for yet another unnecessary product (paracetamol tablets) to undo the damage in an endless cycle of consumptive spending. This is all fine and dandy if you have the money and that's how you want to live. All I'm saying is look deep behind the sexy imagery and celebrity endorsement so you can see clearly what it is you are really paying for, why you want it and can a feckin' bottle of water realistically deliver all that it promises? There's no bloody genie waiting at the bottom of it to grant you your three deepest desires you know. It's just a bottle of water.

82. God is Free

I'm not going to go on a big personal rant here about the merits or otherwise of organised religion, tempting and enjoyable though that might be. That particular indulgence would require a large volume of its own and anyway, the arguments have been done to death by many others before me. If you would enjoy an intelligent biased rant against religion of all creeds you could do a lot worse than reading Richard Dawkins 'The God Delusion'. However here I just want to remind you of a truth that has almost no exceptions, namely: 'absolute power corrupts absolutely'.

We have seen the all too real effects of this truth in Irish society over the past few years. Fianna Fáil simply had too much power for too long. I'm not particularly anti Fianna Fáil by the way, we'd have ended up in a similar mess regardless of who you handed that level of autonomy and power to. Just look at what the Catholic Church, the so called men of God, did with its unquestioned authority in previous generations. You can take your example from any walk of life or any period in history, the Roman Empire, the British Empire, Hitler, the result is always the same, as the power of an individual or organisation increases the level of corruption within that body must by definition increase exponentially alongside it. So if you give anything or anyone too much power you are corrupting them. What has all this got to do with God? Well, all this basically means in the context of organised religion is that the closer you get to the new church roof fund or a mass collection plate the further you are going from that which I think of as God. Bearing in mind that there is no tangible evidence for his, her or its existence in the first place, still I like to think of God existing in the light breeze and the birdsong of a countryside walk; the laughter of a family around the dinner table; the contented comfort as your head reaches your pillow following a solid day's toil; the spontaneous, kind gesture from a stranger and endless other small moments such as those. In other words, if like me, he exists for you, just remember, God is free. He doesn't need to come with an annual (or weekly) subscription fee. He most certainly does not require weekly ceremonial attendances, holy days of obligation, seven sacred sacraments or fancy cathedrals costing hundreds of thousands per year to maintain in which to conduct all this palaver. If that elusive pimpernel known as God is to be found anywhere, he is within. So don't look for him in any manmade organisation or you will be disappointed; instead be still and there he is, the crafty bugger.

83. A Meditated Life

Meditation is at once the simplest and most difficult task you are ever likely to undertake. In its most basic form it involves simply sitting in a comfortable position, usually with your eyes closed and relaxing both mind and body, emptying yourself of all your thoughts and anxieties, perhaps concentrating solely on your breath to achieve this. This theoretically straightforward procedure which in reality is quite tricky and takes a little practice, is credited by devotees with all kinds of benefits from reducing stress, anxiety and even physical ailments to helping concentration levels, promoting contentment and gaining clarity. Wow, sounds like it's got to be worth giving it a whirl, doesn't it? All those benefits and that's only your introductory kindergarten variety for us novices in the western world. But seriously, it's free and logically it can only do you good to sit quietly for ten or fifteen minutes each morning and evening to clear the mind of all its incessant chatter and break the never ending vicious circle of thoughts and anxieties repeating endlessly in our minds. For many of us it doesn't even stop when we are asleep. I'm no expert but that just can't be positive or healthy. So give up the equivalent of one soap episode a day and treat yourself to some TLC in the form of peaceful meditation. With continued practice, over time you should also gain the added advantage of insightful perspective on separating the genuinely important from the inconsequential in life. For some it even becomes a way of life, helping to transform it positively in ways they never dreamed of. In common with most things, once you begin to learn about meditation you discover a whole world previously unknown to you. As it is an area of human activity which has been with us for millennia the good news is there is an endless supply of books, DVD's and groups to educate you. My advice is crawl before you can walk; just enjoy the beauty of its simplicity initially and take it further in time if you so wish. A meditated life has to be better than a medicated one.

Top of the Shops

Here's a list of this tight wad's top ten high street retail outlets for value.

Aldi
Lidl
Penneys
Charity Shops
Dealz
Terryland Fruit and Veg (Galway)
Ikea
Argos
Pawn Shops
Heatons

Check Out the World Wide Web

You've guessed it; this is a list of a few favourite websites of mine for freebies, bargains and financial tips. These are really just a sample selection to whet your appetite, as you know the worldwide web is a new manmade galaxy, a vast, endless, rich, dark, exciting, dangerous and perplexing place which nobody fully understands. I'm hardly the most knowledgeable cyber astronaut around so if you do your own exploring you'll surely uncover gems to beat my finds. May the force be with you!

Freecycle.org
Daft.ie
eBay.ie
Mabs.ie
Citizensinformation.ie
DoneDeal.ie
Askaboutmoney.com
Boards.ie
Swaportrade.ie
Gumtree.ie
Fundit.ie

Further Recommended Reading

Congratulations, you are almost at the end of this course in becoming a qualified Tight Bastard. However, reading and incorporating this book into your lifestyle only confers you with a basic degree. Should you wish to take your studies further to Master's Level, please see the recommended reading list below which includes, with thanks, publications that I have made previous reference to in this text.

The Undercover Economist by Tim Harford (pub: Little Brown 2006).
The Penny Pincher's book Revisited by John and Irma Mustoe (Pub: Souvenir Press Ltd 2007).
No Logo by Naomi Klein (Pub: Flamingo 2000).
Not On The Label by Felicity Lawrence (Pub: Penguin Books 2004).
How to feed your family on less than €10 a day by Elizabeth Bollard (Pub: Orpen Press 2012).

The Power of Now by Eckhart Tolle (GB. Pub: Hodder and Stoughton 2001).

Wild Food Nature's Harvest; How to Gather, Cook and Preserve by Biddy White Lennon and Evan Doyle (Pub: The O Brien Press Ltd 2013)

The Secret by Rhonda Byrne (Pub: Simon and Schuster 2006)

Anything by Patrick Holford (has written numerous books on optimal nutrition)

The Easy way to Stop Smoking by Alan Carr (pub: Penguin 1987)

Bad Pharma by Ben Goldacre (pub: Fourth Estate 2013)

AND FINALLY...

The Tight Bastard's Ten Commandments

I. Look after the pennies and the pounds will look
after themselves

II. Buy in haste, repent at your leisure

III. Never borrow for a depreciating asset

IV. A euro saved is worth two earned

V. Every purchase is optional

VI. You can have anything you want,
but not everything

VII. To owe or own is to be bound

VIII. Spend less than you earn

IX. Invest in what you know

X. Believe only half of what you see and none of
what you hear

Conclusion

So here we are on the home stretch of my marathon undertaking which was to write a book containing at least a couple of relevant, easy to implement money saving tips for anyone who read it. I gave myself a year to do it and I am, as I write this, about two months from my self-imposed deadline. This unfortunately does not mean I am ahead of schedule, the opposite in fact, I will be hard pressed to complete my task on time as there are endless hours of redrafting, editing and spell checking to go through yet, not to mention work on illustrations, cover design and style. God help me, but I'd sooner pick stones in a mountainy Mayo field than go through that final part of the process, but it has to be done or my job won't be complete.

And what has this challenge taught me? Apart from the fact that I now know my abilities of procrastination and avoidance are limitless and indeed would have scuppered my grand project very early on had it not been for another quality which, luckily, I possess by the bucket load, yes sheer, undiluted pig-ignorant stubbornness kicked in to do battle for supremacy with my other charming traits and just about won the day by a short head in the end. So the book has been written and whatever comes of it, I have found it a most enlightening, dare I say life-changing experience. At the outset I believed myself to be a thrifty little so and so and that 'fact' combined with the straitened times we as a nation find ourselves in was what made me think I could offer some useful advice to a few poor sods out there. I quickly discovered as I compared and contrasted my advice with my own actions that there were numerous holes (some gaping) in my own frugality fortress, so the past year has been an adventurous exercise for me to take my own medicine by cutting some of the fat from my personal lardy spending.

As I said, I was already practicing much of what I preached but I built on this foundation in numerous small ways such as baking my own bread, signing up with freecycle, closing a second bank current account which was surplus to requirements and so on. I began to get a kick out of finding new ways to curb costs so I upped the ante by bringing a supply of food (and flask of coffee) with me whenever I was away from home for more than a few hours. This was a bigger challenge as it involved a marked shift in my weekly routine and, as anyone who has ever tried will tell you, changing any longstanding habit is quite difficult as it has become deeply ingrained in your psyche. This adequately explains why the sensible and painless advice to any young person reading this has to be: don't adopt expensive bad habits such as smoking and eating shit take away food in the first place. It also explains why so few people succeed in making the simple (in theory) changes necessary for living a long happy and financially solvent life before the damage has been done. I hope I will have convinced some of you to act sooner rather than later, after all there's no point closing the barn door when the horse has already bolted. So I had reached a point where I had made many minor and a few not so minor financially prudent lifestyle changes whose cumulative effect was saving me a minimum of €60 or €70 per week, on top of which a beneficial side effect was that some of these changes were medically advisable also.

Of course the challenges to the dedicated and ever-vigilant tight bastard are ongoing. I continue to work through my long overgrown list of identified cost cutting measures, large and small, gently pruning a little at a time, maintaining and improving my neat financial garden (if only I could muster the will to pull a fraction of those weeds from my actual garden), whilst at the same time constantly scanning with a furtive eye for previously overlooked opportunities to enhance my frugal landscape. You cannot rest on your laurels lest new, wasteful, parasitic spending habits creep in to replace the old ones you have successfully eradicated which, as sure as the furze is in bloom will happen to the unwary. Any void created must be filled and if it is not filled consciously and creatively then by definition it will certainly be unconsciously piled high with crap.

Even now, here in the late evening, as I pause to formulate my next thought into a coherent written sentence, my ever-vigilant left eye rests its gaze suspiciously upon my mug of coffee and plate of chocolate chip cookies beside the laptop. Having read this book, how many contradictions can you see in that simple picture for this committed skin flint? First of all my choice of beverage and snack have practically no nutritional value; the hour at which I am indulging in my caffeine fix is dubious to say the least and finally and perhaps most importantly, drinking and eating anything while working on your computer is just asking for an expensive accident to happen. Thus in one simple scene is this self-professed master of penury exposed as mere apprentice of his art. Perfection in any discipline is unattainable; this is itself the ironic perfection of pursuit: you can never reach the summit of your obsession. Isn't that a wonderful note to finish on? In other words, you always have new challenges to face and a fascinating journey of discovery awaits with each breaking day. Every hour can bring the excitement of a new goal even if it is only a seemingly mundane, domestic conundrum such as how can I successfully dispense with the task of cutting the bloody lawn to everyone's satisfaction? Just make sure your obsessions are ones which are life affirming and energy enhancing rather than energy draining and depression inducing. It is indeed incredible the insights which are revealed in a plate of biscuits, late at night after you've been staring at a screen for one hour too many. So to finally wrap up my lengthy tirade I sincerely hope all of you dear readers have found some fiscal savings within these pages and perhaps more importantly have at times been given pause for thought about life itself and how you live it.

P.S. A word of caution to the overly dedicated tight bastards among you: Whilst I applaud your diligence this might be an opportune moment to mention that there are no pockets in a habit. Rather than amassing all the savings you have made from cutting out pointless spending into a great big pile to will to your next of kin, it might be better to adopt a more holistic approach by spending it on other areas which will enrich the lives of you and your family today and into the future. As the wise farmer once said, 'money is like manure, it's no use unless you spread it around'. Besides it is worth remembering that nobody appreciates properly that which they receive without effort. Just look at your average, long term social welfare recipient; he thinks his dole payment is an 'entitlement' rather than seeing it for what it truly is: a charitable handout. Equally, your children will see their inheritance as their birthright rather than the generous gift, freely given that it is. They will squander anything which comes too easily which is why we have the disposable society you see all around you today. We acquire so much with negligible effort and therefore are unable to place a value on it. Worse still, we gorge ourselves into early graves while we starve others into theirs. So I'm sorry if the title of my book and even its tone at times mislead you but this was never really a book about being a modern day scrooge, hording your cash in the attic never letting it see the light of day. Rather, it is a gentle push towards reinventing the way we see money. It is a call to treat money with respect and contempt in equal measure. Respect for the power it has in all our lives for good and ill and contempt for the false power attributed to it and the devilishly deceptive illusion of invincibility and happiness it promises its most ardent worshippers.

Contrary to the popular adage, money can indeed buy you happiness, but this is only true to the point where it lifts you out of poverty and up to a certain level of modest creature comfort. Beyond this point numerous studies have shown money does not affect your levels of contentment, either positively or negatively. Therefore, no citizen of Ireland's contentment or happiness is affected to any noticeable degree by their level of income. Rather it is their perception of that income and the incomes of those around them which cause any pain or discontent. Above and beyond what any study states, if you reflect back over your own life, looking at the good, the bad and the downright ugly, you can see the truth of this statement. Ask anyone what their favourite occupation or pastime is or when and where are they happiest and whatever their varied answers might be they almost never necessitate much cash. This is a roundabout way of coming full circle and saying money may not buy you happiness but its lack sure as hell will contribute towards your misery. So handle it with care. Spend it wisely and treat it with just the right amount of gravitas. Not too much, but not too little.